Mometrix
TEST PREPARATION

I0892025

GACE

Marketing Education Secrets Study Guide

Dear Future Exam Success Story

First of all, **THANK YOU** for purchasing Mometrix study materials!

Second, congratulations! You are one of the few determined test-takers who are committed to doing whatever it takes to excel on your exam. **You have come to the right place.** We developed these study materials with one goal in mind: to deliver you the information you need in a format that's concise and easy to use.

In addition to optimizing your guide for the content of the test, we've outlined our recommended steps for breaking down the preparation process into small, attainable goals so you can make sure you stay on track.

We've also analyzed the entire test-taking process, identifying the most common pitfalls and showing how you can overcome them and be ready for any curveball the test throws you.

Standardized testing is one of the biggest obstacles on your road to success, which only increases the importance of doing well in the high-pressure, high-stakes environment of test day. Your results on this test could have a significant impact on your future, and this guide provides the information and practical advice to help you achieve your full potential on test day.

Your success is our success

We would love to hear from you! If you would like to share the story of your exam success or if you have any questions or comments in regard to our products, please contact us at **800-673-8175** or **support@mometrix.com**.

Thanks again for your business and we wish you continued success!

Sincerely,
The Mometrix Test Preparation Team

Need more help? Check out our flashcards at:
http://MometrixFlashcards.com/GACE

Copyright © 2026 by Mometrix Media LLC. All rights reserved.
Written and edited by the Mometrix Exam Secrets Test Prep Team
Printed in the United States of America

TABLE OF CONTENTS

Introduction

Thank you for purchasing this resource! You have made the choice to prepare yourself for a test that could have a huge impact on your future, and this guide is designed to help you be fully ready for test day. Obviously, it's important to have a solid understanding of the test material, but you also need to be prepared for the unique environment and stressors of the test, so that you can perform to the best of your abilities.

For this purpose, the first section that appears in this guide is the **Secret Keys**. We've devoted countless hours to meticulously researching what works and what doesn't, and we've boiled down our findings to the five most impactful steps you can take to improve your performance on the test. We start at the beginning with study planning and move through the preparation process, all the way to the testing strategies that will help you get the most out of what you know when you're finally sitting in front of the test.

We recommend that you start preparing for your test as far in advance as possible. However, if you've bought this guide as a last-minute study resource and only have a few days before your test, we recommend that you skip over the first two Secret Keys since they address a long-term study plan.

If you struggle with **test anxiety**, we strongly encourage you to check out our recommendations for how you can overcome it. Test anxiety is a formidable foe, but it can be beaten, and we want to make sure you have the tools you need to defeat it.

Copyright © Mometrix Media. You have been licensed one copy of this document for personal use only. Any other reproduction or redistribution is strictly prohibited. All rights reserved.
This content is provided for test preparation purposes only and does not imply an endorsement by Mometrix of any particular political, scientific, or religious point of view.

Secret Key #1 – Plan Big, Study Small

There's a lot riding on your performance. If you want to ace this test, you're going to need to keep your skills sharp and the material fresh in your mind. You need a plan that lets you review everything you need to know while still fitting in your schedule. We'll break this strategy down into three categories.

Information Organization

Start with the information you already have: the official test outline. From this, you can make a complete list of all the concepts you need to cover before the test. Organize these concepts into groups that can be studied together, and create a list of any related vocabulary you need to learn so you can brush up on any difficult terms. You'll want to keep this vocabulary list handy once you actually start studying since you may need to add to it along the way.

Time Management

Once you have your set of study concepts, decide how to spread them out over the time you have left before the test. Break your study plan into small, clear goals so you have a manageable task for each day and know exactly what you're doing. Then just focus on one small step at a time. When you manage your time this way, you don't need to spend hours at a time studying. Studying a small block of content for a short period each day helps you retain information better and avoid stressing over how much you have left to do. You can relax knowing that you have a plan to cover everything in time. In order for this strategy to be effective though, you have to start studying early and stick to your schedule. Avoid the exhaustion and futility that comes from last-minute cramming!

Study Environment

The environment you study in has a big impact on your learning. Studying in a coffee shop, while probably more enjoyable, is not likely to be as fruitful as studying in a quiet room. It's important to keep distractions to a minimum. You're only planning to study for a short block of time, so make the most of it. Don't pause to check your phone or get up to find a snack. It's also important to **avoid multitasking**. Research has consistently shown that multitasking will make your studying dramatically less effective. Your study area should also be comfortable and well-lit so you don't have the distraction of straining your eyes or sitting on an uncomfortable chair.

The time of day you study is also important. You want to be rested and alert. Don't wait until just before bedtime. Study when you'll be most likely to comprehend and remember. Even better, if you know what time of day your test will be, set that time aside for study. That way your brain will be used to working on that subject at that specific time and you'll have a better chance of recalling information.

Finally, it can be helpful to team up with others who are studying for the same test. Your actual studying should be done in as isolated an environment as possible, but the work of organizing the information and setting up the study plan can be divided up. In between study sessions, you can discuss with your teammates the concepts that you're all studying and quiz each other on the details. Just be sure that your teammates are as serious about the test as you are. If you find that your study time is being replaced with social time, you might need to find a new team.

Copyright © Mometrix Media. You have been licensed one copy of this document for personal use only. Any other reproduction or redistribution is strictly prohibited. All rights reserved.
This content is provided for test preparation purposes only and does not imply an endorsement by Mometrix of any particular political, scientific, or religious point of view.

Secret Key #2 – Make Your Studying Count

You're devoting a lot of time and effort to preparing for this test, so you want to be absolutely certain it will pay off. This means doing more than just reading the content and hoping you can remember it on test day. It's important to make every minute of study count. There are two main areas you can focus on to make your studying count.

Retention

It doesn't matter how much time you study if you can't remember the material. You need to make sure you are retaining the concepts. To check your retention of the information you're learning, try recalling it at later times with minimal prompting. Try carrying around flashcards and glance at one or two from time to time or ask a friend who's also studying for the test to quiz you.

To enhance your retention, look for ways to put the information into practice so that you can apply it rather than simply recalling it. If you're using the information in practical ways, it will be much easier to remember. Similarly, it helps to solidify a concept in your mind if you're not only reading it to yourself but also explaining it to someone else. Ask a friend to let you teach them about a concept you're a little shaky on (or speak aloud to an imaginary audience if necessary). As you try to summarize, define, give examples, and answer your friend's questions, you'll understand the concepts better and they will stay with you longer. Finally, step back for a big picture view and ask yourself how each piece of information fits with the whole subject. When you link the different concepts together and see them working together as a whole, it's easier to remember the individual components.

Finally, practice showing your work on any multi-step problems, even if you're just studying. Writing out each step you take to solve a problem will help solidify the process in your mind, and you'll be more likely to remember it during the test.

Modality

Modality simply refers to the means or method by which you study. Choosing a study modality that fits your own individual learning style is crucial. No two people learn best in exactly the same way, so it's important to know your strengths and use them to your advantage.

For example, if you learn best by visualization, focus on visualizing a concept in your mind and draw an image or a diagram. Try color-coding your notes, illustrating them, or creating symbols that will trigger your mind to recall a learned concept. If you learn best by hearing or discussing information, find a study partner who learns the same way or read aloud to yourself. Think about how to put the information in your own words. Imagine that you are giving a lecture on the topic and record yourself so you can listen to it later.

For any learning style, flashcards can be helpful. Organize the information so you can take advantage of spare moments to review. Underline key words or phrases. Use different colors for different categories. Mnemonic devices (such as creating a short list in which every item starts with the same letter) can also help with retention. Find what works best for you and use it to store the information in your mind most effectively and easily.

Copyright © Mometrix Media. You have been licensed one copy of this document for personal use only. Any other reproduction or redistribution is strictly prohibited. All rights reserved.
This content is provided for test preparation purposes only and does not imply an endorsement by Mometrix of any particular political, scientific, or religious point of view.

Secret Key #3 – Practice the Right Way

Your success on test day depends not only on how many hours you put into preparing, but also on whether you prepared the right way. It's good to check along the way to see if your studying is paying off. One of the most effective ways to do this is by taking practice tests to evaluate your progress. Practice tests are useful because they show exactly where you need to improve. Every time you take a practice test, pay special attention to these three groups of questions:

- The questions you got wrong
- The questions you had to guess on, even if you guessed right
- The questions you found difficult or slow to work through

This will show you exactly what your weak areas are, and where you need to devote more study time. Ask yourself why each of these questions gave you trouble. Was it because you didn't understand the material? Was it because you didn't remember the vocabulary? Do you need more repetitions on this type of question to build speed and confidence? Dig into those questions and figure out how you can strengthen your weak areas as you go back to review the material.

Additionally, many practice tests have a section explaining the answer choices. It can be tempting to read the explanation and think that you now have a good understanding of the concept. However, an explanation likely only covers part of the question's broader context. Even if the explanation makes perfect sense, **go back and investigate** every concept related to the question until you're positive you have a thorough understanding.

As you go along, keep in mind that the practice test is just that: practice. Memorizing these questions and answers will not be very helpful on the actual test because it is unlikely to have any of the same exact questions. If you only know the right answers to the sample questions, you won't be prepared for the real thing. **Study the concepts** until you understand them fully, and then you'll be able to answer any question that shows up on the test.

It's important to wait on the practice tests until you're ready. If you take a test on your first day of study, you may be overwhelmed by the amount of material covered and how much you need to learn. Work up to it gradually.

On test day, you'll need to be prepared for answering questions, managing your time, and using the test-taking strategies you've learned. It's a lot to balance, like a mental marathon that will have a big impact on your future. Like training for a marathon, you'll need to start slowly and work your way up. When test day arrives, you'll be ready.

Start with the strategies you've read in the first two Secret Keys—plan your course and study in the way that works best for you. If you have time, consider using multiple study resources to get different approaches to the same concepts. It can be helpful to see difficult concepts from more than one angle. Then find a good source for practice tests. Many times, the test website will suggest potential study resources or provide sample tests.

Copyright © Mometrix Media. You have been licensed one copy of this document for personal use only. Any other reproduction or redistribution is strictly prohibited. All rights reserved.
This content is provided for test preparation purposes only and does not imply an endorsement by Mometrix of any particular political, scientific, or religious point of view.

Practice Test Strategy

If you're able to find at least three practice tests, we recommend this strategy:

UNTIMED AND OPEN-BOOK PRACTICE

Take the first test with no time constraints and with your notes and study guide handy. Take your time and focus on applying the strategies you've learned.

TIMED AND OPEN-BOOK PRACTICE

Take the second practice test open-book as well, but set a timer and practice pacing yourself to finish in time.

TIMED AND CLOSED-BOOK PRACTICE

Take any other practice tests as if it were test day. Set a timer and put away your study materials. Sit at a table or desk in a quiet room, imagine yourself at the testing center, and answer questions as quickly and accurately as possible.

Keep repeating timed and closed-book tests on a regular basis until you run out of practice tests or it's time for the actual test. Your mind will be ready for the schedule and stress of test day, and you'll be able to focus on recalling the material you've learned.

Copyright © Mometrix Media. You have been licensed one copy of this document for personal use only. Any other reproduction or redistribution is strictly prohibited. All rights reserved.
This content is provided for test preparation purposes only and does not imply an endorsement by Mometrix of any particular political, scientific, or religious point of view.

Secret Key #4 – Pace Yourself

Once you're fully prepared for the material on the test, your biggest challenge on test day will be managing your time. Just knowing that the clock is ticking can make you panic even if you have plenty of time left. Work on pacing yourself so you can build confidence against the time constraints of the exam. Pacing is a difficult skill to master, especially in a high-pressure environment, so **practice is vital**.

Set time expectations for your pace based on how much time is available. For example, if a section has 60 questions and the time limit is 30 minutes, you know you have to average 30 seconds or less per question in order to answer them all. Although 30 seconds is the hard limit, set 25 seconds per question as your goal, so you reserve extra time to spend on harder questions. When you budget extra time for the harder questions, you no longer have any reason to stress when those questions take longer to answer.

Don't let this time expectation distract you from working through the test at a calm, steady pace, but keep it in mind so you don't spend too much time on any one question. Recognize that taking extra time on one question you don't understand may keep you from answering two that you do understand later in the test. If your time limit for a question is up and you're still not sure of the answer, mark it and move on, and come back to it later if the time and the test format allow. If the testing format doesn't allow you to return to earlier questions, just make an educated guess; then put it out of your mind and move on.

On the easier questions, be careful not to rush. It may seem wise to hurry through them so you have more time for the challenging ones, but it's not worth missing one if you know the concept and just didn't take the time to read the question fully. Work efficiently but make sure you understand the question and have looked at all of the answer choices, since more than one may seem right at first.

Even if you're paying attention to the time, you may find yourself a little behind at some point. You should speed up to get back on track, but do so wisely. Don't panic; just take a few seconds less on each question until you're caught up. Don't guess without thinking, but do look through the answer choices and eliminate any you know are wrong. If you can get down to two choices, it is often worthwhile to guess from those. Once you've chosen an answer, move on and don't dwell on any that you skipped or had to hurry through. If a question was taking too long, chances are it was one of the harder ones, so you weren't as likely to get it right anyway.

On the other hand, if you find yourself getting ahead of schedule, it may be beneficial to slow down a little. The more quickly you work, the more likely you are to make a careless mistake that will affect your score. You've budgeted time for each question, so don't be afraid to spend that time. Practice an efficient but careful pace to get the most out of the time you have.

Copyright © Mometrix Media. You have been licensed one copy of this document for personal use only. Any other reproduction or redistribution is strictly prohibited. All rights reserved.
This content is provided for test preparation purposes only and does not imply an endorsement by Mometrix of any particular political, scientific, or religious point of view.

Secret Key #5 – Have a Plan for Guessing

When you're taking the test, you may find yourself stuck on a question. Some of the answer choices seem better than others, but you don't see the one answer choice that is obviously correct. What do you do?

The scenario described above is very common, yet most test takers have not effectively prepared for it. Developing and practicing a plan for guessing may be one of the single most effective uses of your time as you get ready for the exam.

In developing your plan for guessing, there are three questions to address:

- When should you start the guessing process?
- How should you narrow down the choices?
- Which answer should you choose?

When to Start the Guessing Process

Unless your plan for guessing is to select C every time (which, despite its merits, is not what we recommend), you need to leave yourself enough time to apply your answer elimination strategies. Since you have a limited amount of time for each question, that means that if you're going to give yourself the best shot at guessing correctly, you have to decide quickly whether or not you will guess.

Of course, the best-case scenario is that you don't have to guess at all, so first, see if you can answer the question based on your knowledge of the subject and basic reasoning skills. Focus on the key words in the question and try to jog your memory of related topics. Give yourself a chance to bring the knowledge to mind, but once you realize that you don't have (or you can't access) the knowledge you need to answer the question, it's time to start the guessing process.

It's almost always better to start the guessing process too early than too late. It only takes a few seconds to remember something and answer the question from knowledge. Carefully eliminating wrong answer choices takes longer. Plus, going through the process of eliminating answer choices can actually help jog your memory.

Summary: Start the guessing process as soon as you decide that you can't answer the question based on your knowledge.

Copyright © Mometrix Media. You have been licensed one copy of this document for personal use only. Any other reproduction or redistribution is strictly prohibited. All rights reserved.
This content is provided for test preparation purposes only and does not imply an endorsement by Mometrix of any particular political, scientific, or religious point of view.

How to Narrow Down the Choices

The next chapter in this book (**Test-Taking Strategies**) includes a wide range of strategies for how to approach questions and how to look for answer choices to eliminate. You will definitely want to read those carefully, practice them, and figure out which ones work best for you. Here though, we're going to address a mindset rather than a particular strategy.

Your odds of guessing an answer correctly depend on how many options you are choosing from.

Number of options left	5	4	3	2	1
Odds of guessing correctly	20%	25%	33%	50%	100%

You can see from this chart just how valuable it is to be able to eliminate incorrect answers and make an educated guess, but there are two things that many test takers do that cause them to miss out on the benefits of guessing:

- Accidentally eliminating the correct answer
- Selecting an answer based on an impression

We'll look at the first one here, and the second one in the next section.

To avoid accidentally eliminating the correct answer, we recommend a thought exercise called **the $5 challenge**. In this challenge, you only eliminate an answer choice from contention if you are willing to bet $5 on it being wrong. Why $5? Five dollars is a small but not insignificant amount of money. It's an amount you could afford to lose but wouldn't want to throw away. And while losing $5 once might not hurt too much, doing it twenty times will set you back $100. In the same way, each small decision you make—eliminating a choice here, guessing on a question there—won't by itself impact your score very much, but when you put them all together, they can make a big difference. By holding each answer choice elimination decision to a higher standard, you can reduce the risk of accidentally eliminating the correct answer.

The $5 challenge can also be applied in a positive sense: If you are willing to bet $5 that an answer choice *is* correct, go ahead and mark it as correct.

Summary: Only eliminate an answer choice if you are willing to bet $5 that it is wrong.

Copyright © Mometrix Media. You have been licensed one copy of this document for personal use only. Any other reproduction or redistribution is strictly prohibited. All rights reserved.
This content is provided for test preparation purposes only and does not imply an endorsement by Mometrix of any particular political, scientific, or religious point of view.

Which Answer to Choose

You're taking the test. You've run into a hard question and decided you'll have to guess. You've eliminated all the answer choices you're willing to bet $5 on. Now you have to pick an answer. Why do we even need to talk about this? Why can't you just pick whichever one you feel like when the time comes?

The answer to these questions is that if you don't come into the test with a plan, you'll rely on your impression to select an answer choice, and if you do that, you risk falling into a trap. The test writers know that everyone who takes their test will be guessing on some of the questions, so they intentionally write wrong answer choices to seem plausible. You still have to pick an answer though, and if the wrong answer choices are designed to look right, how can you ever be sure that you're not falling for their trap? The best solution we've found to this dilemma is to take the decision out of your hands entirely. Here is the process we recommend:

Once you've eliminated any choices that you are confident (willing to bet $5) are wrong, select the first remaining choice as your answer.

Whether you choose to select the first remaining choice, the second, or the last, the important thing is that you use some preselected standard. Using this approach guarantees that you will not be enticed into selecting an answer choice that looks right, because you are not basing your decision on how the answer choices look.

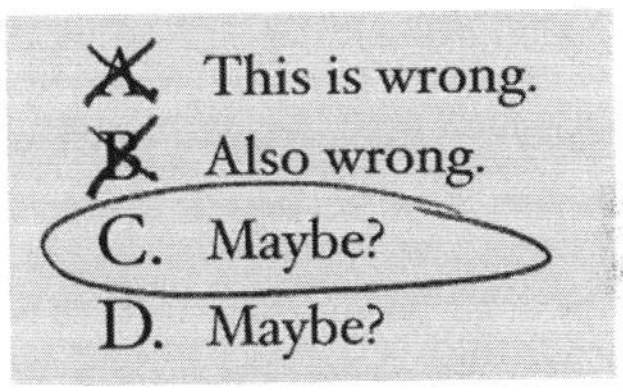

This is not meant to make you question your knowledge. Instead, it is to help you recognize the difference between your knowledge and your impressions. There's a huge difference between thinking an answer is right because of what you know, and thinking an answer is right because it looks or sounds like it should be right.

Summary: To ensure that your selection is appropriately random, make a predetermined selection from among all answer choices you have not eliminated.

Copyright © Mometrix Media. You have been licensed one copy of this document for personal use only. Any other reproduction or redistribution is strictly prohibited. All rights reserved.
This content is provided for test preparation purposes only and does not imply an endorsement by Mometrix of any particular political, scientific, or religious point of view.

Test-Taking Strategies

This section contains a list of test-taking strategies that you may find helpful as you work through the test. By taking what you know and applying logical thought, you can maximize your chances of answering any question correctly!

It is very important to realize that every question is different and every person is different: no single strategy will work on every question, and no single strategy will work for every person. That's why we've included all of them here, so you can try them out and determine which ones work best for different types of questions and which ones work best for you.

Question Strategies

☑ Read Carefully

Read the question and the answer choices carefully. Don't miss the question because you misread the terms. You have plenty of time to read each question thoroughly and make sure you understand what is being asked. Yet a happy medium must be attained, so don't waste too much time. You must read carefully and efficiently.

☑ Contextual Clues

Look for contextual clues. If the question includes a word you are not familiar with, look at the immediate context for some indication of what the word might mean. Contextual clues can often give you all the information you need to decipher the meaning of an unfamiliar word. Even if you can't determine the meaning, you may be able to narrow down the possibilities enough to make a solid guess at the answer to the question.

☑ Prefixes

If you're having trouble with a word in the question or answer choices, try dissecting it. Take advantage of every clue that the word might include. Prefixes can be a huge help. Usually, they allow you to determine a basic meaning. *Pre-* means before, *post-* means after, *pro-* is positive, *de-* is negative. From prefixes, you can get an idea of the general meaning of the word and try to put it into context.

☑ Hedge Words

Watch out for critical hedge words, such as *likely, may, can, often, almost, mostly, usually, generally, rarely,* and *sometimes.* Question writers insert these hedge phrases to cover every possibility. Often an answer choice will be wrong simply because it leaves no room for exception. Be on guard for answer choices that have definitive words such as *exactly* and *always.*

☑ Switchback Words

Stay alert for *switchbacks.* These are the words and phrases frequently used to alert you to shifts in thought. The most common switchback words are *but, although,* and *however.* Others include *nevertheless, on the other hand, even though, while, in spite of, despite,* and *regardless of.* Switchback words are important to catch because they can change the direction of the question or an answer choice.

Copyright © Mometrix Media. You have been licensed one copy of this document for personal use only. Any other reproduction or redistribution is strictly prohibited. All rights reserved.
This content is provided for test preparation purposes only and does not imply an endorsement by Mometrix of any particular political, scientific, or religious point of view.

☑ FACE VALUE

When in doubt, use common sense. Accept the situation in the problem at face value. Don't read too much into it. These problems will not require you to make wild assumptions. If you have to go beyond creativity and warp time or space in order to have an answer choice fit the question, then you should move on and consider the other answer choices. These are normal problems rooted in reality. The applicable relationship or explanation may not be readily apparent, but it is there for you to figure out. Use your common sense to interpret anything that isn't clear.

Answer Choice Strategies

☑ ANSWER SELECTION

The most thorough way to pick an answer choice is to identify and eliminate wrong answers until only one is left, then confirm it is the correct answer. Sometimes an answer choice may immediately seem right, but be careful. The test writers will usually put more than one reasonable answer choice on each question, so take a second to read all of them and make sure that the other choices are not equally obvious. As long as you have time left, it is better to read every answer choice than to pick the first one that looks right without checking the others.

☑ ANSWER CHOICE FAMILIES

An answer choice family consists of two (in rare cases, three) answer choices that are very similar in construction and cannot all be true at the same time. If you see two answer choices that are direct opposites or parallels, one of them is usually the correct answer. For instance, if one answer choice says that quantity *x* increases and another either says that quantity *x* decreases (opposite) or says that quantity *y* increases (parallel), then those answer choices would fall into the same family. An answer choice that doesn't match the construction of the answer choice family is more likely to be incorrect. Most questions will not have answer choice families, but when they do appear, you should be prepared to recognize them.

☑ ELIMINATE ANSWERS

Eliminate answer choices as soon as you realize they are wrong, but make sure you consider all possibilities. If you are eliminating answer choices and realize that the last one you are left with is also wrong, don't panic. Start over and consider each choice again. There may be something you missed the first time that you will realize on the second pass.

☑ AVOID FACT TRAPS

Don't be distracted by an answer choice that is factually true but doesn't answer the question. You are looking for the choice that answers the question. Stay focused on what the question is asking for so you don't accidentally pick an answer that is true but incorrect. Always go back to the question and make sure the answer choice you've selected actually answers the question and is not merely a true statement.

☑ EXTREME STATEMENTS

In general, you should avoid answers that put forth extreme actions as standard practice or proclaim controversial ideas as established fact. An answer choice that states the "process should be used in certain situations, if..." is much more likely to be correct than one that states the "process should be discontinued completely." The first is a calm rational statement and doesn't even make a definitive, uncompromising stance, using a hedge word *if* to provide wiggle room, whereas the second choice is far more extreme.

Copyright © Mometrix Media. You have been licensed one copy of this document for personal use only. Any other reproduction or redistribution is strictly prohibited. All rights reserved.
This content is provided for test preparation purposes only and does not imply an endorsement by Mometrix of any particular political, scientific, or religious point of view.

✓ Benchmark

As you read through the answer choices and you come across one that seems to answer the question well, mentally select that answer choice. This is not your final answer, but it's the one that will help you evaluate the other answer choices. The one that you selected is your benchmark or standard for judging each of the other answer choices. Every other answer choice must be compared to your benchmark. That choice is correct until proven otherwise by another answer choice beating it. If you find a better answer, then that one becomes your new benchmark. Once you've decided that no other choice answers the question as well as your benchmark, you have your final answer.

✓ Predict the Answer

Before you even start looking at the answer choices, it is often best to try to predict the answer. When you come up with the answer on your own, it is easier to avoid distractions and traps because you will know exactly what to look for. The right answer choice is unlikely to be word-for-word what you came up with, but it should be a close match. Even if you are confident that you have the right answer, you should still take the time to read each option before moving on.

General Strategies

✓ Tough Questions

If you are stumped on a problem or it appears too hard or too difficult, don't waste time. Move on! Remember though, if you can quickly check for obviously incorrect answer choices, your chances of guessing correctly are greatly improved. Before you completely give up, at least try to knock out a couple of possible answers. Eliminate what you can and then guess at the remaining answer choices before moving on.

✓ Check Your Work

Since you will probably not know every term listed and the answer to every question, it is important that you get credit for the ones that you do know. Don't miss any questions through careless mistakes. If at all possible, try to take a second to look back over your answer selection and make sure you've selected the correct answer choice and haven't made a costly careless mistake (such as marking an answer choice that you didn't mean to mark). This quick double check should more than pay for itself in caught mistakes for the time it costs.

✓ Pace Yourself

It's easy to be overwhelmed when you're looking at a page full of questions; your mind is confused and full of random thoughts, and the clock is ticking down faster than you would like. Calm down and maintain the pace that you have set for yourself. Especially as you get down to the last few minutes of the test, don't let the small numbers on the clock make you panic. As long as you are on track by monitoring your pace, you are guaranteed to have time for each question.

✓ Don't Rush

It is very easy to make errors when you are in a hurry. Maintaining a fast pace in answering questions is pointless if it makes you miss questions that you would have gotten right otherwise. Test writers like to include distracting information and wrong answers that seem right. Taking a little extra time to avoid careless mistakes can make all the difference in your test score. Find a pace that allows you to be confident in the answers that you select.

Copyright © Mometrix Media. You have been licensed one copy of this document for personal use only. Any other reproduction or redistribution is strictly prohibited. All rights reserved.
This content is provided for test preparation purposes only and does not imply an endorsement by Mometrix of any particular political, scientific, or religious point of view.

⊘ Keep Moving

Panicking will not help you pass the test, so do your best to stay calm and keep moving. Taking deep breaths and going through the answer elimination steps you practiced can help to break through a stress barrier and keep your pace.

Final Notes

The combination of a solid foundation of content knowledge and the confidence that comes from practicing your plan for applying that knowledge is the key to maximizing your performance on test day. As your foundation of content knowledge is built up and strengthened, you'll find that the strategies included in this chapter become more and more effective in helping you quickly sift through the distractions and traps of the test to isolate the correct answer.

Now that you're preparing to move forward into the test content chapters of this book, be sure to keep your goal in mind. As you read, think about how you will be able to apply this information on the test. If you've already seen sample questions for the test and you have an idea of the question format and style, try to come up with questions of your own that you can answer based on what you're reading. This will give you valuable practice applying your knowledge in the same ways you can expect to on test day.

Good luck and good studying!

Copyright © Mometrix Media. You have been licensed one copy of this document for personal use only. Any other reproduction or redistribution is strictly prohibited. All rights reserved.
This content is provided for test preparation purposes only and does not imply an endorsement by Mometrix of any particular political, scientific, or religious point of view.

Copyright © Mometrix Media. You have been licensed one copy of this document for personal use only. Any other reproduction or redistribution is strictly prohibited. All rights reserved.
This content is provided for test preparation purposes only and does not imply an endorsement by Mometrix of any particular political, scientific, or religious point of view.

Marketing-Information Management

Transform passive reading into active learning! After immersing yourself in this chapter, put your comprehension to the test by taking a quiz. The insights you gained will stay with you longer this way. Scan the QR code to go directly to the chapter quiz interface for this study guide. If you're using a computer, simply visit the online resources page at **mometrix.com/resources719/gacemarketed** and click the Chapter Quizzes link.

Goals of Business Correspondence

There are a number of goals commonly seen on business correspondence, and at times they overlap. One of the major goals of business correspondence is to give information. One employee may be providing information to another employee, or the company may be sharing business happenings to customers. Another common goal is to sell the company's goods and services. Many companies create advertisements, blogs, social media posts, and other promotional materials to convince consumers to purchase their offerings. Business correspondence may also be used to convince an audience of something. A person may send a letter to a client to convince him that his product is better. An employee may try to convince another employee to try a new policy. Business professionals often correspond as a response to a question. If a consumer emails a question, customer service will respond with the answer. Businesses will often send out confirmation emails. This may be in response to a purchase or a question. Another form of correspondence may be sent out if an adjustment needs to be made. Correspondence may be through paper, email, the Internet, or other methods.

Communication Modalities

There are many different communication modalities used within a business, including emails, phone calls, and in-person meetings, each with its own uses. **Face-to-face communication** is very important in business, especially when delivering important or serious information. For instance, if there is a serious conflict with an employee, the supervisor is going to want to sit down and talk to him. If a business is going after a big client, a face-to-face meeting can show a lot of effort. Meetings can impart a lot of information to many people very quickly, engage people, and allow everyone to interact. **Email** is used very often for a wide variety of business matters because of its ease, speed, and convenience. This is often used in customer service because many customers prefer it. Also, it allows customers and customer service to interact even when the customer is not available during service business hours. The **telephone** is also commonly used, especially when it is a quick question that needs immediate attention. If there is a lot of back and forth required, a phone call can be quicker than an exchange of emails. Companies generally use many of these forms of communication.

Effective Communication Skills

Effective communication skills are important in business. First, it is important for people to practice active listening. This means perceiving everything about the communication by using all senses. Not only should a person listen, but they should also watch for body language and try to evaluate how the speaker feels. People want to feel like others are really listening to them and processing what they are saying. Eye contact is important. The person shouldn't interrupt or make it seem like he's making judgments. He should display interest. This can be done by nodding or making small comments. Nonverbal communication is also important. The person should appear engaged,

Copyright © Mometrix Media. You have been licensed one copy of this document for personal use only. Any other reproduction or redistribution is strictly prohibited. All rights reserved.
This content is provided for test preparation purposes only and does not imply an endorsement by Mometrix of any particular political, scientific, or religious point of view.

relaxed, and open. He should not be fidgeting. He should use open body language. A person should be aware of what he says and how it comes across, choosing his words carefully. One can easily insult someone, even accidently. He should not argue, but try to work together to communicate effectively. In business, people should think logically and try to keep stress and emotion from influencing decisions. With practice, people can improve their communication skills.

Nonverbal Communication

Nonverbal communication can be just as important as verbal communication in business, thus it is important to know the best strategies to make it effective. First, eye contact is important because it shows that a person is interested, engaged, and actively listening. A person's facial expression can express a lot. When one smiles, she is showing friendliness, encouragement and/or satisfaction with the work. When one frowns or displays an angry face, she is showing displeasure. It is important to show the expression that matches the feelings a person wants to convey when communicating in business, because otherwise the recipient may get the wrong idea. Gestures can show a lot. Someone clenching his fists may show anger. Hand movements can also help convey information. A person's posture tells a lot. Someone who crosses her arms may show resistance. A business professional who is standing or sitting tall may show off confidence. If someone is fidgeting, he may show discomfort or nervousness, which is not good for business. Business professionals should evaluate their nonverbal communication to make sure it enhances what they want to portray.

Proper Etiquette in Personal and Business Communication

Individuals should always practice proper courtesy. Business professionals should ordinarily address each other in a formal way and conduct appropriate cultural moves such as shaking hands. It is important to practice cultural sensitivity and know the rules and traditions of the person being greeted. For instance, in some cultures people may bow, while in another they may hug. People should make every effort not to show any bias or stereotypes as this can be very insulting to business contacts. Sometimes a person can come across as insulting or rude if she is ignorant of cultural customs. It is important to study the culture before interaction to make sure this does not happen. Otherwise, business communication should be formal and free of insults. It should be professional and without errors as well.

Communication Types Commonly Seen in Business

Business letters are sent for a wide variety of reasons and can be very formal. These may contain confidential and important information. Memoranda, also known as memos, are a less formal method of communication and may be used for announcements, information dissemination, and directions. They may be sent to a lot of people at once and are generally short and to the point. Emails are now commonly used in business communications because of their ease of use and speed. These may be less formal than written out business letters, or they can be just as formal. Publicity materials, such as press releases, are used to publicize an event or garner support. Recruitment communications are used in the process of hiring employees. For instance, a classified ad may be made when the company is hiring. Companies also make a lot of advertisements to draw consumers. These may be flashy advertisements or more subdued forms of communication and may appear in places such as newspapers and magazines.

Terminology Commonly Used in Business Communication

A memorandum is a short, informal form of business communication used to disseminate information. When a company writes "Enclosures," it means there is/are one or more enclosures. In email, an attached file is known as an attachment. The return address is the address of the person sending the letter. The inside address, or letter mailing address, is the recipient's address. The

Copyright © Mometrix Media. You have been licensed one copy of this document for personal use only. Any other reproduction or redistribution is strictly prohibited. All rights reserved.
This content is provided for test preparation purposes only and does not imply an endorsement by Mometrix of any particular political, scientific, or religious point of view.

salutation is the greeting used, very commonly "Dear." The body is the main content of the letter. The complementary close is the closing at the bottom of the letter. There may also be reference initials at the end of the letter, which refer to the person who actually typed it, if different than the writer. Knowing these terms can help an individual write a professional business letter.

Writing Business Letters

A business letter should follow conventional professional practices. It starts with the sender's address (but not the name). Sometimes the address will be on the letterhead; otherwise it should be the first part. Next should be the date the letter was finished, written as month, day, and year. It should be two inches below the top and flush left (although some formats allow it to go in the center). Underneath that will be the inside address, or the recipient's address, including the specific name and title of the addressee, always left justified. The salutation is under that and should include the personal title unless it is someone usually referred to by the first name. The body is next. Block format is common and is single spaced and flushed left. There is a line between each paragraph. The content should be succinct, to the point, and logical. It might start with an opening and the main idea of the letter, followed with information supporting or explaining the main point. The final paragraph may reiterate the point and ask for action. Below that is the closing. If there are enclosures, this should be stated under that.

Business Memorandum Format

A business **memorandum** is a relatively informal form of communication used in businesses to spread information, give announcements, explain company happenings, and provide similar functions. It is often sent out to a lot of people at once and does not generally contain confidential information. At the top it should state "Memorandum." Underneath that, flush left will be the word "TO:" along with the addressee(s). Underneath that and still flush left will be "FROM:" with the sender's name. If there are any CCs, this will be under that. Below that will be "DATE:" with the date. "SUBJECT:" is under that. Finally, the body of the memo will be underneath that, written in block format. A properly formatted memo is professional and succinct.

Presentations

Goals

Presentations can have one or more goals, and it is important for presenters to be aware of the specific objectives so they can tailor the presentation for maximum efficacy. One major goal of presentations is to give information to the audience. It might be to employees, the stockholders, the public, or another group, but the company may be presenting information about itself, its products, current news, or more. Reporting data is another common goal of presentations. For instance, a company may be reporting sales numbers to its stockholders. Sometimes presentations are made to convince an audience of something. For example, a company may give a presentation to a potential client in an effort to broker a deal. Inspiring is another common goal. This is often done in employee meetings. For instance, a company may have a meeting to motivate its employees to work harder to reach certain goals. It is vital for the presentation to match its goals and audience for the best chance of success.

Features of Successful Presentations

Presentations play a big part in business, so it is important to know the features of successful ones. First, the audience should be able to understand the presentation. It needs to be tailored to the audience so they can relate to it. It should be concise. The presenter should not carry on too long about the same thing because he or she could lose the audience. A good opening hook is important. It engages the audience from the start. Some people start with a story or quote. The presentation should also look good visually. Visual aids that can enhance a business presentation include graphs,

Copyright © Mometrix Media. You have been licensed one copy of this document for personal use only. Any other reproduction or redistribution is strictly prohibited. All rights reserved.
This content is provided for test preparation purposes only and does not imply an endorsement by Mometrix of any particular political, scientific, or religious point of view.

charts, photographs, and videos. If the presentation contains a call to action, then it should be strong. The audience should be moved to do it. The presenter should be skilled. He should speak loud enough that everyone can hear, keep eye contact, and engage in good body language. He should appear confident. The presentation should flow well and keep the audience's attention. Many business presentations are participative because this can keep people's interest. All of these measures go a long way in making a business presentation successful.

Characteristics of Various Audiences

It is important for presenters to understand the characteristics of the audience for a business presentation because that can greatly influence the best presentation. The size of an audience matters. The presentation will be different for a small room of 10 people compared to a large audience of 500. The cultural composition will matter. People of different cultures have different beliefs and may perceive a presentation differently. The other personal characteristics of the group, such as age, gender, and religion, can also affect how presentations are viewed. The level of knowledge matters. A health presentation on the same subject will be very different if given to a group of doctors as compared to a group of patients. Presenters should evaluate the audience to formulate the best presentation.

Preparation Steps

First, the presenter must understand his or her goals. What does he want to accomplish with the presentation? Once he knows this, he can select the exact topic, narrowing it down to fit the size and timing of the presentation. He will then need to evaluate the audience. The presentation of the same subject will be very different if given to customers as compared to employees or stockholders. The audience should be able to understand the topic, terminology, and references. The presenter should understand what is important to the audience and what they are thinking. Next, he should come up with the main points he wants to cover and make sure they are well illustrated in the presentation. He should find material to support these points such as graphs, charts, tables, photographs, data, and other visual items. This can give the presentation more substance and validity. Finally, the presenter should practice, ideally in front of someone who can evaluate the performance. By taking the time to carefully perfect the presentation, he will be more likely to reach his goals.

Adjusting Based on Needs and Concerns of Audience

To make the most impact, a presenter should adjust his presentation based on the needs and concerns of the audience. First, he or she needs to understand the audience and how they will likely feel about the presentation. He or she should do as much research as possible into the characteristics of the audience, including whether they will accept the presentation with acceptance or hostility and should plan to address their concerns. For instance, if he or she thinks the audience might be potentially hostile, the presenter should right away include things that will help to alleviate their concerns or ease the news to them. He or she should explain things so that they understand and will hopefully accept the content. It is important for the presenter to show empathy to the audience so they feel like the presenter is on their side. Oftentimes, the presenter allows the audience to ask questions and participate so that he or she can address their concerns directly. If they are worried about something that will not happen, then the presenter should be reassuring, personable, and friendly. The more the presenter comes off as a caring and competent individual, the better the presentation will proceed.

Delivery Strategies

Different strategies can make presentation delivery more effective. One decision is whether to use an extemporaneous (unscripted) speech or a scripted one. If the person is knowledgeable enough

Copyright © Mometrix Media. You have been licensed one copy of this document for personal use only. Any other reproduction or redistribution is strictly prohibited. All rights reserved.
This content is provided for test preparation purposes only and does not imply an endorsement by Mometrix of any particular political, scientific, or religious point of view.

and wants to engage the audience without looking at a paper or prompter, he or she might choose the unscripted version. If he thinks he would be too nervous or forgetful without it, he might choose to use a script. Anyone might need it for a very technical speech with a lot of statistics. No matter what, it is important for the presenter to display only positive body language. He should make eye contact with members of the audience and not just look down. He should use positive gestures, facial expressions, and enthusiasm. He should watch his words to make sure nothing can be interpreted as biased or inappropriate. It is important for the presenter to be aware of the audience at all times and respond as necessary. If he senses that they do not understand something, for instance, he should go into more detail. If they are upset about something, he should try to address their concerns. With the right strategies, the presentation has a greater chance of success.

Visual Aids

Visual aids can enhance a business presentation. Graphs and charts can give a visual representation of the subject. For instance, if a person is talking about how sales numbers have changed, a line graph can make this very clear by showing how sales have changed over time or in response to certain variables. Diagrams can give a visual explanation of a concept. They can make a technical subject easier to understand. For instance, if someone is explaining a new product to investors, a diagram can help explain how it works. Slideshows are commonly used in business presentations. They can reinforce what the presenter is saying and draw interest. If a company is talking about its charity work, a picture of a smiling child the company helped would be more compelling than just talking about it. Videos can also show people a great deal. For instance, a company can make a video showing its factories or a new design. Computer projections are used as well. Most presentations use one or more visual aids.

Whiteboards, Presentation Software, and Multimedia Equipment

Whiteboards are often used in presentations. These are dry erase boards that the presenter can write on as he is speaking. This is also useful for a participative presentation in which the presenter asks the audience a question and writes down the answers as they are given. He can show step-by-step how something is done. Presentation software is also very commonly used. PowerPoint is one of the most commonly used presentation software programs and allows presenters to create detailed slides of photographs, charts, graphs, and more to enhance the presentation. They can make it easier to understand numbers and statistics. There are also various types of multimedia equipment a presenter might use. They might use a projector or a television. All of these can catch the audience's attention and bring the presentation to life.

Telecommunication Modalities Used in Business

The telephone is one form of telecommunication modalities. Individuals can get immediate access to someone to ask a question or have a discussion. A disadvantage is that there is no record of it (unless the call is recorded) and someone may not be available for a phone call. Another common form is a fax machine. This allows someone else to see a document. It is almost immediate. Both locations must have faxing ability, and it creates a physical document instead of a digital record, which many businesses prefer. Videoconferencing is commonly used. Individuals can discuss matters in real time. They can also share charts, graphs, and other visual aids. It has lowered the need for many business trips. Network email is also commonly used in business. It is delivered almost immediately and leaves a record. It can take longer to explain something than a simple phone conversation, however. An advantage is that it can be less intrusive and sometimes quicker.

Internet Modalities Used in Business

Email can be used to communicate with other businesses and with customers. Many customers prefer to email a company and it can be less time consuming for the company than a phone call.

Copyright © Mometrix Media. You have been licensed one copy of this document for personal use only. Any other reproduction or redistribution is strictly prohibited. All rights reserved.
This content is provided for test preparation purposes only and does not imply an endorsement by Mometrix of any particular political, scientific, or religious point of view.

People like the convenience of being able to do it at any time. Message boards are also used. This is advantageous because customers can look up threads with topics similar to their issues and might get the answer to the problem without needing to contact customer service themselves. Mailing lists allow businesses to send out emails to many people at once. It is a great way for a company to disseminate information. Many companies also have instant messaging, both between its employees and for customers. This can be a great way to give customer service because customers like getting answers right away. One employee can be on several chats at once, which lowers the number of employees needed as compared to phone support. Chat rooms are also convenient because multiple people can see the answers. Many businesses use a combination of these.

Communication Technologies Used in Business

Many businesses have switched to solely wireless technology use, such as tablets and phones that use wireless internet. Cell phones are advantageous because people can take them while they're on the go and be reachable even when not sitting at a desk in the office. Of course, they do not always get service everywhere. Fax machines are used to communicate a document over long distances. They are almost instantaneous, inexpensive, and create a hard copy. Bluetooth is a wireless technology that provides convenience by letting data travel over short distances. It has lowered the need for wires. Streaming technology has allowed multimedia to be constantly delivered and received from one party to another. For instance, a person can watch a live newscast on a phone. Voice over Internet Protocol (VoIP) allows voice and multimedia to go over the Internet and other Internet Protocol Networks (IP). An example is Skype. It is advantageous for businesses because it is inexpensive and offers high bandwidth efficiency. Because voice and data communications can use one network, infrastructure costs are lower. In addition, it can be run on inexpensive standard interfaces like personal computers. It can be less reliable, however.

Etiquette in Electronic Communications

It is important to use professionalism in electronic communications, especially if it is a business letter. Just because a message is sent via email does not mean it should be sloppy. Of course, how professional it is will depend on the recipient, but if it is to a professional contact, it should be formed professionally. The sender should make a proper introduction and closing and avoid emoticons, writing in all capitals, and using excessive exclamation marks. It is very important to make sure it is free of typos and grammatical errors. Senders should proofread it just as they would proofread a regular letter. It is also important to not bombard people with unnecessary emails. Senders should be careful about including someone in a chain of unnecessary emails. They should make use of BCC and not share people's addresses with others. They should write an appropriate subject line so people know what it is. Senders should be careful about confidential information because users can easily forward them. By following these rules, the email will be more professional.

Chapter Quiz

Ready to see how well you retained what you just read? Scan the QR code to go directly to the chapter quiz interface for this study guide. If you're using a computer, simply visit the online resources page at **mometrix.com/resources719/gacemarketed** and click the Chapter Quizzes link.

Copyright © Mometrix Media. You have been licensed one copy of this document for personal use only. Any other reproduction or redistribution is strictly prohibited. All rights reserved.
This content is provided for test preparation purposes only and does not imply an endorsement by Mometrix of any particular political, scientific, or religious point of view.

Market Planning and Channel Management

Marketing Management

Marketing Aspects and Strategy

Niche marketing is a subset of a market sector that deals with marketing towards a specific group of highly interested people due to limited resources. A niche market is an area that has not been filled by a large company because it is not profitable enough for a large company and no other small company has filled the need. Better said, niche marketing is finding an area where there is demand but no supply. In business, it is often more important to be the first business, not the best. An example of niche marketing would be the creation of NetFlix.

There are four main aspects to marketing:

1. **Promotion** -- This is anything that you do to make customers aware of your product or company. There are several different ways to promote your product; the best one for your company will depend on several different factors.
2. **Product management** -- This is a very difficult term to define because there are several different methods of management. Generally product management consists of market research, product definition and design, and managing the product as it goes through its life cycle
3. **Distribution** -- The distributor is usually the middleperson between the manufacturer and a retailer.
4. **Pricing** -- One of your most important questions to answer in marketing is, "How much can I charge for my product?" Pricing is the process of applying prices to your products based on several different factors.

Marketing strategy is a companies plan to achieve its objectives. It is the blueprint for how a business will use their finite resources to obtain their goals. Marketing strategy is an integral part of a marketing plan. If your company's strategy were to provide the highest quality product on the market, your plan would contain specific goals and dates related to the strategy. The goal of an effective marketing strategy is to integrate all of a company's abilities, resources, and tactics into a whole. Once this is completed, this strategy will become the foundation for the marketing plan. You can have a marketing strategy without a plan, but you can't have a plan without a strategy. The best marketing strategies often come from being able to think like a customer.

Market

A market is a field where sellers compete within a framework of rules to provide a certain product to buyers. The word market has evolved with the market concept. Originally, it was a place where buyers and sellers met to barter over goods. As technology evolved, the market did as well. Now it simply refers to groups of buyers and sellers due to the fact that supply and consumption have separated. There are different types of markets. Some include: consumer, business, global, and government or non-profits. Each market has its own legal framework and niches. Differences in markets usually involve how the product is sold and who is selling it. A company serves a different market when its sells its products to businesses, directly to consumers, overseas, etc. Companies must navigate the differences between each market in order to have a successful product.

Copyright © Mometrix Media. You have been licensed one copy of this document for personal use only. Any other reproduction or redistribution is strictly prohibited. All rights reserved.
This content is provided for test preparation purposes only and does not imply an endorsement by Mometrix of any particular political, scientific, or religious point of view.

Economic Systems

Capitalism is an economic system where the means of production are privately owned and run with the objective of turning a profit. In this type of economy, goods, services, and prices are determined largely in a free market; that is containing minimal government intervention. A capitalist economy differs from a communist or socialist economy because the majority of businesses are owned and run by its citizens. In a communist or socialist economy, business is owned and/or regulated by the government. As a result, the government instead of private citizens sustains profits and losses. This often results in less motivation to innovate and work hard. Note that while most developed nations have capitalist economies, there is no such this as a pure capitalist economy. While it may be minimal, the government is involved in the economy just by existing.

Communism is an economic system used by only a few countries in the world that strives to create equality by giving total control over means of production to the government. They control almost every aspect of the economy, and as a result control the will of their people. Since business is owned and/or regulated by the government they also sustain profits and losses. As a result, there is less motivation to innovate and for people to work hard. This factor is often what is blamed for the fall of the Soviet Union. Communism exists in only a handful of countries today. Cuba, North Korea, and China are the most well-known communist countries. China is somewhat of an exception because while its government is communist, there are several "special economic zones" that are free from government regulation. As a result, their economy has quickly grown to be large enough to challenge the United States for economic supremacy.

A socialist economy is a mixture of communist and capitalist economic systems. While many citizens may own their own business, they may face strict regulation from a government or worker's union. The level of socialism varies according to the culture of the area. In some places, government may protect infant industries; others may offer generous healthcare or welfare benefits to citizens. This system is commonplace in Europe, largely because people expect the government to provide benefits to its citizens. For example, there is a tradition of generous welfare and unemployment benefits. It is much more acceptable in Europe to receive services from the government than it is in the United States. Due to the high levels of government intervention and emphasis on workers instead of profits, socialist economies tend to not be as profitable as capitalist economies, but more profitable than communist economies.

GDP and GNP

Gross Domestic Product (GDP) is one of the most popular ways to measure the size of a country's economy. GDP is the market value of all the goods and services produced within a country's borders during a set period (usually one year). This statistic is very useful because it enables someone to compare the value of all production between two countries. GDP differs from GNP in the fact that GNP measures all economic activity of a country. An example would be that the profits of a Honda factory in the United States would count towards Japan's GNP. As a result, the GNP of a country will be higher than its GDP. The easiest way to find a country's GDP is the formula:

$$\text{GDP} = \text{Consumption} + \text{investment} + \text{government spending} + (\text{exports-imports})$$

Business Types

A sole proprietorship means that one person runs and owns the business. Better said, the owner is the business. Eighty-five percent of businesses in the United States are sole proprietorships. While they are risky, there are many reasons why this type of business is the most popular. With a sole proprietor, there is no need to come to a consensus. As a result, things tend to run more smoothly

Copyright © Mometrix Media. You have been licensed one copy of this document for personal use only. Any other reproduction or redistribution is strictly prohibited. All rights reserved.
This content is provided for test preparation purposes only and does not imply an endorsement by Mometrix of any particular political, scientific, or religious point of view.

when there is one owner. The business can start and stop whenever the owner chooses. The owner carries the risks, but also obtains the reward.

Sole proprietorships do have their limitations. They tend to die with the owner, due to the fact that there is no one to take the owner's place. In addition, all the assets of the company are in the owner's name. Companies that worked with the owner often take their business elsewhere. The only way a proprietorship outlives its owner is if it becomes a partnership, involving other members of the family.

A partnership is a relationship between two or more people with the purpose of owning and operating a business. It is run similar to a sole proprietorship with the difference being that decisions about the way the business is run are shared. The benefit to a partnership is that the risks and burdens of operating a business are lessened with each partner. However, when the business turns a profit, the reward is lessened as well.

There are three types of partnerships: **general, limited liability, and limited**:

- In a **general partnership**, two or more people enter into an agreement (contract) and are personally liable for all debts and liabilities of the business.
- In a **limited liability partnership**, all participants give up some control of their company in the form of stocks in order to limit their liability except for the negligence of their partner(s) and people supervised by their partner(s).
- **Limited partnership** participants agree to give up all control (in form of stocks) to manage their business in exchange for limited liability of the companies' debts.

A corporation is a legal entity that exists separate from its owners. Shareholders own it, which may be people or legal entities. As a result, it has several unique powers different from a partnership or sole proprietorship. For example, one could sue the owner of a proprietorship, but couldn't sue the owners of a corporation. They own many of the rights that human beings have such as the right to sue, own property, and pay taxes; however, they also have other privileges not afforded to individuals. Examples include: Treaty rights, tax exemptions, and the right to stockpile certain products.

A corporation exists as a stockholder or non-stockholder corporation. Whether it sells stock or not usually determines whether the business is run for a profit or not. In either case, a board of directors usually exists to make decisions on behalf of its members.

A limited-liability company is a form of partnership that offers limited liability to its owners. An LLC is very similar to a corporation in the way that it is run and in the flexibility it offers to its owners. All members have an equal stake in the company that creates a partnership structure similar to a board of directors that run a corporation. The advantages to a LLC are that owners don't lose their power to a board of directors. There is less paperwork and record keeping. The business will carry on despite the death or incapacitation of one of its owners. Economic and tax benefits are plentiful, and members are protected from the debts and actions of the LLC. The disadvantages of an LLC are that a franchise fee is levied in many states. The income that members receive is taxed as income tax and not as other taxes. Sometimes it can be more difficult to raise capital when members have different goals about company growth.

Entrepreneurship is the process of starting a new business. Someone who does this is known as an entrepreneur. Their presence is one of the most important factors in a capitalist economy as the majority of businesses are sole proprietorships where the owner is the business. Entrepreneurship

Copyright © Mometrix Media. You have been licensed one copy of this document for personal use only. Any other reproduction or redistribution is strictly prohibited. All rights reserved.
This content is provided for test preparation purposes only and does not imply an endorsement by Mometrix of any particular political, scientific, or religious point of view.

is a very risky field. Its activities and level of risk differ depending on the scale of the project and the market being entered. The majority of start-up businesses fail within the first few years. Since this is a very risky field, the people that tend to be most successful possess certain characteristics. They tend to be dynamic individuals that have a vision, are enthusiastic, and charismatic. The most successful people in the United States are entrepreneurs whose vision changed the way that we live our lives. Examples include: Bill Gates, Henry Ford, and Mark Cuban.

Marketing Research

Test marketing is used to see how a product will be perceived when it is released on a larger scale. To do this, the product is first tested on a smaller market to determine if people will like it. Mystery shopping is when an employee or paid representative anonymously shops at a store and later records their experience for later analysis. This tool is used to find many things about a store. The mystery shopper may be observing employee behavior or purchasing their or their competitor's products among other things. Concept testing is where a concept is presented to an audience to see how it is perceived. This is an important part of research and development because it helps businesses decide to invest more money into the product.

Market Competition

Market positioning -- This term refers to how the consumer perceives a product in relation to a specific market segment. A company seeks to change its market position by creating advertisements that make their products compete head-to-head with their competitors. It will explain what makes their product unique or better than the other product.

Competitive analysis serves to answer the question, "how well is a business doing compared to its competition?" It measures many factors besides sales. Product, price, quality, customer satisfaction, service, and delivery are just some of the things that are measured in a competitive analysis.

Business Cycle

The business cycle is the name used to describe the fluctuations that are associated with local, national, and world economies. The economy goes through periods of growth, known as recovery and prosperity. Growth periods are followed by times of decline or low activity known as recessions. It is not a cycle in the fact that its phases occur at regular times; rather it can be brought on by many unpredictable patterns. Non-business factors such as war, weather, or politics can influence the ups and downs of the business cycle. What economists do agree on is that the business cycle goes through four phases:

1. **Contraction** (When the economy slows down, if it slows enough it is known as a recession)
2. **Trough** (A low point in the business cycle when a contraction begins to become an expansion.)
3. **Expansion** (Growth in the pace of economic activity)
4. **Peak** (The highest point of the business cycle)

Four P's of Marketing

Product, price, promotion, and place are the four elements of marketing. These factors make up the **marketing mix**, or all the actions that go into selling a product. People do studies of consumers to find out what they want and need. Once this is established, companies take steps to create a **product**. Using the information provided by market researchers, businesses customize their products to meet the demands of their consumers. The **price** of the product is determined by the business. This is a very tricky job because the price has to be set at just the right level to satisfy many different demands. The price must be high enough to turn a profit, but low enough for a

Copyright © Mometrix Media. You have been licensed one copy of this document for personal use only. Any other reproduction or redistribution is strictly prohibited. All rights reserved.
This content is provided for test preparation purposes only and does not imply an endorsement by Mometrix of any particular political, scientific, or religious point of view.

customer to want to purchase it. **Promotion** is every action that a business takes to let customers know about their product, where to buy it, and why they should buy it. A successful promotion will make customers excited to purchase a product. **Place** refers to the location that the product is sold. Businesses want to sell their goods in the easiest way possible for their customers. Place can also refer to where a product is sold at the store. Several studies have been conducted that prove that where an item is located can have a direct influence on its sales.

International Marketing

International marketing can provide many benefits that are not available in national markets. However, it also comes with a whole new set of problems that are unique to its market. There are three main challenges associated with working in foreign markets.

- Communication is the first barrier. Americans take for granted that everybody should speak English, but the need to know other languages is greater than it has ever been. There are several amusing stories of American companies whose English slogans translated into something completely different in another language.
- A country's traditions and customs can be a problem with your business. Budweiser and Absolut do not sell well in places like the Middle East where alcohol is forbidden. It is also important to know the business customs of the area that you are doing business in. For instance, bribes are taboo in some cultures, but are embraced in others.
- Other cultures can also have different buying habits that should influence a businesses decision to enter a foreign market. Sometimes there are items in certain products that foreigners look for that Americans don't. It is important to understand these differences.understand these differences.

Causes of Price Changes

There are three main factors that create price fluctuation: changes in supply, changes in demand, and change by an outside force controlling a market. A change in supply usually happens due to weather phenomena, production costs, or increased efficiency. Floods, droughts, and heat waves are some of the things that can create a change in the supply of items. Price can be affected when an item is in such demand that the manufacturer cannot keep up with the supply. Shortages or an abundance of a product will cause the price of it to rise or fall accordingly. Sometimes a price will change because a force outside the market influenced it. For instance, when lawmakers decided that it is harmful for people to smoke, they levied large taxes on the purchase of cigarettes. As a result, many people could not afford to smoke the brand of cigarettes that they preferred.

Business Types

The easiest way to classify businesses is by the products that they make. Producers take raw goods from the earth and export them without any processing. Examples are fishermen, miners, and forestry businesses. Processors take the raw goods from the producers and turn them into a useful product. Note that sometimes their products may require further processing before it reaches the consumer. Manufacturers take raw or processed goods and turn it into a final product. Intermediaries move products from one business to another. Service businesses provide services instead of goods. These are intangible goods, something that you can't hold. Getting a massage, going to see a movie, and having your house cleaned are examples of intangible goods.

Monopoly

A monopoly is a business that controls all of a market with its product. As a result, they can charge whatever price they want for a good or service because the consumer has no other choice to meet their need. Most monopolies are illegal in the United States due to the fact that price setting is

Copyright © Mometrix Media. You have been licensed one copy of this document for personal use only. Any other reproduction or redistribution is strictly prohibited. All rights reserved.
This content is provided for test preparation purposes only and does not imply an endorsement by Mometrix of any particular political, scientific, or religious point of view.

counter-productive to a capitalist economy. Some monopolies do exist, however only in markets in which competition would make the market hurt consumers. For example, a city may allow only one company to sell electricity because high infrastructure costs make competition difficult and drive prices up. In exchange, the company agrees to be regulated and to charge a fair price for its services.

Purposes of Business

Businesses are the lifeblood of the United States economy. 85 percent of businesses are small companies owned by one to three people. Everything that they do in order to produce their goods and services and provide them to consumers can be defined as business. Business involves many different functions such as organizing, managing, producing, marketing, and advertising. Businesses need resources to provide their goods and services. The most successful businesses use their finite resources in innovative ways. By coming up with new and efficient ways to develop their business, they grow and evolve with the American economy.

Economic Resources

The economic resources that a country possesses is one of the most important factors that determines their economic health. If a country has an abundant supply of a scarce resource (like oil) they can use it to influence the political and economic behaviors of another country. For example, Japan imports almost 100 percent of its energy due to lack of resources. As a result, they are at the mercy of market fluctuations and the demands of energy-rich countries. Abundant economic resources are not always a benefit. Relying on one resource can keep an area from diversifying its economy. The Middle East is the best example. These countries rely so much on their oil wealth that the rest of their businesses make up 1-2% of its GDP. As a result, when the oil wells dry up, they will be left without any other businesses to rely on and their economies will crash.

Factors of Production

When economic resources are used by companies to become goods or services, they become factors of production. There are four major factors of production. They are: capital resources, entrepreneurial resources, human resources, and natural resources.

- Capital resources are items that are necessary to run a business that are not natural resources. They include: buildings, supplies, tools, machines, and equipment.
- Entrepreneurial resources are the initiatives to use natural, human, and capital resources to the best of their ability.
- Human resources are the people that contribute physical and mental resources to a business.
- Natural resources are things that come from the earth that are converted into goods and services.

Circular Flow

The circular flow of economic activity refers to the constant exchange of money between businesses and the public. Some of the ways that businesses send funds to people in the form of wages, rents, interest, and dividends. The people send money back to businesses in the form of purchases, mortgages, payments, loans, etc. This is a simple version of the economic activity model. Economic activity is much more complicated when you add the influence of government. They change the flow of economic activity by requiring people and businesses to pay money in the form of taxes. Government also distributes money in the form of business contracts, welfare, social security, etc.

Copyright © Mometrix Media. You have been licensed one copy of this document for personal use only. Any other reproduction or redistribution is strictly prohibited. All rights reserved.
This content is provided for test preparation purposes only and does not imply an endorsement by Mometrix of any particular political, scientific, or religious point of view.

Economic Indicators

Economists may use several different statistics to understand the strength of the economy. The information they use may differ according to what exactly they are looking for. The United States Department of Commerce releases statistics for almost 250 different economic indicators. The 3 most widely used are Gross Domestic Product, inflation, and unemployment. GDP measures the value of all goods and services produced by a country in a year. Inflation is the extended rise in the prices for goods and services. This is a useful statistic because you can measure the rise of prices compared to the rise of people's wages to see how the change is affecting people's incomes. The other statistic that most economists use is the unemployment rate. If large numbers of people are unemployed, then chances are that the economy is not going well.

How Government Influences Economy

The government influences the economy two ways: its monetary policy and fiscal policy. Monetary policy refers to how the government manipulates the economy by controlling the amount of money in circulation, how much credit is available for people, and the amount of business in the economy. Fiscal policy is how the government uses its revenue to influence the economy through military spending, taxation, and government spending. In times of recession, it is not uncommon for the government to stimulate the economy by creating jobs. They pay for these jobs with the revenue from tax dollars and other sources. Some level of local, state, or federal government employs almost half of the United States workers, so people have come to rely on the government to to stimulate the economy.

Franchising

Franchises are the most recognizable businesses in the world. One can start a franchise by obtaining a right to sell or operate a parent company's product or service in a given area. The benefits of a franchise is that most of the hard work is done for you. The products, materials, and business planning have been developed ahead of time. All the franchisee needs to do is hire employees and open the doors. Franchisees are required to run their operation in a certain way that is uniform with other franchises. The benefits to owning a franchise is that it is usually already a recognizable, profitable name. This makes it easier to get started. The disadvantages are that most franchises require a large licensing fee to be paid up front along with an annual fee. The franchise may also severely restrict the freedom that the owner has to run their business.

Credit

Companies need credit for a number of reasons, mostly the same reasons that individual consumers do. Companies make money by offering credit to their clients. Stores that allow payment by installment plans or credit cards make it easier for consumers to buy expensive products. If they supply their own credit then they can make money from the interest as well. Businesses need credit to give them the financial ability to grow without sacrificing capital. They can use credit to do a variety of things such as buy more machinery, pay salaries, or purchase property. Credit allows them to do this without siphoning money from other parts of the business.

Seeking Capital

When starting a new business, all the ways money can be raised fall into two categories: **debt capital and equity capital**. Debt capital is borrowing money that must be repaid in the future. This is a risky but often necessary part of doing business. Equity capital refers to money raised by selling equity (ownership) of the company or raising the money from within the company. Most businesses use a mixture of both to minimize financial risk.

Copyright © Mometrix Media. You have been licensed one copy of this document for personal use only. Any other reproduction or redistribution is strictly prohibited. All rights reserved.
This content is provided for test preparation purposes only and does not imply an endorsement by Mometrix of any particular political, scientific, or religious point of view.

Market Segmentation

Certain groups of people are so attractive to businesses that companies will create unique advertising, promotions, and sales to cater to these specific groups. For instance, to attract women and people that were no longer able to smoke indoors, Skoal created a unique brand of fruit-flavored smokeless tobaccos. This division of the market is called **segmentation**. There are an almost unlimited number of markets that a company can choose to enter. The segment they choose is called their **target market**. The third step in segmentation is to determine its market **position**. They design the competitive positioning for their product and a detailed marketing mix. Companies can no longer market a one-size-fits-all product because they lose their influence after a short period. Even companies like Coke and Pepsi that grew large with one product release new variations of their flavors every year.

Concepts of Marketing

There are five concepts that businesses use to carry out their marketing activities: the production, product, selling, marketing, and societal concepts. The **production concept** is the theory that consumers value affordability and availability over anything else. **Product concept** is the theory that consumers value quality, performance, and general improvement from their products above anything else. **Selling concept** believes that consumers will not buy a product unless they are bombarded by advertising and sales promotions. The **marketing concept** attempts to create a profit by targeting distinct markets and being better than their competitors. Not all companies value profit above people or quality. **Societal marketing** is the concept that businesses products and services can benefit the world in a positive way and turn a profit without sacrificing their ethics.

New Market Thinking

The way that businesses market to their consumers has rapidly evolved as consumers are exposed to more information about product choices. Old ways of marketing consisted of little more than advertising and selling. Now companies need to connect with customers on deeper levels. Marketing is much more customer based than it used to be. Companies are not just selling a product; they are selling an experience. Companies must gear their products to ensure customer loyalty for the present and the future. They must market locally and globally. They must know which companies to work with and which to work against.

Strategic Planning

Strategic planning consists of a company's long-term goals and its path to achieving them. There are four steps to this plan: Defining a mission statement, supporting goals and objectives, designing a business portfolio, and developing detailed marketing plans. The mission statement is a short message to consumers as to what this company stands for, its goals, and how it will go about obtaining them in relation to the market. The supporting goals and objectives guide the company. A business portfolio helps companies decide how to best allocate their limited resources. Finally, detailed marketing plans are developed to work in line with the company objectives.

Marketplace Environments

The marketing environment can be divided into two categories: macroenvironments and microenvironments. Macroenvironments are outside forces that influence markets that people or businesses have little or no control over. They can be political, cultural, natural, economic, or many other forces that may affect a market. Microenvironments are any internal factors that impede a companies ability to get their goods or services to their customers in the most efficient way. Things such as suppliers, competitors, prices, and markets are some of these things. A company is much

Copyright © Mometrix Media. You have been licensed one copy of this document for personal use only. Any other reproduction or redistribution is strictly prohibited. All rights reserved.
This content is provided for test preparation purposes only and does not imply an endorsement by Mometrix of any particular political, scientific, or religious point of view.

more likely to control or respond quickly to change in its microenvironment. For instance, a company can change suppliers if there is a problem, but they cannot change the weather.

Customer Markets

When deciding how to market their products, companies need to decide which of the five types of markets to compete in. They are: **customer markets**, **business markets**, **reseller markets**, **government markets**, and **international markets**. Each market has different and unique characteristics that companies need to understand before they enter. Customer markets consist of the individuals and households that purchase products for personal use. Business markets purchase goods and services for the use of their company to process or use for their business. Reseller markets are for companies that buy goods and services for resale. Government markets are agencies that buy goods and services for distribution to citizens or use for producing pubic services. International markets are buyers that come from other countries including governments, buyers, resellers, and producers.

Information Systems

With all the information that businesses accumulate about consumers and markets, an information management system is needed. A marketing information system (MIS) is the process that a company uses to take all incoming data from marketing research, determine what is relevant, distribute the findings to marketing decision makers, and decide what to do with the results. The MIS revolves around people successfully interpreting data, therefore it is very important that a company have the right personnel capable of accomplishing that.

Types of Publics

One of the most worrisome parts of business is that there are so many outside factors affecting your company that you have little or no influence over. These factors are called publics. There are seven categories that they are divided into:

- **Citizen-action publics** are usually non-profit groups that advocate for a special interest. Examples include: environmental, minority, or labor groups.
- **General public groups** pertain to the public image of the company. How people view the actions, products, and behaviors of a company can directly influence its sales
- **Government publics** are groups that influence governmental policy. They may be advocacy groups that make sure that a business behaves in an ethical way.
- **Financial publics** are the companies that lend money, set interest rates, own stock, and hold sway over how a company gets money.
- **Internal publics** are the people inside the company. By motivating them and keeping them happy, they project a positive image of the company that spreads to the public.
- **Media publics** are groups that report and provide opinions about a company and its practices. Blogs, newspapers, magazines, and television are examples.
- **Local publics** are local or grassroots organizations that have interests in a company.

Risk Management

Risk management is the process of assessing and minimizing risks in the business process. Risk management focuses on factors that can hurt a business such as fires, theft, lawsuits, and deaths. It also focuses on the financial risks that can hurt a company. These risks are things such as identity theft, intellectual property theft, and other damages that can be caused using financial instruments. Risk management also calculates opportunity costs to give companies get a better idea of where to best allocate their resources.

Copyright © Mometrix Media. You have been licensed one copy of this document for personal use only. Any other reproduction or redistribution is strictly prohibited. All rights reserved.
This content is provided for test preparation purposes only and does not imply an endorsement by Mometrix of any particular political, scientific, or religious point of view.

Making a Sale

There are seven steps that salespeople use to increase their odds of making a sale. Each step is in response to the five steps that a buyer goes through when deciding whether to make a purchase. The **approach** is where the salesperson is essentially "selling themselves." They communicate and establish rapport with the customer. The way a salesperson presents themselves greatly affects how a customer perceives a product and whether to make a purchase. **Qualification** is the second step and involves working to maintain the rapport established with the customer and the conversation shifts to more sales specific topics. This is where the seller is obtaining as much information about the buyer as possible to help them make a sale.

Buying

The people that make the purchases for business are divided into five categories: users, influencers, buyers, deciders, and gatekeepers. Users are the people that will use the things that the buyers bought. Influencers define specific things and give input as to what purchases should be made. Buyers are the employees that have the authority to pick suppliers and negotiate prices. Deciders make the final purchase. In smaller businesses, the deciders are often buyers as well. Gatekeepers are the ones that communicate information to other employees.

Purchases by a business are much more complex than decisions made by a consumer. A business cannot just pick an item off a shelf. It must factor many different things before buying goods and services.

- The process begins with the recognition of a need or a problem.
- Once the need or problem is acknowledged, the buyer creates a general need description that explains the number and characteristics of what is needed.
- The buyer then decides the specific things they are looking for in order to find the best value.
- Then they go on a supplier search to find the best prices from various places.
- After the supplier search, the buyer will submit bids from suppliers called the proposal solicitation stage.
- After the bids have been submitted, the buyer will compare and contrast each bid to find the best fit. Companies usually compare price, reputation, and delivery among other things.
- Once a supplier has been chosen, the buyer will prepare an order-routine specification. This will include the final order and include things such as quantity, product specifications, and availability. After they have received the product or service, the buyer usually gives a performance review to the supplier and determines if the two will do business again in the future.

Target Marketing Steps

When a business is deciding where to sell their products, they need to decide what markets their product or service will be appealing to. This process is called target marketing. It is a three-step process. The steps of target marketing are*:* **market segmentation**, **targeting marketing**, and **marketing positioning**. Market segmentation means to divide the market according to distinct groups. Each group usually requires a unique marketing mix of promotions, advertisements, and products. The most profitable markets that a company enters are called their target markets. Marketing positioning is creating and finalizing a marketing plan and competitive positioning.

Segmentation

There is no one way to segment a market. A marketer has to try several different variables before they find a marketing mix that is successful for their company. The different variables that are used

Copyright © Mometrix Media. You have been licensed one copy of this document for personal use only. Any other reproduction or redistribution is strictly prohibited. All rights reserved.
This content is provided for test preparation purposes only and does not imply an endorsement by Mometrix of any particular political, scientific, or religious point of view.

in segmenting markets can be divided into four categories: **behavioral**, **demographic**, **geographic**, and **psychographic**.

- **Behavioral segmentation** separates buyers into groups based on certain variables related to a product. Behavioral segments can be divided even further into occasion segmentation (tracking when buyers make specific purchases) and benefit segmentation is grouping people by the specific benefits that they look for in a product. For instance, people with less income may be looking for value while higher-income buyers may be looking for quality.
- **Demographic segmentation** is the most popular form of segmentation because it divides markets by variables such as age, income, sex, education, religion, race, occupation, and several other factors. Customer needs are often based on these factors. For instance, if you sell lipstick, your company won't do very well in the male segment.
- **Geographic segmentation** divides markets up by their location. For instance, McDonald's restaurants in the South may sell items such as grits and biscuits with gravy that are not available in other parts of the country.
- **Psychographic segmentation** identifies buyers by factors such as wealth, lifestyle, and social standing.

In evaluating different market segments, companies take three steps.

1. First, they analyze the segment size and growth. This helps them identify markets that would be profitable for them to enter.
2. The second step is to segment structural alternatives. This means that they need to weigh in several things such as the strength of its competitors, the purchasing power of buyers, and the strength of alternatives to their products. If one of these factors is significant, they may choose not to enter that segment.
3. Finally, companies factor in their objectives and resources available to them. The best market may not be the most profitable to them. For instance, if a company is small it might not be the best idea to enter a certain segment where a larger company dominates the competition.

Consumer Product Types

Products are the tangible or intangible things that a company produces that can be offered in a market. They can be broken down into two categories: **consumer and industrial products**.

- **Consumer products** are products and services consumers purchase that will not be used again.
- **Convenience** products are products like fast food or newspapers that require a minimum of effort and product comparison.
- **Shopping** products are purchased less frequently than convenience products. Consumers often compare similar products when shopping for things such as used cars, furniture, and clothing.
- **Specialty** products are products and services that have unique characteristics that a person does not purchase regularly.
- **Unsought** products are things that a consumer usually doesn't purchase because they don't think about them. Life insurance and cemetery plots are examples of unsought purchases.
- **Industrial products** are products and services purchased by companies for further processing or to use in their business. The three types of industrial products are materials and parts, supplies and services, and capital items.

Copyright © Mometrix Media. You have been licensed one copy of this document for personal use only. Any other reproduction or redistribution is strictly prohibited. All rights reserved.
This content is provided for test preparation purposes only and does not imply an endorsement by Mometrix of any particular political, scientific, or religious point of view.

- **Capital items** are products that help companies run their day-to-day operations. They can be large purchases like buildings and land or small items like computers and furniture. Material and parts include raw materials, natural products, farm products, and components. Supplies and services are the operating items that make a business run like pencils, repairs, and advertising.

Social and Organizational Marketing

Organizational marketing is all the activities that a business makes to shape, change, or influence the way the public perceives an organization. This could be to influence sales, or to change an unfavorable image. **Societal marketing** is the promotion of social ideas in order to get the public to change their behavior in a manner that makes society better. They could be ads encouraging people to quit smoking, gambling, or drinking. They could try to get you to wear your seat belt or to recycle.

Decision-Making

Whom a marketer chooses to do business with is a very important decision because they usually have limited resources. They go through a five-step process when deciding how to market their products.

1. A company decides which **product attributes** they will promote of their product that will separate it from competitor's products in the same market.
2. The company then chooses a logo, motto, sign, and/or symbol to promote their product called **branding**. This is how people will identify the product.
3. **Packaging** is how a company decides the product will be presented to customers. This includes the package the product is sold in. Its purpose isn't just to carry the product; it's to help sell the product.
4. **Labeling** identifies the brand and includes any warnings or information that the consumer may need to know.
5. **Product support** services are the supports in place that help the customer after the product has been purchased.

Product Line

In an effort to appeal to all types of customers, companies create several products for a diverse marketplace. Reebok doesn't make just one shoe and McDonald's doesn't make just one type of hamburger. However, all their products are slightly different. This is referred to as a company's **product line**. The major product line decision companies face is how many different products they will make. Often a company will add products to its line to enter a more expensive, or less expensive market, or to sell to protect against economic swings.

Product Mix

A company's product mix are all the products and lines that a company sells. Product mixes are often limited to large companies or corporations due to the large costs associated with creating several products. A product mix has four levels: consistency, length, width, and depth. Consistency measures how similar certain factors are in a company's product mix. Length mix is how many products are in a company's product line. Some companies have a few products; others have several thousand. Width is the variety of different product lines a company carries and depth refers to the number of different versions of a product in a product line. For example, while Burger King sells fast food, it sells at least ten different types of hamburgers.

Copyright © Mometrix Media. You have been licensed one copy of this document for personal use only. Any other reproduction or redistribution is strictly prohibited. All rights reserved.
This content is provided for test preparation purposes only and does not imply an endorsement by Mometrix of any particular political, scientific, or religious point of view.

Brand Equity

A brand conjures up positive or negative feelings in a consumer. For example, many Americans boycott Wal-Mart without ever having been in one because it has received large amounts of negative media attention about how they treat their workers poorly and drive out small businesses. Fortunately for Wal-Mart, more people associate seeing the brand with saving money and low prices. What a company means in the eyes of its consumers is called brand equity. Basically, it is the positive effect that companies' receive from their reputation. A good way of measuring brand equity is to see how much more a consumer would pay to have a certain brand. Customers make this trade-off in return for the quality they believe comes from that product.

Markets for Services

The service industry is the largest sector of the American economy, accounting for almost 70 percent of total jobs. Service industries in the country are broken down into the following areas.

- **Government** services are the largest sector of the service industry. Almost half of the employees in the United States work for some branch of the government. These are the teachers, police officers, fire fighters, doctors, soldiers, postal workers, etc. While they don't produce anything, the country could not exist without them.
- **Non-profit** organizations offer services to the public for a minimal cost. These businesses often seek to create enough revenue to keep their business running. These are the churches, museums, hospitals, charities, etc.
- Business organizations offer services to their clients and their employees in the form of banks, insurance, flights, entertainment, real estate, etc.

Marketing strategies are unique for service industries as opposed to businesses that create products. Companies consider four factors when designing a marketing plan for their service.

- **Service intangibility** means that a consumer cannot see the results of the service before it is purchased. An example would be cosmetic surgery. This presents a unique challenge to the company in how they market their service. They may show before and after pictures of satisfied clients.
- **Service inseparability** means that the service can't be separated from its producer, usually because the producer is giving the service. An example is a message or pedicure.
- **Service variability** means that the service will vary depending on who is providing the service.
- **Service perishability** means that a service cannot be saved for later use or resale.

The way a service company markets its products differs greatly from a company that produces tangible goods. A good can sit on a shelf for as long as it needs to until it is sold. This is not true for a service. Since a service is provided, there is a large level of interaction between a service firm and its clients. Internal marketing trains and motivates employees to take pride in teamwork and outstanding customer satisfaction. External marketing is how a company promotes its service to the public. Interactive marketing puts a large emphasis on the quality of the interaction between the consumer and producer in a service encounter.

Copyright © Mometrix Media. You have been licensed one copy of this document for personal use only. Any other reproduction or redistribution is strictly prohibited. All rights reserved.
This content is provided for test preparation purposes only and does not imply an endorsement by Mometrix of any particular political, scientific, or religious point of view.

Concept Testing and Development

Once a company has a good idea for a product or service, they develop it into a concept. This is a much more detailed version of the idea that may include colors, prices, and specific sizes and shapes.

- The company develops the concept further until it is ready for testing. The product or service is sampled by a small group of consumers who give their feedback on the product. From their feedback, the concept is further edited and evaluated to decide if this is a product that could be profitable.
- Once a company decides on a concept to develop, they need to figure out a way to market it. Companies create a marketing strategy development that consists of three parts. First, they identify their target market. Next, they figure out all the logistics of the product or service. Price, distribution, and marketing strategy are some of the things that are decided on. The last part of development consists of profit goals, long-run sales, and their marketing mix strategy.
- After the product has been developed, they then conduct an in-depth business analysis, which reviews the sales, costs, and profit projection.

Price Changes

Price changes are unavoidable in business. When one company in a market changes its price, it affects every one of its competitors. Companies raise and lower prices for many reasons. Price cuts may occur to compensate for loss in market share, to boost struggling sales, or to dominate a market. They may increase costs to compensate for inflation or the costs of their own business. Prices may be raised due to an increase in demand. Companies raise prices in subtle ways. They could take away discounts or promotions or gradually raise the price a small amount over an extended period of time.

Channel Levels

A product often changes hands several times before it reaches its final buyer. Each person or business it goes through is referred to as a channel. **Channel levels** are the names for levels of intermediaries that get products to the consumer. The numbers of channels used are referred to as the length of a channel. Some companies such as Tupperware save costs by selling a product directly to a consumer. This is a company's **direct marketing channel**. **Indirect marketing channels** contain one or more intermediaries.

Following are various methods of getting products to consumers:

- A **conventional distribution channel** is the traditional method for getting products to consumers. A different company with their own goals and business models owns each channel.
- This is different from a **vertical marketing channel** that is a structure where producers, retailers, and wholesalers cooperate because one channel member owns the other members or controls their means of production.
    - A **corporate VMS** combines successive stages of production by owning all of them.
    - A **contractual VMS** is the type of structure commonly known as a franchise. Contractual agreements are made between each channel enabling everybody involved to reach more customers than they would independently.
    - An **administered VMS** occurs when one of the channel members has significant influence over the others and uses it to influence the other members to cooperate.

Copyright © Mometrix Media. You have been licensed one copy of this document for personal use only. Any other reproduction or redistribution is strictly prohibited. All rights reserved.
This content is provided for test preparation purposes only and does not imply an endorsement by Mometrix of any particular political, scientific, or religious point of view.

- A **horizontal marketing channel** is when two marketing channels decide to collaborate on a marketing campaign to increase their profits. These partnerships have become much more commonplace in the global market as companies partner up to increase worldwide appeal.
- A **multichannel distribution system** is a method of distributing goods in which a single firm organizes many different marketing channels to reach customer segments. Today, consumers can reach companies by phone, e-mail, mail, or by text message.
- **Disintermediation** is a developing marketing system in which companies bypass intermediaries completely and sell directly to the final consumer. This is proving to be an efficient way to reduce costs to the consumer.

Logistics System

The goal of a logistic system is to reach a target level of customer satisfaction at the most affordable price. The functions of the logistics system are to manage inventory, manage information, transport materials, and store materials. Inventory management affects customer satisfaction because it is very important that a company's products are on the shelf. If they are not there, a customer could decide to purchase an alternative product. Managing information is vital to the logistics system. This has become much easier in the last decade. Many companies now use computer programs to constantly update inventory. They use the Internet to order more products automatically. The ability to get products to stores quickly affects the price and customer satisfaction of a product.

How Marketing Channels Behave

Even though different channels have different goals and objectives, generally they work together for a common good. The retailer needs the producer for new quality products. The producer needs the retailer to generate sales and buzz about the product. Both need the distributor to get the products from one place to another. Everybody's success in the channel market system generally depends on the work of each individual channel member. Sometimes disagreements occur, called channel conflict. This is when channel members disagree over roles and objectives. This is problematic because there is usually no mediator to resolve conflicts and it affects the other businesses involved in the channels as well.

Retail Stores

There are several different types of retail stores.

- **Department stores** carry several different product lines.
- **Supermarkets** are designed to sell food and household products to consumers.
- **Superstores** are large stores that are aimed at meeting consumers' total needs. They will contain food, household items, electronics, and furniture.
- **Discount stores** carry basic merchandise at a lower price.
- **Specialty stores** have a narrow product line but have a large assortment. GAP and Barnes & Noble are examples.
- **Convenience stores** are small stores that are generally open all night and are located near neighborhoods.

Retail Organizations

In order to reach more people, some retail stores collaborate in order to lower prices or to increase market share. **Corporate chain** stores are multiple stores that are owned and operated by one person or group. This allows them to buy large quantities of goods and sell them at a discount. **Voluntary chains** are wholesale groups that buy in bulk and common merchandising. Retailer

Copyright © Mometrix Media. You have been licensed one copy of this document for personal use only. Any other reproduction or redistribution is strictly prohibited. All rights reserved.
This content is provided for test preparation purposes only and does not imply an endorsement by Mometrix of any particular political, scientific, or religious point of view.

cooperatives are groups of independent retailers that set up joint promotion offers and set up a central buying organization. **Franchises** are contractual associations between a parent company and independent business owner who pay for the right to own and sell products or services of the parent company. Franchises make up over 30% of retail stores. **Merchandising conglomerates** are corporations that unite several different types of retail stores under one ownership.

Retailers have several decisions to make about how to best allocate their resources. Before a store is opened, the retailer needs to find a great location that will be accessible to consumers. Retailers must define their target markets and how they will present themselves to these markets. They need to decide what products will be put on the shelves and how much inventory to have. They need to decide what services they will provide to consumers. Prices need to be set. They need to decide how they will promote their store and products and what methods they will use to do it.

Wholesaling

Wholesalers are the activities related to selling goods and services to people who buy them for use in their own business or resale. A wholesaler is someone who sells products and services to other people of businesses. Retailers use wholesalers because they add value to marketing channels. They perform several activities that reduce costs to retailers. Wholesalers keep inventories, break up bulk purchases into smaller groups, distribute, sell, and promote goods, select items for retailers to sell, and offer financing to retailers.

Direct Marketing

Direct marketing is type of selling that features direct communications with a target individual to get an immediate response. Companies customize their sales approach to fit the needs of individuals to build a stronger, more personal relationship with its customers. Buyers like direct marketing because it's personal, fast, and private. For example, a consumer can browse a company's website at their convenience and but at any time they would like. There is no pressure from a salesperson. The business saves money on employees and spaces. Some companies like Dell and Amazon do all their business using direct marketing. There are several different forms of direct marketing.

- **Direct-mail marketing** uses the mail to send letters, advertisements, and offers to prospective customers.
- **Telephone marketing** has become the most used form of direct marketing. It uses the telephone to contact consumers or for them to contact businesses.
- **Online marketing** uses the Internet to sell to customers.
- **Catalog marketing** uses print or electronic catalogs to sell to customers.
- **Kiosk marketing** is the use of small information booths located in malls, airports, and other places where crowds gather.
- Salespeople who sell directly to customers use **face-to-face marketing**.

Integrated Direct Marketing

Integrated direct marketing uses several diverse advertising methods to improve response rates and profits. By coordinating all the different forms a company uses to market, they can increase efficiency and decrease repetition. For example, a direct-mail piece can be more effective if it is linked to a web site and a toll-free number. This gives prospective customers more opportunities to purchase products because not every person has access to Internet or phone.

Copyright © Mometrix Media. You have been licensed one copy of this document for personal use only. Any other reproduction or redistribution is strictly prohibited. All rights reserved.
This content is provided for test preparation purposes only and does not imply an endorsement by Mometrix of any particular political, scientific, or religious point of view.

Direct Marketing Ethics

While direct marketing offers customers and businesses many conveniences and benefits, there are many potential avenues for abuse. Every American knows the inconvenience of late night or dinnertime phone calls from telemarketers or the loud, annoying direct response commercials on TV. These issues are small compared to new direct marketing issues. With advanced technology, companies can find and track all of a person's personal information without them even knowing. Besides an invasion of privacy, this can leave people vulnerable to credit card fraud or identity theft. How much information businesses should be able to keep about people will be debated for years to come.

Competitive Marketing Strategies

For a company to win in specific markets, they need to use their **competitive advantages** over their competitors. This is a value or benefit that they can offer that their competitors cannot. They need to build and manage customer relationships. They also choose their **competitor analysis**, which is the process where they identify their competitors and assess their strengths, weaknesses, objectives, market share, and business patterns. With this information, they form their **competitive marketing strategy** and decide which companies to attack, which to avoid, and where they want to be in the marketplace.

Interacting with Competitors

In a crowded marketplace a company needs to know everything it can about its competitors. They need to know information about their rivals products, prices, sales, growth, and promotions. Analyzing competitors is a three-step process in which a company first identifies who their competitors are: assesses their strengths, weaknesses, reaction patterns, and objectives, and then chooses which competitors to attack and which to avoid. Companies choose to look at rivals from either an industry or a **market point of view**. An example is that McDonald's sees its rivals from an industry P.O.V. as other fast food companies. It sees rivals from a market P.O.V. as all restaurants, eating at home, supermarkets, or any way that people eat.

Marketing Strategy Approaches

With so many different companies in the same markets with very similar products, it is not uncommon for companies to have the same business strategy. This is referred to a **strategic group**. When a company is competing against other companies run just like it they have to know about almost every aspect of a company such as: their pricing, sales force strategy, strengths and weaknesses, advertising and sales promotion, manufacturing, and purchasing strategies. In a crowded market where all the products are the same, companies need to figure out what they can beat their competitors at to seize a larger market share. The marketing strategy a company chooses will vary according to the diverse needs and objectives of it. Most companies use one of three different marketing strategies at some point in their lives. They are: **entrepreneurial marketing, formulated marketing**, and **intrepreneurial marketing**. Most companies start off in the entrepreneurial marketing stage. This is when an individual with an idea starts a company at a grass-roots level. When the company grows and becomes more successful, it moves towards formulated marketing. They begin to develop formal strategies, goals, and objectives and follow them. When a large company has become less competitive and strayed from what made it successful, they turn to an intrepreneurial strategy and try to rediscover what made them great.

Target Markets

Most companies tend to focus on competing against weaker competitors. This is because it takes fewer resources and is easier. However, a company gains little from beating up on smaller

Copyright © Mometrix Media. You have been licensed one copy of this document for personal use only. Any other reproduction or redistribution is strictly prohibited. All rights reserved.
This content is provided for test preparation purposes only and does not imply an endorsement by Mometrix of any particular political, scientific, or religious point of view.

businesses. When they choose to attack larger companies, they gain valuable expertise and usually become more efficient from the competition. Companies need competition for the sole reason that most market monopolies are illegal in the United States. The government would not let companies exist in the marketplace without some competition. To assess the strengths and weaknesses of competitors, companies use **customer value analysis** to determine what target customers value in their products and how they rate versus their competitors.

Competitive Positioning Strategies

There are four basic competitive positioning strategies that a company can use in a market.

- **Differentiation** -- This is when a company focuses on creating a product and strategy that is unique to all other products on the market.
- **Focus** -- The focus of a companies competitive positioning strategy is to identify which target markets they would be most successful in and how to enter them.
- **Overall cost leadership** -- This is when a company attempts to achieve the lowest costs to themselves and the consumer, thus winning the market share by having lower prices than its competitors.
- **Middle-of-the-road** -- This is an unsuccessful competitive position strategy that happens to companies that do not attempt to stick out from its competitors and instead be good at all segments of the market. As a result, they often become an afterthought to consumers and lose money.

Value Strategies

Created by marketers Michael Treacy and Fred Wiersema, *value disciplines* are the different ways that companies can produce customer value. There are three basic strategies that companies can use in delivering superior value.

- Creating **customer intimacy** provides great value by tailoring markets and segments to the exact needs of it customers.
- **Operational excellence** is a strategy where companies create and sell reliable products and services, but with an emphasis on low prices.
- **Product leadership** is when a company creates value by creating a continuous stream of new, innovative, products that define the future market. Apple is a good example of a company that leads its market.

Marketplace Positions

There are four different positions a company can take in a market. They are either **the market leader**, **one of the market challengers**, **a market follower**, or a **market nicher**. A company's position in a market helps determine what types of strategies it will employ.

- The **market leader** is the company with the largest share of the market.
- The **market challengers** are the companies that are competing to become the market leader.
- A **market follower** is a company that is content with its position in the marketplace and wants to keep the status quo.
- A **market nicher** is a company that serves all the small segments in the market that larger companies are not interested in.

Copyright © Mometrix Media. You have been licensed one copy of this document for personal use only. Any other reproduction or redistribution is strictly prohibited. All rights reserved.
This content is provided for test preparation purposes only and does not imply an endorsement by Mometrix of any particular political, scientific, or religious point of view.

Market Leaders

In every market there is one company that all the others aspire to be or to beat. When you are the leader there are three things that you try to do to stay on top. Market leaders try to expand total demand of a market because new consumers most often go with the product made by the industry leader. They try to protect their market share by fixing weaknesses and fulfilling value promises. They also to expand their market share because it usually means higher profits. This can be done through better sales or by acquiring smaller competitors in the market. It is important to note that in some markets, a 1 percent increase can be worth hundreds of millions of dollars.

Market Challengers

The strategies that a market challenger uses are more important than the ones made by the market leader because if they are not successful, then they risk losing more market share to the leader and other market challengers. Some of the largest companies in the world are market challengers. Pepsi, Ford, Target, Sears, and Best Buy are some of the largest companies in the world and they do not lead their respective market. They employ one of two strategies; they aggressively challenge the leader or they play along with competitors and keep the status quo.

Market Followers

Sometimes a company knows that it cannot match the market leader in price or value so they are content to follow. There are several advantages to being a follower. First, they can learn and gain experience from the precedence that the leader takes. If they create a successful new product, they release their own later. If a leader's strategy fails, then the follower attempts a different strategy. They can improve on the leader's products. In some markets, having a 10 or 15 percent share can mean revenues of millions of dollars.

Market Nichers

Market nichers fill in the gaps in a market that no other company has filled because it is either unprofitable or not worth pursuing. Niche marketers are successful because they get to know their customers on a more personal level than a large company. The main idea in niche marketing is specialization. By focusing on a small, loyal group of target customers in one or two markets, they focus on making a profit, not controlling market share. Some nichers sell directly to one larger company. Others sell to specific customers.

Orientation

There are three different ways that a company tries to be oriented.

- A **customer-centered company** focuses on customer development when designing its marketing strategies and tries to deliver value to them.
- A **competitor-centered company** focuses on what its competitors do and then react to it.
- A **market-centered company** is a company that tries to focus on all aspects of business.

Every company should focus on their competitors and their customers, but it is very difficult do lead the way in both; therefore companies are forced to choose an orientation. Sometimes companies focus on one of these aspects too much causing a decline in sales. Home Depot and Wal-Mart are two companies that have recently received scrutiny for neglecting their customers by not having enough employees.

International Trade

A **tariff** is a tax on imports by a government to encourage its citizens to buy goods made in their country. A **quota** is the exact number of products that is allowed to be imported into a country. An

Copyright © Mometrix Media. You have been licensed one copy of this document for personal use only. Any other reproduction or redistribution is strictly prohibited. All rights reserved.
This content is provided for test preparation purposes only and does not imply an endorsement by Mometrix of any particular political, scientific, or religious point of view.

embargo is when a country prohibits doing business with certain countries until they meet certain demands. Exchange controls prohibit inflation by capping the amount of foreign exchange and the exchange rate with certain countries. Sometimes companies face non-tariff barriers, which are usually cultural differences between countries that prevent another business from exporting there.

International Marketing

Before a company decides that it wants to operate in foreign countries, there are many complex decisions that they have to make. First, they need to decide if there is a market for their product or service. While many American companies have great success abroad, many products and services do not sell well because of cultural differences or little interest. Once they have decided that they are going to go international, they need to figure out which market they are going to enter and how they are going to do it. The company then needs to figure out how it will work in the international community. They will need foreign companies to purchase supplies and interact with. There are three ways a company sells its products internationally: **exporting**, **joint venturing**, and **direct investment**.

- **Exporting** is the easiest way to enter a market. To export all a company has to do is sell its goods to a foreign distributor.
- **Joint venturing** is when a company joins forces with a foreign country in order to share costs and learn about the market. It is different from exporting because the company is actually joining with the foreign company to sell the product.
- **Direct investment** is the riskiest way to enter a foreign market, but also the most highly profitable. When a company directly invests in an international market, they build and maintain assembly or manufacturing plants and a foreign workforce.

Analyzing Economic Environment

When deciding whether to do business in a country, a business will study two major economic factors: their *industrial structure* and their *income distribution*. There are four types of industrial structures:

- **Subsistence economies** exist in countries where the majority of the people are farmers. These are the poorest areas of the world.
- **Raw material exporting economies** exist in countries that have abundant natural resources but have high amounts of poverty.
- **Industrializing economies** are the economies of the world that import raw materials and have a large level of manufacturing business.
- **Industrial economies** are in countries with well-developed economies and a high level of specialization.

The way that income is distributed in a country gives a business insight as to whom they should market their products to.

Analyzing Political Environment

In international marketing, it does not matter how large a potential market is if a country's government makes it too difficult to conduct business there. Before a business enters a country, they need to understand the countries attitude towards international companies. Some countries welcome foreign investment, others set quotas or unreasonable demands. **Government bureaucracy** is another factor. Officials in many countries commonly demand bribes for things to get done. The **political stability** of a country can keep a business out. There is a reason why there are not many businesses in Iraq. Businesses also need to understand a country's **monetary**

Copyright © Mometrix Media. You have been licensed one copy of this document for personal use only. Any other reproduction or redistribution is strictly prohibited. All rights reserved.
This content is provided for test preparation purposes only and does not imply an endorsement by Mometrix of any particular political, scientific, or religious point of view.

regulations. Artificial exchange rates or investment rules can make certain countries unappealing for investment.

Joint Ventures

There are several types of joint ventures, each with their own risks and rewards. **Joint ownership** is a venture where a company joins forces with foreign investors to create a local business that they share. Companies sell **licensees** for fees or royalties of the company in exchange for using the company's name, logo, and products. **Contract manufacturing** is a joint venture where a company contracts with foreign manufacturers to produce its product. **Management contracting** is where the domestic company gives management and leadership while the foreign company supplies labor and capital.

Global Marketing Programs

Companies have to decide how they are going to adapt their marketing mix for each foreign market that they enter. Companies that do little to change their marketing mix use a **structured marketing mix**. This is effective in countries that have similar cultures such as the United States, Canada, Britain, and Australia. An **adapted marketing mix** is an international marketing strategy where companies adjust their strategies to gear them towards a target market. This strategy is initially more expensive due to the adjustments, but the hopes are that it will make the company more profitable in the long run.

Long-Term Financing

In order to expand their business and purchase more materials, companies need to obtain long-term financing. This is used to pay for things such as new facilities, equipment, or renovations as opposed to a short-term loan used to pay bills and salaries. Companies have three options for long-term financing: **long-term loans, bonds, and equity financing**. A long-term loan is paid off in small amounts over an extended period. The bank profits by charging interest on the loan. A bond is a certificate exchanged for a loan. The bondholder becomes a creditor for the company because the bond represents their debts. Equity financing is the action of a company selling shares of stock in order to raise capital for their business.

Short-Term Financing

When a business needs money that can be repaid in a short period of time, they usually do it one of two ways. They receive **trade credit** from a company. This is a payment delay that gives the business around 30 to 60 days to pay their bills. If a company needs money for purchases they can go to the bank and get either a **loan** or a **line of credit**. A loan is given when the company signs a *promissory note* promising to pay the loan back in full in the expected time period. A line of credit gives the company the convenience of being able to borrow however much money they need up to a certain limit, provided they pay it back.

Buyer Decision Process

When a prospective buyer is deciding to make a purchase, they go through five steps to decide if they are going to make the purchase.

1. **Want recognition** -- A buyer decides what it is that they want to buy and how much they have to spend on it.
2. **Information search** -- The buyer gathers as much information that they can about different products in a market.

Copyright © Mometrix Media. You have been licensed one copy of this document for personal use only. Any other reproduction or redistribution is strictly prohibited. All rights reserved.
This content is provided for test preparation purposes only and does not imply an endorsement by Mometrix of any particular political, scientific, or religious point of view.

3. **Alternative selection** -- Alternatives to products including not making the purchase are taken into consideration.
4. **Product decision-making** -- The buyer decides on whether they will make a purchase or not and on which product will be purchased.

Post-purchase behavior- The steps the buyer takes after making a purchase including deciding whether they will buy again.

Consumer Bias

Whether we are aware of it or not, people carry biases with them that steer them towards the purchases they make. Some of the more common biases are:

- **Anchoring** -- Decisions made by sticking to a first impression of a product or service.
- **Group think** -- The tendency to do the same thing as the majority because it is the majority.
- **Source credibility** -- We tend to accept information from people or things that we like and not from people or things that we dislike.
- **Regency** -- Relying too heavily on current information while neglecting older important information.
- **Conservatism** -- Unwillingness to change perceptions in the face of new ideas or information.
- **Selective perception** -- Only using information that supports an objective and neglecting information that contradicts it.
- **Premature selection** -- Accepting the first alternative that works.

DECA and ME Programs

DECA stands for Distributive Educations Clubs of America. At colleges the group goes by the Greek name, Delta Epsilon Chi. This club is for people interested in having careers in the fields of management, business marketing, and entrepreneurship. Teachers in these fields can also be members. Their mission statement as found on their website reads as follows: "DECA, Inc. is to enhance the co-curricular education of students with interest in marketing, management and entrepreneurship. DECA helps students to develop skills and competence for marketing careers, to build self-esteem, to experience leadership and to practice community service. DECA is committed to the advocacy of and the growth of business/education partnerships." The organization provides ample opportunities for its members to gain valuable experience in their future fields. They provide scholarships and awards for its top members in the field of .

Personal Finance Rules

The six golden rules of personal finance:

- You will never get ahead financially if you spend more than you earn. Try to put 10% of your income into a savings account.
- Stay up-to-date about current economic trends and conditions. Read news websites and magazines to know what is going on in the world. Understand the economic views of politicians whose choices affect your life.
- Map your financial future by creating goals and making realistic plans to obtain them. Set 1-year, 5-year, 10-year, and 25-year goals for your financial future
- Take advantage of employer benefits like a 401(k) plan or life insurance and opportunities to shelter income through a tax-deferred retirement savings program. Many companies offer nice financial packages to go with employment. It is important to take advantage of them and take them with you when you leave your job.

Copyright © Mometrix Media. You have been licensed one copy of this document for personal use only. Any other reproduction or redistribution is strictly prohibited. All rights reserved.
This content is provided for test preparation purposes only and does not imply an endorsement by Mometrix of any particular political, scientific, or religious point of view.

- Develop expertise in financial matters. Even if you don't become an investment banker, you should know the basics of micro and macro economics.
- Remember that you are responsible for your own financial success. In the end, you control your own financial destiny by the choices that you make.

Evolution of US Economy

The US economy is by far the largest and most diverse in the world. During its history, it has evolved four times and continues to grow and reinvent itself. In the early years, almost seventy percent of Americans were farmers. The country was an **agricultural economy**. As the Industrial Revolution swept the US during the 1800's, the country became an **industrial economy** as fewer people were needed to farm and more were needed to work in factories. By the 1950's, the US evolved into a **service economy** where many people to earned a living by buying and selling services, as other countries began to manufacture products cheaper. With the creation of the Internet and global communication, the US economy is still a service economy but depends on the buying and selling of current accurate information, called an **information economy**.

Organizing Businesses

Any business that is not a sole proprietorship needs structure and people that explain to its employees what its goals are and how to carry them out. But how do you delegate authority and communicate your goals to thousands upon thousands of employees? There are a few different ways.

- **Centralization** puts the authority in one place. Usually that person is the president of the company or the owner.
- **Decentralization** delegates authority to managers and supervisors that report to people above them. The delegates are given autonomy over their employees and report to their bosses.
- In larger companies, different functions are **departmentalized**. This means that the company is divided into different units where specialized employees work on their specific tasks. An organized company is usually a successful company.

Interview Process

The human resources department at a company deals with the application process of hiring new employees. After recruiting potential applicants, they read through their applications to see which people are worth interviewing. An application should ask for the following information: Name, address, phone numbers, email address, work history, education, training, special awards, and three references. Prospective applicants will send their résumé with all of that information plus any other qualifications that they may have for the job. After reducing the pool of applicants, people are contacted to set up interviews with the company. There may be more than one interview with more than one level of employee as well. During this process, the company tries to learn about the attributes and qualifications of the employee to determine if they would help the company. The employee may be asked to perform certain tests; either physical, psychological, or drug. From there, an employee is hired.

Accounting

Accounting is a vital part of marketing because it helps a business keep track of its money. This is the system that classifies, records, and interprets all the financial data of a company. Anything of value that the company owns is called an asset. This would include equipment, buildings, capital, and land. Any debts or obligations that they have are called a liability. The daily financial activities that occur involving the company are called transactions. All the transactions that occur in a 12-

Copyright © Mometrix Media. You have been licensed one copy of this document for personal use only. Any other reproduction or redistribution is strictly prohibited. All rights reserved.
This content is provided for test preparation purposes only and does not imply an endorsement by Mometrix of any particular political, scientific, or religious point of view.

month period are called a fiscal year. These transactions are recorded on a balance sheet. The balance sheet is usually a spreadsheet or database.

Business Plans

It is very important that a business plan includes every aspect of the potential business. There are eight parts to a good business plan. They are:

- The **Summary** is an overview of the general business plan. It is usually only a few pages and is designed to hook the reader into continuing.
- The **Company Description** describes the type of company and describes it if it already exists.
- The **Product and Services** *plan* describes what it is that the company will sell. It also explains why people would want to buy the product or service.
- The **Marketing plan** explains the potential client base, competition, and marketing strategy.
- The **Legal plan** points out any legal concerns of liabilities that the company may have.
- The **Management** *plan* describes the people that will run the company.
- The **Operating plan** explains how the company will produce the good or service that it wants to provide.
- The **Financial plan** specifies the company's financial needs and how it will turn a profit.

"White-Collar" Jobs

White-collar jobs refer to jobs that are mostly in the service industry. In a white-collar job, you are more likely to perform a specialized task rather than do some sort of manual labor. They are four basic categories for white-collar jobs: Administrative support, Sales and clerical, managerial, and professional.

- **Administrative jobs** are the people that keep and maintain records. Sales and clerical workers sell goods and services.
- **Managerial workers** guide and supervise workers.
- **Professional workers** are the doctors, lawyers, teachers, actors, and writers of the world. They create new information and usually have more contact with people than other workers do.

Blue-Collar Jobs

If a white-collar worker uses their brain, then a blue-collar worker uses their hands. About 1 in 4 workers in the United States are considered blue-collar workers. A blue-collar worker is more likely to produce a good than a service. However, there are many service jobs such as chefs, hair stylists, police officers, firefighters, and day-care providers. The United States has seen a dramatic decrease in the number of blue-collar jobs over the last few decades for several reasons. Modernity has enabled companies to use machines for jobs that were once done by humans. Many factory jobs have been shipped overseas because of cheaper labor and more demand. The biggest reason is that more people do not want to do physical labor all their lives.

Good Resumes

A good resume should leave an employer only asking one question, "when can we set up an interview?" Your resume should provide your contact information, work experience, level of education, references, specialized skills, and awards and recognitions. Your resume should be clear, uniform, and believable. 50% of all Americans embellish on their resume. While it is okay to tout your qualities, going overboard could cost you the job or get you in trouble later down the road. Most businesses will check your references, so it is important to have people that can talk about you

Copyright © Mometrix Media. You have been licensed one copy of this document for personal use only. Any other reproduction or redistribution is strictly prohibited. All rights reserved.
This content is provided for test preparation purposes only and does not imply an endorsement by Mometrix of any particular political, scientific, or religious point of view.

in detail. Stay away from family, and use someone like a former employer or co-worker, teacher, or someone who can assess your work experience.

Looking for a Job

A job is much more satisfying when it is something that you enjoy doing. Figure out what jobs are suited to your talents and abilities. Once you have identified a job that you would like to do, you need to find that job. There are many places to look. While newspapers are no longer a great source of job postings, the Internet provides many opportunities to find employment. Places like monster.com, jobs.com, and careerbuilder.com offer jobs across the country. If you are graduating from college, the guidance office will have connections to companies that want to hire students upon graduation. Word-of-mouth is still a great way to find employment because it can give you a way into a job that doesn't come from a want ad.

Job Interviews

A job interview is the first face-to-face contact with a business and a potential employee. Before the interviewee comes in, they should learn some information about the company that they are interviewing for. It is important to be on time for the interview. You should even be there a few minutes early. Your dress should reflect the job that you are interviewing for. Appropriate dress is one of the most important parts of the interview. At the interview, ask good questions. It shows the interviewer that you are interested in the job. It is not inappropriate to ask about pay or benefits if the employer does not bring them up.

Internet Domains

Business web sites can be divided into four categories: Business to consumer, business-to-business, consumer to consumer, and consumer to business. Business to business (B2B) are e-marketplaces where businesses sell directly to other businesses. They can be auction sites like ebay.com, but are also places where companies can learn and purchase products to better run their companies, like sun.com. Business to consumer (B2C) websites are the most popular types of business websites. These sites are where companies sell to the final consumer. Almost every company has a website where a customer can research and/or purchase goods online. These sites accounted for over $112 billion dollars in 2005. Consumer to consumer web sites (C2C) are similar to the want ads in the local newspaper except on a global scale. Consumer to Business (C2B) websites are sites where consumers enter a market and search for a business that they want to do business with. Priceline.com would be an example.

Legislative Acts

Influencing Marketing

Since businesses cannot be trusted to operate in an ethical manner without supervision, the federal government has intervened on behalf of consumers by creating legislation to protect their interests. While there have been too many acts passed to name, here are some of the major ones. The Sherman Antitrust Act was passed in 1890 and made monopolies illegal without the consent of the government. The Federal Food and Drug Act in 1906 created the Food and Drug Administration, which regulates the safety of products designed for human consumption. The Federal Trade Commission Act of 1914 created the Federal Trade Commission, to be a watchdog for unfair labor practices.

Marketing to Children

As children become a larger part of the marketplace, legislation has been designed to protect them from being exploited by companies looking to profit from them in unethical ways. The Child Protection Act of 1966 banned the sale of products and packaging that may be harmful to children.

Copyright © Mometrix Media. You have been licensed one copy of this document for personal use only. Any other reproduction or redistribution is strictly prohibited. All rights reserved.
This content is provided for test preparation purposes only and does not imply an endorsement by Mometrix of any particular political, scientific, or religious point of view.

The Children's Television Act of 1990 limited the amount of commercials aired during children's programming. In 2000, the Children's Online Privacy Protection Act was passed to prevent companies from obtaining information from children without their parents permission.

Supply Chain Management

Supply chain management is the ability to manage and distribute information traveling both ways in a company. SCM involves **marketing logistics**, which is the work involved with planning and controlling the flow of goods and materials from the company to the consumer. The logistics manager's job is to try to coordinate the all activities in all the different channels from start to finish. They have to get suppliers, purchasers, retailers, distributors, and customers all on the same page. Their other jobs include: taking inventory, warehousing, forecasting, planning transport, shipping, and many other things. Businesses put a large emphasis on logistics because shipping represents a significant portion of a product's price. By reducing these costs, they can be passed onto the consumer.

Shopping Centers

A store's location is one of the most vital factors that determine its success. Because of its proximity to other stores, the shopping center is a favorite location of retail stores. A shopping center is a large group of stores that are organized, developed, and managed as a unit. The largest type of shopping center is the regional mall. This can have from 40 to over 200 stores. A community shopping center has about 15 to 40 stores. Strip malls are made of 5 to 15 stores that usually contain a supermarket and service stores. A power center is a new type of shopping center. It revolves around one or two superstores, like Wal-Mart or Home Depot, with four or five stores surrounding it.

Selecting Salespeople

Since so many resources are invested in hiring, training, and evaluating new employees, it is very important to select new hires carefully. Companies want as little turnover as possible because it leads to lost sales and productivity. The top 30 percent of a sales force can account for over 60 percent of sales. Once a company decides what traits they are looking for in an employee to fill their specific opening, they recruit prospective employers using advertisements, current employees, and headhunters. When a company has a few prospects, they interview them until they have selected the right person for their job.

Free Trade Zones

Many economists believe that the best way for the global economy to grow is by encouraging free trade. Certain countries in the world have been cooperating in creating **economic communities** that try to reduce tariffs and regulate trade. One example is the European Union, which is a group of several European countries that use a single currency, collaborate on policies, and trade with each other. No single European country could pose an economic threat to the US, but all of them together do. This is one of the goals that the EU seeks to accomplish. Europe is not the only place where free trade exists. In North America, the North American Free Trade Agreement exists between the US, Canada, and Mexico. This agreement created a market that did almost 20 trillion dollars worth of business in 2013, according to the IMF.

Panel and Behavioral Interviews

A **panel interview** is a type of interview where there is more than one interviewer. Typically, there are between three and ten people. They will usually be different levels of management present at the interview. A person may be asked to demonstrate their problem solving skills to see what they might do in various situations. Interviewers looking to see how an applicant's previous work

Copyright © Mometrix Media. You have been licensed one copy of this document for personal use only. Any other reproduction or redistribution is strictly prohibited. All rights reserved.
This content is provided for test preparation purposes only and does not imply an endorsement by Mometrix of any particular political, scientific, or religious point of view.

history makes them qualified for the job conduct a **behavioral interview**. Applicants are asked behavior-oriented questions that need to be answered with facts.

Vocational Education History

Vocational education got its start with the passing of the Morrill Act in 1862. This granted land in almost every state for colleges and universities to create agricultural and mechanical schools. These A & M schools are also referred to as land grant colleges. Vocational schools mainly focused on trades such as auto mechanics or carpentry. As the economy has become more specialized these schools have adjusted their programs to meet these new demands. Now vocational schools offer many diverse programs from cosmetology to funeral services. Vocational schools have shed their image as "blue-collar factories" for people that could not attend four-year universities. Demand has increased the pay of several vocational careers to levels that rival or surpass those that require college degrees.

Packaging

It is not uncommon for a consumer to buy a product on an impulse because the package was appealing. In fact, companies consciously make an effort to package their product in a way that separates them from their competitors. Making a good package requires a lot of work. A company first establishes its **packaging concept**. This is what the package should say or do for the product. Then they design a label that is used to identify the brand. The package will also contain warnings and product information required by law. Food packages will contain nutritional information that the company will either tout or downplay depending on the nutritional information given.

Brand Name and Generic

A **brand name** is a symbol of a company that distinguishes it from other products. Examples include the Nike Swoosh, the McDonald's Golden Arches, and design of a Coke or Pepsi can. A **generic product** is similar to the brand name but has no logo or symbol. It is usually a cheaper, knockoff brand that appeals to customers seeking value. Companies make all sorts of generic products like: cereals, condiments, sneakers, or paper towels. It is important to note that because the brand name product is always of higher quality does not mean that it is the better purchase.

Product Life Cycle

Products go through five stages. They are: new product development, market introduction, growth, maturity, and decline or stability. Each stage contains unique characteristics that separate it from the other stages.

1. The **new product development stage** is where research and development occurs. During this stage, companies experiences no sales revenue and incur high costs due to getting the product ready for the market.
2. The **market introduction stage** is when the product is introduced to the public. Costs are still high, but mostly because of advertising. Sales volume tend to be low as businesses wait to see how the product is received by the public.
3. The **growth stage** is when your business should start to profit. Costs are reduced due to economies of scale. Due to advertising, the public is aware of your product. There will be more competition due to new businesses trying to establish themselves in the market.
4. The fourth stage is known as the **mature stage**. By this time the product is well established in the market. Because of this, costs are at their lowest of the product life cycle. The product should be very profitable, but its price tends to drop due to competition.

Copyright © Mometrix Media. You have been licensed one copy of this document for personal use only. Any other reproduction or redistribution is strictly prohibited. All rights reserved.
This content is provided for test preparation purposes only and does not imply an endorsement by Mometrix of any particular political, scientific, or religious point of view.

5. The final stage is the **decline** or **stability stage**. Here sales volumes will either stabilize or decline. Profitability lessens or disappears completely as the product has run its course through the market.

Consumer Goods

Consumer goods are products and services sold to families and individuals. They can be divided into three categories:

- **Convenience goods and services** are products that people use on a regular basis without much effort. These goods tend to be inexpensive and are widely available. Examples include: gasoline, milk, and candy bars.
- **Shopping goods and services** are products that consumers buy after comparing similar products. These tend to be more expensive items such as cars, electronics, or a house
- **Specialty goods and services** are products that are purchased because of their association with a certain brand or label. Items in this category tend to be expensive. Examples include automobiles, specialty clothing, and electronics. An example of a specialty service would be taking a car to a specific mechanic like Midas.

Channels of Distribution

One of the most important decisions that marketers can make is where and how consumers will purchase their product and/or services. The answer to this problem is called **channels of distribution**. They are all the people that guide products to consumers. Even though it is growing due to the Internet, it is still rare for a company to sell directly to its consumers. When a product is distributed, the process usually involves an intermediary called a middleman. There are three types of middlemen:

- A distributor represent a manufacturer in a certain geographic area
- A wholesaler buys large amounts of different products and sells them in smaller bunches to retail stores
- A retailer sells the goods directly to the consumer

Effective Advertising

To have an effective advertisement, your message should:

- **Be clear** -- The message should be delivered in an easy, unambiguous way so that anyone can understand your point
- **Be creative** -- Your message should be something that is fresh and new in order to separate yourself from your competitors
- **Be hard-hitting** --The font, graphic, or headline should make a reader stand up and take notice.
- **Be informative** -- The more information you give your prospective audience, the more comfortable they will be buying a product from you. Information helps the customer remember your product.
- **Be memorable** --Leave a lasting impression in their head that keeps the audience thinking about you all day. You want them to be thinking about why they need to purchase your product.

Merchandising

Merchandising is a difficult term to define because the meaning of the term changes according to the context of what is being spoken about. Basically, it is a broad term for the practices, methods,

Copyright © Mometrix Media. You have been licensed one copy of this document for personal use only. Any other reproduction or redistribution is strictly prohibited. All rights reserved.
This content is provided for test preparation purposes only and does not imply an endorsement by Mometrix of any particular political, scientific, or religious point of view.

and operations related to promoting certain categories of commercial activity. The most common form of merchandising is selling a product with a company's logo that is different from the product that they sell. The selling of a logo, brand name, or image to a company is called licensing. This gives a company the right to use an item on a product for their own profit. This helps the company increase awareness of its product while helping the other company make more money than what the product sold without the image. Better said, a T-shirt with a recognizable image will sell better than a blank T-shirt.

- **Children's merchandising** -- one of the most profitable areas of merchandising. With low overhead costs and very loyal customers, selling the right image can make a company very profitable. Children's merchandise tends to consist of toys that are likenesses of characters from television and movies. Once a character is a hit, you can be sure to see it as a toy, on a cereal box, and at a fast food restaurant, among other places. Money is a large factor in children's merchandising. Often products are made first and the shows are made to revolve around the merchandise. Other times, the merchandise lives on long after the show has disappeared. This is because consumers have remained loyal to the product since they were children.
- **Adult merchandising** -- As people get older, the way that businesses promote merchandise changes with it. Most adults are not longer interested with toys (though many are), so promoters need to meet adult interests to create interest in their product. The most popular form of adult merchandising is related to sports teams and their players. Billions of dollars are exchanged every year between companies and the right to be the officially licensed product of a major league sport. This is because it means guaranteed sales and that their product will be the only one sold at events. A new trend in marketing is for non-media products to sell their image on products completely unrelated to what they are known for. For instance, Harley-Davidson has a clothing line even though they sell motorcycles.
- **Retail merchandising** -- In an effort to cut costs for retailers, manufacturers, wholesalers, or merchandisers will stock the shelves of the retail store for that business. This is commonplace in several industries, especially beverages, books and magazines, and packaged baked goods. This relationship has many advantages on both sides. The retailer saves on costs enabling it to offer the product at a lower cost to the consumer. The manufacturer gets valuable insight as to how its product is selling in different stores. Merchandisers are also more likely to take the time to create an appealing display than the vendor selling many products. In many fields, merchandisers are the largest employee group of a company. Coca-Cola and Pepsi employ thousands of merchandisers to move their product.

Marketing Principles

Psychological Factors

The choices that a buyer makes are based on four factors: **beliefs and attitudes**, **learning**, **motivation**, and **perception**.

- A person's **beliefs and attitudes** shape how they think about a product.
- **Learning** changes the more experience a person has with a product. If they have good experiences, they usually learn to like the product.

Copyright © Mometrix Media. You have been licensed one copy of this document for personal use only. Any other reproduction or redistribution is strictly prohibited. All rights reserved.
This content is provided for test preparation purposes only and does not imply an endorsement by Mometrix of any particular political, scientific, or religious point of view.

- **Motivations** are factors that drive a person's specific need to have a product. The higher the person's motive is to purchase a product, the more likely they are to purchase it. Companies spend a lot of resources trying to figure out what motivates consumers.
- **Perception** is the process that people use to select the information they have available to form a meaningful image of the product.

Buying Situations

There are three types of buying decisions: straight re-buy, modified re-buy, and new task.

- A **straight re-buy** is the most common type of purchase. This is when a consumer buys a product, as is without any modifications.
- A **modified re-buy** is when the buyer wants to change something about a product whether it is the size, price, terms, etc. An example would be going to McDonald's and getting a Big Mac but with no lettuce or tomato.
- The other extreme of a straight buy is a **new-task situation**. This is when a person is purchasing a product for the first time. This is both a challenge and opportunity for the company because it gives a chance to create a loyal customer or lose their business.

Branding Decisions

Major brands have to make four large decisions about how to market their brand to the public.

1. **Brand positioning** is the promotion of specific attributes, benefits, and values of a product. It is here where a company decides what emotions they want to try to evoke from the consumer.
2. A company then comes up with a name for its brand. A successful product usually has a name that suggests something about the companies' benefits or qualities.
3. Once the company has its brand name, it then decides who will sponsor it. Products and services can be sold as **manufacturer's brands** or **private brands**. Each type of brand has unique advantages depending on the company's marketing plans.
4. Finally, a company decides how to develop its brand. It has four options for developing its brands:
    a. line extensions
    b. brand extensions
    c. multibrands
    d. introduce a new product completely

Developing New Products

Companies must constantly create and sell new products in order to keep up with the evolving tastes, preferences, and technological advances in the marketplace. There are two ways to do this. One is by buying an existing company that produces the product or service that a business wants to sell. The other way is through the creation of new ideas. **Idea generation** is the process of taking an idea and turning it into a new product or service. It takes several different ideas before any of them becomes a product or service.

Retailers Manage Product Variables

Once the store is in place, retailers have to decide how the store will be presented to the consumer. They need to decide what type of atmosphere they are going to create. This is the feel one gets when they walk into the store and browse. Some places encourage people to sample products while others have lots of sales associates on hand to help customers with their shopping. The **product**

Copyright © Mometrix Media. You have been licensed one copy of this document for personal use only. Any other reproduction or redistribution is strictly prohibited. All rights reserved.
This content is provided for test preparation purposes only and does not imply an endorsement by Mometrix of any particular political, scientific, or religious point of view.

assortment they carry should separate them from their competitors. This means they need to either offer merchandise that no one else carries or sell it for less.

Integrated Marketing Communications

Integrated marketing communications is a concept that businesses create a concise message about itself for use on all its products. The need for this has arisen from the specialization of markets. Rather than two or three companies leading the way in a market, the marketplace now often has smaller, specialized companies competing in target markets. While companies see each individual market, consumers see all the different messages as a reflection on the company as a whole. Therefore, it is very important that a company have a consistent image among all its products.

Communication Process

The way business has evolved means that the communication process has taken on much more importance. Communication used to mean having a 1-800 number that customers could call when something broke. Now marketers view communications as a long-term method of managing the customer relationship over time. There are nine elements to effective communication. First, there are the parties involved in a communication, the **sender** and the **receiver**. There are the methods of communication: the **message** and the **media**. These are the major functions: **encoding**, **decoding**, **response**, and **feedback**. The last element is **noise**.

Effective Communication

Effective communication begins with the **sender**; which is the company. **Encoding** is the process of putting the message into an advertisement. The **message** is the advertisement that the company puts out. The **media** is the communication channel that the sender puts the message through. **Decoding** is the process that the receiver goes through giving meaning to the message. The **receiver** is the party that receives the message. The **response** is how the receiver reacts to the message. **Feedback** is the response that the receiver gives back to the sender. Finally, **noise** is the term for anything that contributes to the distortion of the message.

Personal Communication Channels

No type of communication channel takes more precedence within a company than its **Personal communication channels**. They are channels in which groups of people speak with each other about a product instead of using an intermediary. They are so important because no matter how effective an advertising campaign a company runs; nothing creates more sales than **word-of-mouth influence**. People hearing from someone they trust about the effectiveness of a product is more likely to influence them to purchase a product than any advertisement. This is especially true for expensive or risky products like automobiles, electronics, and appliances.

Designing Effective Messages

When putting a message together it is important to know what you want to say and how you are going to say it. Most marketers follow the AIDA model. This means that the message should get the reader's **attention**, hold their **interest**, arouse their **desires**, and get them to take **action**. The message attempts to appeal to the reader rationally or emotionally. Often products offer safety and security, patriotism, or family closeness. By appealing to readers' emotions, companies hope to evoke a strong enough response to make the reader want to go buy that product.

Nonpersonal Communication Channels

Nonpersonal communication channels are channels that do not have any feedback or personal contact with its consumers. Companies communicate their messages three ways. They create an **atmosphere** that encourages a buyer to make and feel good about a purchase. They have **events**

Copyright © Mometrix Media. You have been licensed one copy of this document for personal use only. Any other reproduction or redistribution is strictly prohibited. All rights reserved.
This content is provided for test preparation purposes only and does not imply an endorsement by Mometrix of any particular political, scientific, or religious point of view.

that communicate their messages to target audiences. This could be anything from a press conference, tour, opening, exhibit, etc. Companies also communicate through different forms of **media**, such as: print media (online or written), broadcast media, and display media. Examples of print media are: mail, newspapers, or magazines. Broadcast media is radio and television. Display media are signs, billboards, and posters.

Culture

Certain cultures can affect the strategy that marketers employ. American companies especially have to worry about cultural backlash that can occur when a country feels that it is becoming "Americanized." Many countries love foreign investment, but others associate globalization with the invasion of Western values. To be successful, American companies have learned that it is important to understand the local customs of an area and adapt instead of forcing their own customs on the population. For instance, McDonald's signature items are its hamburgers, but in India the cow is sacred and never eaten. As a result, Indian McDonald's offer the Maharaja Mac, which is made from mutton.

Socially Responsible Businesses

Socially responsible business means putting a company's principles before its profits. While capitalism has brought the world more prosperity than any other type of economic system, there are many major criticisms of it. Many people are exploited in the process of bringing products to the store shelves. There are many consumers that want to purchase products that are made in an ethical way. This is where the market for socially responsible business was created. An example is ice cream company Ben and Jerry's. They cared so much about their environmental and social responsibilities that they did things like buy hormone-free milk and organic fruits and nuts. They bought locally whenever possible. As a result, consumers could feel guilt-free buying their product and they turned a handsome profit.

Social Criticisms of Marketing

Marketing receives criticism from many people for several different reasons. While some of them are deserved, many of them are not. Some people feel that high prices are a result of marketing and the methods that marketers use to sell their products. They point to the high costs of distribution, advertising and promotion costs, and excessive markups as the cause of higher prices. Other critics see the deceptive practices that some marketers use such as selling dangerous or low-quality products or using high-pressure or deceptive sales practices. The materialism that excessive marketing can cause affects all people in many different ways. Some corporations have become so powerful that they wield powerful influence over politicians who manipulate or overlook laws and regulations so that they may profit. It is common knowledge about the influence that "Big tobacco, food, and oil" hold sway in Washington. Many media outlets are loathe to report on certain consumer products because those companies are paying their bills through advertising. As a result, the truth often does not get told. Other people worry about the "cultural pollution" caused by excessive marketing. By the time an average American child reaches 13, they have seen 100,000 advertisements. Some people feel that this pollutes people's minds with materialism.

Impact of Marketing

While marketing has brought society many great things, it has caused us many great problems as well. The biggest problem that marketing has brought to Americans is **materialism**. This is an infatuation with material things and judging people by what they own rather than whom they are. Critics of materialism see this as created by the marketers of the world so people will consume more and keep industrial output high. If people don't covet goods, then marketers will have a hard time selling them.

Copyright © Mometrix Media. You have been licensed one copy of this document for personal use only. Any other reproduction or redistribution is strictly prohibited. All rights reserved.
This content is provided for test preparation purposes only and does not imply an endorsement by Mometrix of any particular political, scientific, or religious point of view.

Deceptive Practices

There are many different ways that marketing fraud is committed. Some people use **deceptive pricing** which is falsely advertising price reductions or incorrectly labeling a product. **Deceptive packaging** is misleading a consumer about a product's size, not filling a bag completely, or exaggerating a product through a design. Examples of **deceptive promotion** are running rigged contests, using a bait-and-switch technique, or exaggerating a product's service. While deceptive marketing practices will hamper a company's business in the long run, many are willing to do it in exchange for short-term profits.

Marketing's Impact on Businesses

There are three major ways that one company's marketing practices can hurt another's. The recent trend of acquisitions of smaller companies has narrowed the number of competitors in a market and given some companies larger resources. For example, in the pharmaceutical industry it is common for a corporation to purchase a smaller company that has made a generic version of their drug rather than face the competition. Some people feel that it is too difficult for new businesses to enter a market because of the actions of their established competitors. Large companies can use their resources to price out smaller, fledgling companies. Other companies engage in unfair business practices such as bundling products or creating monopolies.

Consumerism

Consumerism is a movement created in response to illegal or unfair marketing practices. The movement started in the 1960's and found its voice behind leading advocate Ralph Nader. Consumerists have successfully lobbied the government to give consumers more information to make right choices. Because of them, there are nutritional labels on food, the actual interest rates on loans, and truth in advertising laws. They have established rights for sellers and consumers in the marketplace. Consumers have the right to not buy, expect a safe product, and for it to work as advertised. Companies have the right promote their products, charge what they want, and sell products however they want provided they do it in an ethical way.

Environmentalism

Environmentalism is a growing movement for people all over the world to conserve the Earth's resources, reduce and remove pollution, and improve the quality of life for people. Environmentalism started in the 1960's in response to the growing wave of health problems of people but also the effects of pollution, litter, acid rain, and strip mining, etc. were having on the planet. Eventually, government became more involved in the movement by passing laws regulating pollution and cleaning the environment. Today, companies are realizing that it is profitable to be recognized as an environmentally friendly company. It reduces overhead costs passing savings on to consumers, and people feel good about buying products from companies with good reputations.

Environmental Sustainability

Environmental sustainability is a strategy where a company tries to adopt eco-friendly policies while still focusing on profits. This is a large challenge for a company, but also a large opportunity. Consumers are choosing to buy more products from companies who businesses do little damage to the environment. So, it is not just a moral choice to be environmentally sustainable, it is a business choice. Companies start by practicing **pollution prevention**. They clean up waste they created and recycle where possible. They can practice **product stewardship**, and design their products to minimize waste throughout their life cycle.

Copyright © Mometrix Media. You have been licensed one copy of this document for personal use only. Any other reproduction or redistribution is strictly prohibited. All rights reserved.
This content is provided for test preparation purposes only and does not imply an endorsement by Mometrix of any particular political, scientific, or religious point of view.

ENLIGHTENED MARKETING

Enlightened marketing is a belief that a company should strive to strike a medium between making a profit and adhering to strict social and environmental ethics. There are five principles to enlightened marketing:

1. **Consumer-oriented marketing** -- Means that a company should market its products or services in a way that empathizes with a consumer.
2. **Innovative marketing** -- Means that a company should always focus on improving and innovating its products.
3. **Sense-of-mission marketing** -- Means that a business should define who it is in broad social terms with a mission statement instead of a business plan.
4. **Societal marketing** -- Means that a company tries to encompass some part of all the strategies of enlightened marketing. They consider the needs, wants, and short- and long-term interests of the consumer.
5. **Value marketing** -- Means that a company should put its resources into building value, not ineffective and expense promotions.

CORPORATE MARKETING ETHICS POLICIES

Companies know that transparency in business is becoming more important with each corporate scandal that makes the headlines. In addition, when employees of a company commit crimes, it causes consumers and investors to lose faith in the company's ability to do honest business. Rather than wait for a problem to occur, many companies are becoming proactive and creating corporate ethics polices for their business and employees to follow. By doing this, it forces employees and the business to work towards having standards for socially responsible and ethical behavior.

ADVERTISING

Advertising is an integral part of American society. The average American has seen 100,000 advertisements by the time they are 13. An advertisement is paid for by a company in order to promote the benefits of their product. As consumer's habits and tastes have evolved, advertising has managed to keep up with them. Advertisers have evolved the delivery of their message to use methods such as the Internet, e-mail, and other forms of electronic communication. Celebrities often advertise products to supplement their income. In many cases, such as with pro athletes, the money they make from advertisements is more than they make playing their sport. Advertisers attempt to have consumers associate their product with their favorite athletes or celebrities. When that person does well, sales of that product usually rise.

There are many different types of advertising.

- **Product advertising** is the most common. It refers to promoting goods and services.
- **Advocacy advertising** is when an advertiser touts the company's stance on a public issue. This is done to enhance the image of a company.
- **Comparative advertising** shows the difference between two products with the advertiser promoting certain attributes that make it better than its direct competitor.
- This is similar to **competitive advertising** points out the things in its product that are not available in its competitor's brands.
- **Defensive advertising** attempts to diminish the effects of a competitor's on-going advertising campaign.
- **Institutional advertising** promotes a political or organizational image or idea.
- **Reinforcement advertising** tries to retain customers by reassuring them that they made the best choice buying their product.

Copyright © Mometrix Media. You have been licensed one copy of this document for personal use only. Any other reproduction or redistribution is strictly prohibited. All rights reserved.
This content is provided for test preparation purposes only and does not imply an endorsement by Mometrix of any particular political, scientific, or religious point of view.

- **Reminder advertising** reminds customers about all the uses and benefits of their product.
- **Pioneer advertising** is used to create a need for a product by informing the public what their product is, how it is used, and why they need it.

Sales Promotions

Formally, sales promotion is the marketing activities that motivate consumer purchasing, other than personal selling, advertising, and publicity. Sales promotion might include distributing samples, planning contests to promote a product, developing store display materials, and designing product deals (like rebates or two-for-one offers). Point-of-purchase display units, like cardboard racks next to the cash register in a supermarket, try to encourage immediate sales. Another common sales promotion device are coupons sent by email, which offer small discounts. The cost of these coupons is often shared by the product manufacturer and the retail store that sells the product. Other common sales promotions include company t-shirts, pens, or any other item bearing the name of the company.

Cradle-to-Grave Advertising

Cradle-to-grave advertising is a marketing scheme that is designed to hook consumers at the youngest possible age until they die. By making them loyal to their product when they are young, corporations ensure future profits. McDonald's is one of best examples of this type of advertising. At many of their locations, playgrounds are available for free use. In many inner cities, this may be the only safe place for many children to play. When parents take their children to use the facility, they purchase a Happy Meal. As the consumer grows older, McDonald's wants them to associate their food with the happy times that they had as a child. GAP is another example with its Baby GAP, GAP Kids, and GAP stores nationwide. With three different types of stores, they can create brand loyalty with their consumers.

Cooperative Advertising

Cooperative advertising is when a retail store collaborates with a national manufacturer to share advertising costs of a product to be sold by the retail store. The manufacturer and the retail store agree to share costs to promote and advertise a product. This relationship has many benefits for both sides. National manufacturers tend to have very large advertising budgets while a retail store has a small, limited budget. By sharing the costs of advertising, retail stores will experience an increase in sales, while keeping costs down. The national company spends only a fraction of its large budget, while reaching a niche market with the retail stores loyal customers.

Guidelines of Surveys

It is important to know what the objective of your survey is. It should be designed in a way that can be turned into a measurement or a question as well. The surveyor needs to decide how the survey will be conducted. What will it measure, how will it be measured, and how the results are recorded are all things that need to be answered before you can start. Next a control group needs to be found. It is usually important that the group is picked to represent a realistic part of the population. If you can't then you should attempt to understand how this would influence your results. When you have finished the survey, be sure to differentiate between the numerical and factual results and how you interpreted the results. The purpose of the survey is to give you useful and accurate data.

Company's Microenvironment

There are six main factors in a company's microenvironment: the company, suppliers, marketing intermediaries, customers, competitors, and publics. Marketing success depends on how well a company responds to these different factors. Even though the many branches of a company may have different goals, it is up to the marketing department to take them all into account. Suppliers

Copyright © Mometrix Media. You have been licensed one copy of this document for personal use only. Any other reproduction or redistribution is strictly prohibited. All rights reserved.
This content is provided for test preparation purposes only and does not imply an endorsement by Mometrix of any particular political, scientific, or religious point of view.

help get the product out to the consumer in an efficient way. Marketing intermediaries are the businesses that help a company distribute, advertise, and help sell products. Companies need to study and decide what types of customers they want to market their products towards. They need to make sure that they are providing a better service and value than their competition. Publics are the name given to any individual or group that has a vested interest in the activities of a company.

Cultural Factors

The days of companies being able to market a one-size-fits-all product and advertising campaign are over. When companies are deciding how to market products they have to take into account several different cultural factors. All these things can be categorized into a buyer's culture, subculture, and social class. For instance, the way that McDonald's promotes their products are going to be different in Vermont than they are in Los Angeles. Their menus in the south may have popular regional items on the menu that would not be featured in the northern part of the US. While this causes more overhead, it does help business and ensure customer loyalty when it appears that a company cares about the diverse needs of a population.

Adoption Process

What makes a consumer purchase a new product? Or more likely, consider an existing product that is new to them? The process that a consumer goes through from learning about a product to purchasing it is called the **adoption process**. Consumers go through five stages in adopting a product:

1. **Awareness***:* The consumer learns about the product, but doesn't know anything about it.
2. **Interest***:* Through advertising and word-of-mouth the consumer finds out about the product.
3. **Evaluation***:* The consumer makes a decision about whether to try the product
4. **Trial***:* The consumer takes the product on a trial basis to decide if it is something that they want to become more invested in.
5. **Adoption***:* The consumer decides to purchase the product regularly.

Target Marketing Strategies

A target market is a group of buyers that a company decides to enter because they have certain common needs and characteristics. There are four common strategies related to marketing.

1. **Undifferentiated marketing** is also known as mass marketing. This is when a company ignores market segments and sells products to an entire market.
2. **Differentiated marketing** is also known as segmented marketing. A company will target different segments of a market and create a unique product for each one.
3. **Concentrated marketing** is when a company goes after one niche and tries to dominate one small segment. This is a good strategy for small businesses. Many companies started by catering to niches that had not been realized or deemed unprofitable by larger companies.
4. **Micromarketing** is customizing products to individuals and locations.

Product Positioning

Product positioning is how its customers perceive a company's product in relation to its competitor's products. Positioning involves communicating the specific benefits of a product in relation to others. For example, Subway encourages customers to "Eat Fresh" as an alternative to fast food. Domino's Pizza defines itself as providing fast, hot, food delivered to your door. Once a company has established how it wants to define itself in the segment, it tries to find its **competitive advantage**. This is an advantage over its competitors by offering something that they don't such as:

Copyright © Mometrix Media. You have been licensed one copy of this document for personal use only. Any other reproduction or redistribution is strictly prohibited. All rights reserved.
This content is provided for test preparation purposes only and does not imply an endorsement by Mometrix of any particular political, scientific, or religious point of view.

better value, lower price, higher quality, and several other attributes. It is very important to choose the right competitive advantage. It is almost impossible to have advantages over every aspect of a company; therefore companies need to carefully choose where to allocate their resources. This is called **value proposition**.

BRANDING

Branding is one of the most important parts of marketing. A successful brand sells itself. It changes the way that people think about a product in a positive or negative way. A brand is a combination of logos, signs, designs, and symbols, that a company uses for people to associate with their product and differentiate themselves from their customers. There are many reasons why a company should invest resources in its brand. The uniqueness or prestige of a brand may enable companies to charge more for its product. A successful brand name may enable a company to enter new markets and have success based on the reputation of their brand. A manufacturer has four options when decided how to sponsor its product.

1. A **manufacturer's brand** is when a company sells a product or service under their own name.
2. A **private brand** is also known as a **store brand**. These are products sold by companies by other names. For example, Wal-Mart sells many products in its stores under the name Sam's Choice.
3. A **licensed brand** is when companies sell the use of their brand logo for use on other products. This is market is growing rapidly because it is highly profitable and costs the parent company nothing and gains their logo more exposure.
4. **Co-branding** is when two companies collaborate to use their names on the same product. An example is XM radio being installed in Honda trucks.

The four options a company has in developing its brand:

1. **Line extensions** are when a company introduces new products to an already existing brand line using the same name. The new product is usually a slight variation to an existing product. For instance, a food company may introduce a new product that has less fat, a different color, or is a better value than its existing product in the market.
2. **Brand extensions** use the name of the brand to sell products in a new market. For example, several soda companies such as Mountain Dew and Coke used their name to successfully sell energy drinks.
3. **Multibrands** are different products a company introduces into the same market. The drawback to this is that it makes the products compete against each other and may reduce a company's overall profitability.
4. **New brands** are completely new products a company produces that are nothing like the products they are known for selling. This is done usually when a company's brand name is getting stale or they want to enter a new market but feel that the existing brand would not be effective.

PROMOTION MIX

A company's promotion mix is the blend of advertising, public relations, promotion, personal selling, and direct marketing that a business uses to pursue its advertising and marketing goals.

- **Advertising** is how a company pays to promote their goods and products.
- **Public relations** is the image and relationships that a company has with its customers and the community.

Copyright © Mometrix Media. You have been licensed one copy of this document for personal use only. Any other reproduction or redistribution is strictly prohibited. All rights reserved.
This content is provided for test preparation purposes only and does not imply an endorsement by Mometrix of any particular political, scientific, or religious point of view.

- **Promotions** are incentives that company's use to give people incentives to buy. **Personal Selling** is how the company presents itself for the purpose of making sales and creating customer relationships.
- **Direct marketing** is contacting single consumers directly and getting instant feedback from them.

Each one of these things requires specific tools and skills. Integrated marketing requires that a company blend their promotional tools carefully into their promotion mix. Companies must decide how important each characteristic of each tool is to their goals and objectives. Advertising, direct marketing, public relations, sales promotion, and personal selling are the parts of the promotion mix. Each one of these tools contains several different choices a company must make. For instance, industrial companies will spend much less on advertising than a retail company, but will spend much more of their resources on personal selling than a retail company due to the nature of their business. With their promotion mix in place, most companies use either a **push or pull** strategy towards promotion. A **push strategy** involves using a sales force and promotion mix in a trickle-down promotion where every channel from producer to wholesaler to retailer promotes the product. They promote the good to wholesalers and retailers and they push the product to the consumer. **Pull strategy** creates a demand for a product through advertising and promotion that hopefully gets consumers to demand the product from retailers. They will then pull the product from wholesalers or the company.

Promotion Budget

Determining how to spend its money and resources is one of the hardest decisions that a company has to make because it is so hard to determine if its promotions are successful or not. There are generally four methods a company uses to determine how it will allocate its resources. Some companies use the **affordable method**, which is to set their promotion budget at a level that the company can afford. Others match their budgets to their competitors, called **competitive-parity method**. Some dedicate a certain percentage of their sales towards promotions called, **percentage-of-sales method**. Some companies base their budgets on logic and specific objectives, called the **objective-and-task method**.

Ethics of Promotion

When creating their promotion mix, companies must understand that there are many ethical and legal issues that they must consider. Companies must avoid false or deceptive advertising. They cannot use bait-and-switch tactics, which advertises a deal to get people into a store only to try to entice them to a more expensive product. In personal selling, companies now have to offer a cooling-off period of three days for all major purchases made at customer's homes. This gives the buyer a chance to think about the purchase they made and make sure that it was not just an impulse buy. Although abuses are still common, many businesses have realized that ethical promotion and selling can be an effective way to promote their business in itself.

Advertising Campaigns

When developing an advertising program, businesses have four important decisions to make:

1. **Their objectives** are usually based on what markets they want to enter, positioning, and their marketing mix.
2. Their **budget** usually depends on what part of the life cycle their product is in. This helps determine how much resources they should allocate on their product.

Copyright © Mometrix Media. You have been licensed one copy of this document for personal use only. Any other reproduction or redistribution is strictly prohibited. All rights reserved.
This content is provided for test preparation purposes only and does not imply an endorsement by Mometrix of any particular political, scientific, or religious point of view.

3. Their **strategy** is how they are going to develop their message and who it will be marketed to.
4. Finally, they **evaluate their results** to find out if their advertising was effective or not.

Advertising Budget

One of the major factors that determines the amount of advertising a company invests into its budget is determined by what stage the product is in its life cycle. More money is needed for advertising a product when it first comes on the market and when it is competing against rivals than when it is an established product. A company also needs to know how much market share its product has. Companies that dominate a market require less advertising than companies that are establishing their product or expanding a market.

Advertising Strategies

There are two major elements to advertising strategy: how to create the message and how to distribute it. Advertisers create a **message strategy** that explains how the message will be given to consumers. They create a *concept* for the message that will bring it to life. The concept should be believable, distinctive, and meaningful so that consumers will remember the message. The message is then delivered using one of several **execution styles**. The tone of the message is important because it nonverbally communicates important information about the product.

Advertising Objectives

An advertising objective is a specific communication task that a company wants to accomplish in a specific timeframe with a specific target audience. Objectives can be broken down into three categories: **Informative**, **persuasive**, and **reminders**. Informative advertising is used when introducing new products to consumers. Persuasive advertising is used more when there is competition in a market between two or more companies. This type of advertising is often called **comparative advertising** because companies will tout certain characteristics of their products and show how it is superior to its competitors. Reminder advertising is used on well-known brands to keep consumers thinking about certain products.

- **Informative advertising** is used when a product or service is at the beginning of its life cycle. Its main purpose is to make consumers aware of the product or service and their need for it. Informative advertising is also used to explain how the product works and where it can be purchased. It is also used as a promotional tool used to build a company's image, to reduce fears and concerns about the product or service, or to explain new uses for it to reinvigorate sales.
- **Persuasive advertising** is often used in the middle of a product's life cycle. This is the time that companies often allocate the largest part of their advertising budget. Once a demand has been established, companies begin to change their advertising message to explain to consumers why their product or service is better than their competitors. Persuasive advertising is also used to create and build brand loyalty or to encourage people to switch to their brand. It is also used to persuade consumers to buy immediately while this market is popular.
- It is a good sign for a company if they use **reminder advertising** because it usually means that their product or service is/was a success. Reminder advertising occurs at the end of a product's life cycle and is used to revive stagnant sales or to remind people about mature products. For instance, long-running companies like Coca-Cola don't need to persuade people to drink Coke, they just need to remind people to drink it. It is also used to tell people where to buy, and by mature seasonal companies to keep their products in people's thoughts in the off-season.

Copyright © Mometrix Media. You have been licensed one copy of this document for personal use only. Any other reproduction or redistribution is strictly prohibited. All rights reserved.
This content is provided for test preparation purposes only and does not imply an endorsement by Mometrix of any particular political, scientific, or religious point of view.

Media Production

There are four major steps involved in deciding what forms of media to use: deciding on the **frequency, reach and impact, the type of media, specific media vehicles,** and **timing.**The frequency of media is how many times a person in a market is exposed to a message. The reach is how many people in a market a message is trying to reach. Impact is how strong an impression the product's message provided through the medium it was delivered. Advertisers have to choose among the many forms of media. They have to choose among different media vehicles and specific media within each larger channel. An example is deciding which magazine to advertise in after deciding to advertise in magazines. The timing of a media campaign is important because there are many different variables that can hurt a product's sales momentum if they are released at that time.

Advertising Agencies

Large companies often hire advertising agencies because they offer several advantages over doing their own. They are specialized in what they do, bring in an outside point of view, and have years of experience. Ad agencies have four departments:

- The **creative** department creates the advertising campaign.
- The **business** department handles the financial aspects of the company.
- **Research** studies what people want and are looking for in a product, and communicate the results to media and creative.
- The **media** department selects its media channels and places advertisements.

Specific Media Vehicles

Once a company decides what basic type of media they are going to invest in, they have to choose which specific **media vehicles** they are going to advertise through. These are often large investments so marketers compute the costs per person in the market. For example it can cost $2 million dollars for a 30-advertisement during the Super Bowl. If 50 million people watch the game then the cost to reach each person is will cost about $25 dollars. A company must also consider the high cost of these types of advertisements. While a print ad is cheap to make, a high-quality commercial can cost millions of dollars for something that may only be shown a few times.

When to Advertise

A well-known quote in business is, "timing is everything." If a product is released at the wrong time, it may never get the momentum needed to establish itself in the marketplace and turn a profit. Companies have to anticipate things such as downturns in the economy, rival product release dates, holidays, weather, etc. A company first decides on how it is going to time its ads. It **continually** releases them at regular intervals throughout the year, or it releases its ads in bursts, called **pulsing.** Mostly seasonal companies that make their money one or two months out of the year use this method.

Sales Promotions

Sales promotions are short-term incentives provided by companies to encourage people to purchase their products or services right now. Promotions come in many forms: a one-day sale, a $1.00 off coupon, free shipping if you spend $25 dollars or more, etc. Sales promotions make up an ever-increasing part of companies expenditures due to the high demand of sales and the increase of promotions from rival competitors. As a result, **promotion clutter** has occurred in the marketplace. This means that the amount of sales promotion is so high, that customers have begun to tune them out.

Copyright © Mometrix Media. You have been licensed one copy of this document for personal use only. Any other reproduction or redistribution is strictly prohibited. All rights reserved.
This content is provided for test preparation purposes only and does not imply an endorsement by Mometrix of any particular political, scientific, or religious point of view.

There are many different types of tools that companies use to increase sales. Coupons, samples, cash refunds, sweepstakes, games, rebates, and contests are some of the many different ways that companies promote their products. These promotions are very popular. Consumers clip almost five billion coupons a year. Samples are small amounts of the product given to customers for trial. Contests, games, and sweepstakes offer the consumer a chance to win a prize through luck or little effort. Cash refunds give customers the feeling of money back in their hands directly after a purchase.

Public Relations

Companies have been investing in public relations much more as they realize the importance of good relationships with their customers and the public. Promotion is used to promote people, products, services, ideas, activities, and several other aspects of a company. Public relations departments perform the following functions for a company. They control **press relations** by creating information and placing it in the news media to attract attention. They control **public affairs**, by building and maintaining relationships with the community. **Lobbyists** are used to influence politicians and government officials. **Investor relations** are maintained to keep shareholders informed and happy.

Public relations play a vital role in the image of a company. While they may perform some of the same duties as marketers, PR is different from marketing because their main job is to communicate within the company and to the public. They are the ones that build up the image of a business or attempt to repair it when an unfavorable story or rumor is being circulated. Public relations can create marketing buzz on a very small budget. Speeches, news conferences, and educational programs are some of the inexpensive and highly effective ways that PR can create demand for a product or service.

Global Market

There are several strategies companies can choose from when adapting their products to the global market that generally depend on the level of product adaptation. **Straight product extension** means to market a product in a foreign market without any change. **Product adaptation** means to adapt a product to meat the specifications of a foreign market. **Product invention** is when a company creates a completely new product for sale in a foreign market. This usually happens with large food companies that want to operate in places where the people do not eat the same things that Americans eat.

Empathy

Empathy is the ability to understand what a person is feeling because they have experienced it themselves. A good salesperson is one who is empathetic to their customers because it makes their sales pitch seem more legitimate. Understanding a situation the way a customer sees it is a valuable tool because it enhances the ability to understand what a customer may be looking for in the product, enabling the seller to adjust their pitch accordingly.

Management

Management uses material and human resources to obtain business goals. There are usually three levels of managers. Top-level managers usually have titles like: CEO, president, vice-president, or CFO (chief financial officer). They are most concerned with the direction that the company is going in the future and set long-term goals and objectives. Middle-level managers carry out the vision and goals of the top-level managers. They take these goals and turn them into short-term goals for their employees. First-line managers directly oversee employees and assign duties to entry-level employees. They are often referred to as foremen, managers, or supervisors.

Copyright © Mometrix Media. You have been licensed one copy of this document for personal use only. Any other reproduction or redistribution is strictly prohibited. All rights reserved.
This content is provided for test preparation purposes only and does not imply an endorsement by Mometrix of any particular political, scientific, or religious point of view.

Customer Relationships

There are many levels of customer-consumer business relationships. It mostly rests on the size of the market and its margins. In a **basic relationship**, companies seek to keep customers satisfied, but not get to know them personally. A **full partnership** exists in markets where there are few customers and high margins. The company will work to ensure that the consumer is completely satisfied and may even seek input from them on the product. Many other levels exist between these two extremes. Companies strive to build and keep customer loyalty. There are several ways that they do this. By offering **financial incentives**, businesses try to add value to their relationships. Programs like frequent flyer miles, point systems, and cash-back programs are examples of the incentives.

Buying-Decision Behavior

A person behaves differently when they decide what type of soda to buy as opposed to what type of car to buy. Generally, as purchases become more expensive, the consumer put more thought and deliberation into their decision-making progress. **Complex-buying process** refers to customers getting very involved with a purchase and looking for distinct differences between brands in the marketplace. **Dissonance-reducing buying behavior** is when customers still make a large investment in comparing products, but find little difference between them. **Habitual buying behavior** is when consumers make low-involvement low-cost buying decisions. For example, if you need a notebook, you may just reach for one and buy it without thinking. **Variety-seeking buying behavior** features low customer involvement, but they constantly try different brands because of low cost. Food and drinks are an example.

The Buyer Decision Process

There are five stages that a buyer goes through when deciding what to purchase.

1. **Need recognition** is the name for when a buyer realizes that they need to purchase a product to satisfy a need, want, or to solve a problem.
2. **Information search** is the stage when the buyer will search different avenues to figure out what they need to purchase or to find out information comparing products.
3. **Evaluation of Alternatives** is when the consumers use the information they obtained to decide whether they should buy another brand, put off the purchase, or not make it at all.
4. **Purchase decision** is when the buyer decides which product to purchase.
5. **Post-purchase behavior** is how the buyer acts after the purchase. Depending on their level of satisfaction, these are what actions they take. A buyer might decide to purchase this product in the future, tell friends, or take negative actions if they are dissatisfied.

Customers

Customers come in many different forms. By understanding the different needs of different types of customers, a salesperson can greatly increase their sales. For instance, families tend to look for safe, quality products and services, but may have a limited amount of money to spend. Someone who is single usually tends to have more disposable income than a family consumer but may have needs that are harder to match. Sellers also need to take into account the market segment that they are competing in and how that will influence the potential purchases a customer will make. For instance, a travel agent does not sell many Spring Break packages to families, but will be able to sell them to young, single customers.

Channels, Supply and Value

The **supply chain** is the control of goods, ideas, and materials that flow between producers and consumers. The **distribution channels** are how the company gets the product or service to the

Copyright © Mometrix Media. You have been licensed one copy of this document for personal use only. Any other reproduction or redistribution is strictly prohibited. All rights reserved.
This content is provided for test preparation purposes only and does not imply an endorsement by Mometrix of any particular political, scientific, or religious point of view.

consumer. **Marketing channels** are a set of organizations that make products and services available for use. A **value delivery network** are all the people who make up the company. They are suppliers, distributors, and customers that improve the performance of the product or service with their input.

Copyright © Mometrix Media. You have been licensed one copy of this document for personal use only. Any other reproduction or redistribution is strictly prohibited. All rights reserved.
This content is provided for test preparation purposes only and does not imply an endorsement by Mometrix of any particular political, scientific, or religious point of view.

Economics

Transform passive reading into active learning! After immersing yourself in this chapter, put your comprehension to the test by taking a quiz. The insights you gained will stay with you longer this way. Scan the QR code to go directly to the chapter quiz interface for this study guide. If you're using a computer, simply visit the online resources page at **mometrix.com/resources719/gacemarketed** and click the Chapter Quizzes link.

International Business, Marketing, and Trade

Benefits of International Trade

There are many benefits to international trade. One advantage is that a company has an entirely new market to which to sell. It can increase its sales and thus its profits tremendously by reaching these customers. A company may have surplus supply that would otherwise not be utilized. Customers can enjoy products that are not available domestically. If international trade was not available, they may not be able to get that product. Also, opening up international trade can make those products available for less money. They may get the foreign product for less, and even domestic companies may lower their prices to become more competitive. Consumers who wouldn't have been able to afford the products may now do so. Also, there is less dependence on a single market, so if something goes wrong, the item will still be available. A foreign market may be more profitable for a domestic company.

Drawbacks of International Trade

There are a lot of arguments against free trade. It can lead to job losses and company failures domestically. New domestic companies may not have a chance to catch up with foreign companies. Some feel that getting products from rival countries is risky, and there are concerns about working conditions. In some countries, there is little regulation and people work in unsafe and unsanitary conditions. Workers, including children, may work many hours for little pay. Also, the manufacturing processes may damage the environment. There might not be the same quality control for the products, and some of the products may be of lower quality or even hazardous. Also, when jobs are outsourced, there will be less opportunity in the United States. Domestic companies that have good practices and fairly compensated employees may have difficulty competing with international companies that do not. A company may also face barriers to trade such as quotas, tariffs, and cultural resistance.

Historical Patterns of International Trade

The United States has engaged in international trade for many centuries. The **triangular trade system** was a system that ran from the late 1500s to the early 1800s. It connected Africa, the American colonies, and the Caribbean and consisted of slaves, crops, and manufactured goods. Many countries export raw goods and import manufactured materials. The United States trades with a wide variety of countries, and many companies have gone international through trade. The

Copyright © Mometrix Media. You have been licensed one copy of this document for personal use only. Any other reproduction or redistribution is strictly prohibited. All rights reserved.
This content is provided for test preparation purposes only and does not imply an endorsement by Mometrix of any particular political, scientific, or religious point of view.

United States used to practice protectionism, but has gravitated towards free trade in modern days. Still, protectionism is not eradicated and can be seen in policies today.

Review Video: The Triangular Trade
Visit mometrix.com/academy and enter code: 415470

Modern Trends in International Business

There have been many trends in international business. Much of the manufacturing has moved internationally to areas where the cost of labor is lower. China has emerged as a significant exporter, with many of the goods in the United States and other countries coming from there. Multinational businesses have a great impact on the growth and health of the economy, especially given their size. They add a lot to the growth of the GDP. Trade also plays a large part in economic growth, both in the United States and other countries. There have also been some trends specific to the United States. The US has increased the importation of oil. Approximately half of the oil import originates from the Western Hemisphere. Also, the United States currently has a negative balance of trade, also known as a trade deficit. This means the United States is importing more than it is exporting.

Economic Factors That Influence International Trade

There are various economic factors that influence international trade. One is opportunity costs. **Opportunity costs** are what a producer gives up by choosing a different option. For instance, if a producer can make a dozen cookies in an hour or a dozen brownies in an hour for the same cost and he chooses to make the cookies, then the dozen brownies are the opportunity cost. Someone who has a higher opportunity cost for making a product may want to import that product so they do not have to incur the opportunity cost. **Comparative advantage** is given to the party with the lowest opportunity cost. It makes sense for them to produce and export the product. **Absolute advantage** is when a producer can make more of something with smaller inputs. For instance, if one country can make 10 shirts for the cost and effort that another country uses to make five shirts, then the country that can make more has the absolute advantage. It makes sense for the producer who can make it with the least inputs to make it.

Government Policies That Create Obstacles to International Trade

There are many government policies that create obstacles to international trade. These are done for different reasons, including protecting domestic businesses and raising revenues. **Quotas** put a restriction on the number of imports. Beyond that number, the products must be made by domestic means. This can make products more expensive because it may be more expensive to make domestically, although domestic companies gain because they can charge more. The government also wins with more tax revenues. **Tariffs** are taxes that apply to goods that are imported. Because the cost of imports is increased, domestic production is cheaper. This is advantageous for domestic manufacturers. **Voluntary export restraints** are self-applied rules that restrict what a country can export to another country. Oftentimes the importing country has requested the limit. **Embargoes** occur when a country restricts trade with a specific foreign country, often for political or economic reasons. These measures are often done concurrently.

Effects of Currency Exchange Rates on Trade

When a country purchases items from another country, they first change their money over to that currency. When the foreign currency is weaker, they can purchase more of it for their own money. They will then have more money and the items will be relatively cheaper. They will import more from the country with the weaker currency because these items are less expensive. Alternatively, if a country is trading with a country that has a stronger form of currency, then they will be able to get

Copyright © Mometrix Media. You have been licensed one copy of this document for personal use only. Any other reproduction or redistribution is strictly prohibited. All rights reserved.
This content is provided for test preparation purposes only and does not imply an endorsement by Mometrix of any particular political, scientific, or religious point of view.

less of that foreign money and thus the goods will be more expensive. They might import less in this case. Exchange rates change constantly, thus so does trade.

Benefits and Drawbacks of a Weak/Strong Dollar

Whether the dollar is weak or strong can make a big difference for the economy and everyday people. If the dollar is weak, it has less purchasing power and it becomes more expensive to import from foreign countries. As prices increase, consumers spend less. Fuel costs tend to go up, too. Inflation can occur because of this. Central banks might raise interest rates to attract investors, but this can be problematic for the economy. A benefit of a weak dollar is that a trade deficit could decrease and domestic job growth can occur, especially in industries like manufacturing. Demand will also increase for exports because they are cheaper, which will also increase jobs. There could be some lost jobs, however, from businesses that are paying more for supplies. A strong dollar makes the opposite occur. Foreign goods cost less, so importing may increase while exporting or domestically-produced items go down. Prices can go down as well. One is not necessarily bad or good. Overall, a strong economy will have a strong dollar, but sometimes a weak dollar is best.

Elements That Influence International Trade

The **balance of trade**, the differential between a nation's imports and exports, can influence international trade. So can the **balance of payments**, which is a compilation of economic transactions of a nation and the global companies with which it trades. It includes loan repayment, capital movements, money spent by tourists, and more. International trade is also affected by changes in the supply of labor as well as demand for labor. If a lower supply of labor exists, a country may need to import more and vice versa. Some countries also have practices such as **dumping**. This is where a country exports products at an extremely low price compared to what they would be available for domestically. This can be catastrophic for manufacturers in that country. Sometimes countries will also take retaliatory actions that can affect international trade. The exchange rates and values of the different currencies also matter. If a country's currency is strong, it has more power and might import more; if it is weak, it might import less. All of these factors combine to affect international trade.

GATT

The **General Agreement on Tariffs and Trade (GATT)** is a treaty that was formed after World War II to help the economy. It strives to lower obstacles to global trade such as quotas, tariffs, and subsidies. It played a huge part in increasing free trade throughout the 20th century. The main part was for trade to occur without discrimination. A country had its markets opened equally to other countries. If a country made an agreement to lower tariffs with the countries it had a significant trade with, then those went to other GATT members, too. The nations would specify the tariff rates they would provide to the other member countries. GATT also strove to promote tariffs rather than a limit on the number of items traded. There was an escape clause in case a country lost a lot because of concessions in trade. It was in effect until the World Trade Organization took over in 1995, at which point it had 125 nations signed to it and governed 90 percent of international trade.

NAFTA

The **North American Free Trade Agreement (NAFTA)** became active in 1994 and has had a profound effect on trade ever since. The agreement was signed by the United States, Mexico, and Canada and, as part of it, number restrictions and duties were terminated on January 1, 2008. The largest international free trade area was formed, and trade between the three countries increased tremendously, going to 1.2 trillion for US goods and services in 2012. Canada benefited economically from the agreement. Mexico has a lot of factories known as maquiladoras that take raw goods and make them into finished products. The United States has seen trade increase

Copyright © Mometrix Media. You have been licensed one copy of this document for personal use only. Any other reproduction or redistribution is strictly prohibited. All rights reserved.
This content is provided for test preparation purposes only and does not imply an endorsement by Mometrix of any particular political, scientific, or religious point of view.

tremendously, but there has been loss of manufacturing jobs to Mexico. There were some issues about environmental concerns, thus the North American Agreement on Environmental Cooperation (NAAEC) was formed to address this. Despite some increases in pollution, there have been many benefits overall.

WTO

Started in 1995 by the Marrakesh Agreement, the **World Trade Organization (WTO)** is an international organization related to trade rules between different countries. WTO agreements are negotiated and created to form agreements that benefit producers, importers and exporters. It provides a place for companies to negotiate trade and work through problems, such as trade restrictions. It has formed trade rules. It works to promote safe and effective trade without conflicts between nations. If there is conflict, WTO works to resolve disputes and ensure nations comply with the agreements they have made. It also helps nations come up with their own trade agreements. The WTO has a staff of more than 600 people in Geneva, Switzerland.

IMF

Part of the United Nations, the **International Monetary Fund (IMF)** promotes economic stability in 188 member countries. It strives for international growth by giving policy advice and helping developing nations reduce their level of poverty. Some of its primary roles are to keep exchange rates stable, balance international trade, provide financing to struggling countries, and give training and technical assistance. It also works with research and tries to keep the international financial system stable and looks at worldwide economic trends. The IMF performs surveillance to keep track of economic or financial problems. It will appraise financial situations and help countries create policies that are best. There is some criticism of the organization based on several issues, like reports that the loan conditions are too intrusive and intervene too much by forcing privatization, for instance. Critics also argue the policies of the Washington consensus are put forth without considering the special needs of that country, that policies are expected to be implemented together right away, and that the organization doesn't take criticism well.

World Bank

The **World Bank** works to reduce poverty by loaning money to developing countries for capital programs. This international financial organization is part of the United Nations and is based in Washington, D.C. It promotes foreign investment, international trade, and capital investment. It also works to improve health and fight diseases such as AIDS, tuberculosis, and malaria by sending vaccines internationally, along with other measures. It has also fought for environmental causes such as preventing climate change. It is now focused on 14 centralized global practices, including health and water. There has been some criticism, with some based on upcoming layoffs and lowered budgets.

Conducting International Business Through Licensing

International business is often conducted through licensing. **International licensing** occurs when one business makes an agreement with another, giving special permission to make the product in a foreign country. It might involve the resources to do it or the right. This might include a copyright, skills of managers, patents, technology, and more. It is advantageous in that companies can get into new markets they may not have been able to enter otherwise, because of restrictions in trade. It is also a way to enter another market without spending too much money or incurring too much risk because the company is just giving the rights and resources to make the product and not actually going in and doing it itself. The disadvantage is that there is a risk that the foreign firm will not adhere to the agreement. Also, with lower financial involvement and risk comes a lower expected financial return.

Copyright © Mometrix Media. You have been licensed one copy of this document for personal use only. Any other reproduction or redistribution is strictly prohibited. All rights reserved.
This content is provided for test preparation purposes only and does not imply an endorsement by Mometrix of any particular political, scientific, or religious point of view.

Conducting International Business Through Franchising

One way to conduct international business is through franchising. This is where an individual leases the ability to replicate a business model and brand. Generally, the individual will create a business that is a replica of a successful one. For instance, a franchise restaurant will have the same look, food, etc. McDonald's is a common franchise. There are both advantages and disadvantages to conducting international business through franchising. The model has already been successful and people are accustomed to it, so it may already have a built-in audience, which can stimulate business from the beginning. Domestic success may not translate to international success, however. Tastes and preferences are different in other countries. One advantage is that much of the work is done—the person will already have the branding, products, and so forth created. The franchisee may be subject to laws and regulations in other countries, however. Also, the franchisee may have little control and be unable to change things. Entrepreneurs should consider all these factors when deciding whether to franchise.

Conducting International Business Through Contract Manufacturing

Contract manufacturing is a popular method of entering a foreign market. With contract manufacturing, the company designs the product but then hires another company to manufacture and ship it. This can be a very cost effective way of doing business, especially in foreign markets where it might be more expensive to do business. Also, companies can find a manufacturer that is able to make a product that they do not have the ability to make. It will also free the company to focus on designing the products and other things. There are risks as well. The company will not have as much control over the product and it may not come out with the desired quality. Also, some foreign companies have poor practices with regard to working conditions or the environment. The company will also be sharing their intellectual property, which they risk losing. If there is a problem with the manufacturer, it will reflect on the company. Also, sometimes there are contract disputes or other issues with the relationship. Overall, contract manufacturing can be a great way to enter a foreign business as long as the risks are considered.

Conducting International Business Through Joint Ventures

One common method for conducting international business is through **joint ventures**. In this strategy, a company will form a partnership with a company in the international market it wants to enter. Both inputs and outputs, such as profits or losses, are shared. It can be short or long term, but is often temporary. It is advantageous in that the risk is shared, making it less risky to a business entering the foreign market. In addition, the business can take advantage of the fact that the foreign business is already familiar with the market in the other country. Also, consumers may be less resistant to them because they will seem to be part of the local business and not a foreign entity. Sometimes there are laws and regulations that would make it difficult for a foreign business to enter the market otherwise. The downside is the company will share the profits from the venture. Also, the company may have to give up some decision-making power. Sometimes disagreements arise from partnerships. With proper research it can be an excellent way to enter an international market.

Conducting International Business Through Strategic Alliances

A common method of conducting international business is through **strategic alliances**. It is similar to a joint venture in that two companies—one domestic and one foreign—come to an agreement to work on a project to benefit both of them, perhaps sharing resources or knowledge. Whereas in a joint venture the company may form an actual business entity together, with a strategic alliance they work together on a project, but the firms remain independent. Also, it is typically not as long or involved as a joint venture. It is advantageous because a company can get into a foreign market it

Copyright © Mometrix Media. You have been licensed one copy of this document for personal use only. Any other reproduction or redistribution is strictly prohibited. All rights reserved.
This content is provided for test preparation purposes only and does not imply an endorsement by Mometrix of any particular political, scientific, or religious point of view.

may otherwise have difficulty entering. It can use the benefits of the foreign company's knowledge and reputation in that country and help avoid resistance to a foreign business. The businesses can also share the risk. Of course, the company will not have full control over the project and may be responsible if the other company does something wrong. They will also have to share the rewards, such as profit.

Conducting International Business Through Foreign Subsidiaries

When a company opens a new subsidiary in a foreign country, either by starting one or buying an existing company, it is called a **foreign subsidiary**. The advantage is that the parent company stays in charge of the subsidiary and makes the decisions. They can get the rewards of it, and also enjoy cost savings when the parent and subsidiary share the same resources, such as the same financial processes. A disadvantage is that they can be liable for the subsidiary's problems. If the parent company starts a business from the beginning, it will have to deal with the difficulties of establishing a business in a foreign country such as finding customers and suppliers. Buying an established business can ease some of these difficulties. It can be very expensive to get into international business this way, and it is a large commitment. Still, it can expand a business' customers, sales, and profit.

Factors to Consider When Entering International Business

There are many factors that businesses should consider when entering international business. First, they should think about how their product is likely to do overseas. Consumers have different tastes and preferences in different areas. The company should make sure there is a demand for their product by conducting market research. Sometimes a product can be successful but only with changes to the product, branding, pricing, or marketing. They should also consider the competition. Businesses should look at the laws, regulations, and licensing requirements, which may be very different from those in the United States. The company should consider the logistics and costs of expanding internationally. It may cost a lot more to ship products overseas. The company needs to consider exactly how it will penetrate the international market. There are many methods for international penetration; the company should research these to find out what is best for them. They may want to research alliances with others in the foreign area. They should make a clear business plan for penetrating the market.

Influences of Cultural, Economic, Sociopolitical, and Language Differences

Laws and regulations, including those pertaining to business, can be different in different countries. Business professionals need to be sure to understand the laws in the country in which they are doing business. The culture can have a significant effect. Some cultures are much more formal than others. Certain practices, such as touching someone, are taboo in certain cultures. Business professionals need to know what is acceptable. Also, there can be language barriers, and someone may accidently convey the wrong meaning. It is important to have someone who knows the language well and can translate successfully. There can also be political issues as well. Some countries are more restrictive on what can be advertised and how. Businesses should understand how distribution channels work. When a business plans to enter a foreign market, they should do research to make sure they understand the cultural, economic, sociopolitical, and language factors at play.

Ethnocentrism and Stereotyping

Cultures across the globe are very different, and it can be difficult to communicate across these lines. This has led to some mistaken beliefs and practices. **Ethnocentrism** occurs when a people believe that they and their culture are superior to those of others. It is extremely common and can affect international business greatly. People of one culture may be very resistant to businesses from

Copyright © Mometrix Media. You have been licensed one copy of this document for personal use only. Any other reproduction or redistribution is strictly prohibited. All rights reserved.
This content is provided for test preparation purposes only and does not imply an endorsement by Mometrix of any particular political, scientific, or religious point of view.

other countries because they feel they are not as good. Stereotyping can occur in which people believe certain things about a people just because of who they are. They may believe everyone from a certain country is bad, for instance. When consumers are ethnocentric and have stereotypes, they may reject products from international companies and prefer those from their country. Certain countries display these characteristics more than others. This can affect international business greatly.

Review Video: Stereotypes
Visit mometrix.com/academy and enter code: 569262

Foundations of Marketing

Economies of Scale

An economy of scale is a term used to describe how an increase in the number of units produced leads to a decrease in the average cost of each unit produced. This term is used in conjunction with the third phase of the product life cycle. During this phase, a product is at its most profitable and therefore its production is at its highest. Diseconomies of scale refers to just the opposite. This causes companies to increase costs despite increasing production. This phenomenon occurs mostly in larger companies that are top-heavy with many levels of well-compensated management. When these two forces are balanced, it is known as the constant returns to scale. In the graph below, the company achieves the lowest cost per unit, C_1, when they produce a quantity Q_2 of units. If they produce a greater or smaller number of units, the **long-run average cost (LRAC)** goes up.

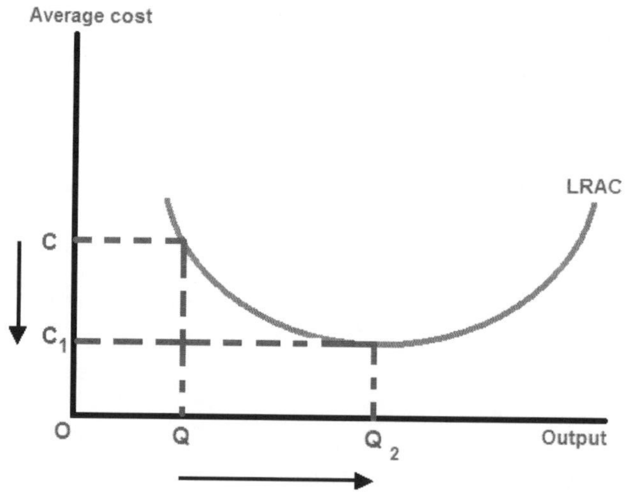

Supply and Demand

Supply and demand refers to the relationship between producers and consumers regarding the price and sales of a product in a certain market. This theory is one of the basic principles of microeconomics. Both supply and demand are directly affected by price. The law of demand states that demand will be inversely proportional to price. As the price goes up, demand goes down. The law of supply states that it is directly proportional to the price. If the price goes up, the supply of the good will go up. This law assumes that as factors affect the market, these laws will move the price towards an economic equilibrium where businesses supply exactly the demand wanted.

Copyright © Mometrix Media. You have been licensed one copy of this document for personal use only. Any other reproduction or redistribution is strictly prohibited. All rights reserved.
This content is provided for test preparation purposes only and does not imply an endorsement by Mometrix of any particular political, scientific, or religious point of view.

Measuring Inflation

Inflation is measured using what is called the **Consumer Price Index**, (CPI) This measurement takes a number of products from a broad number of markets that urban households consume and measures the fluctuations in their prices. A **personal inflation rate** is the rate of much prices increase for the items of one particular person. For instance, the personal inflation rate of a person that frequently uses their vehicle will be higher than a person who doesn't due to the fluctuations in the prices of products related to the vehicle. (gas, oil, service checks)

Price Elasticity Formula

Companies need to plan ahead of time for economic fluctuations. One of the ways they do this is planning for price elasticity. This is a measure of how the demand for goods and services will be affected by a change in price. Many factors influence price elasticity such as: time of year, weather, demand, supply, and price. The formula looks like this:

$$\text{Price Elasticity of Demand} = \frac{\%\text{ Change in Quantity Demanded}}{\%\text{ Change in Price}}$$

Salespeople

In order to attract the best candidates, companies need to offer appealing compensation packages that offer not just good pay, but benefits such as health care and retirement and vacation benefits. A company must first decide what type of financial mix it is best suited for the job. They decide whether the job should be paid based on salary, commission, bonuses, or a combination of the three. It is managers whose job it is to motivate and give direction to the salespeople. The amount of supervision needed depends on the company, employee, and type of job. Salespeople are evaluated by sales reports and feedback from coworkers and customers.

Market Demand

Total market demand is measure of sales of a product or service in a hypothetical situation. For example, the total market demand of baseball equipment would depend on how many companies are making equipment, the weather, marketing, and many other factors that may manipulate sales. The ceiling of market demand is called market potential. The formula to estimate total market demand is:

$$Q = n \times q \times p$$

Where:

Q = Total market demand

n = number of buyers in the market

q = quantity purchased by an average buyer per year

p = price of an average unit

There are two different methods companies use when attempting to determine where the best sales territories are and how much of their resources they need to allocate. The **market buildup method** is a method marketers use to predict market potential and using certain factors. The **market factor index method** is used by marketers to figure out which markets to enter and

Copyright © Mometrix Media. You have been licensed one copy of this document for personal use only. Any other reproduction or redistribution is strictly prohibited. All rights reserved.
This content is provided for test preparation purposes only and does not imply an endorsement by Mometrix of any particular political, scientific, or religious point of view.

estimate how much money customers would spend on their product. The **buying power index** (BPI) is based on three factors: an area's population, buying income, and retail sales.

BPI = 0.2 x percentage of national population in the area
+ 0.5 x the percentage of effective buying income in the area
+ 0.3 x percentage of national retail sales in the area

Forecasting

Forecasting is a method of estimating future demand by anticipating the actions of buyers under various conditions. Forecasting the future sales of a product or service is very difficult because it is impossible to foresee what events may happen in the future. Companies usually use a three-step process to determine a sales forecast. First, they make an **environmental forecast**. At this step they predict external factors that they have little control over like: inflation, unemployment rates, and interest rates. Their findings are used to provide an **industry forecast**. A **company sales forecast** is all the methods a business uses to figure out what the sales of their products in a certain market might look like.

Forecasting Future Sales

There are several different ways in which companies attempt to figure out what their future sales might look like. Companies are trying to figure out what people say, what they do, and what they have done in relation to the market. Some of the common techniques used to figure out what people are saying about products are: surveys, expert opinions and getting the opinion of salespeople and other people in the sales force. To figure out what people are doing, companies put products into test markets and observe how buyers react to it. Forecasters analyze records of past buying behavior, statistics, and other leading indicators to figure out what buyers have done before.

Operating Statement

Balance sheets and operating statements are the two mains ways that companies keep track of their financial records. A **balance sheet** is a financial statement of a company that shows all its assets, liabilities, and value. Marketers use **operating statements** more than balance sheets. They show figures like company sales, cost of goods sold, and expenses during a specific time period. Operating statements are also known as income statements and profit-for-loss statements. An outline of an operating statement looks something like this:

Net sales	$100,000
Cost of goods sold	- 25,000
Gross margin	$ 75,000
Expenses	- 30,000
Net profit	$ 45,000

The **net sales** are compiled using three numbers: the gross sales, returns and allowances, and net sales. **Gross sales** are the amount of total sales a company charged to customers during a specific time period. Not every customer keeps their product. Sometimes a customer **returns** a product and receives cash or store credit. Other times a customer is given an **allowance** by keeping the product for a reduced price. Adding returns and allowances and subtracting it from the gross sales gives the **net sales**.

Operating Ratios

Once a company has the figures it needs from its operating statements, it then puts them into an operating ratio. This is a ratio that is found by taking select operating statement items to net sales

Copyright © Mometrix Media. You have been licensed one copy of this document for personal use only. Any other reproduction or redistribution is strictly prohibited. All rights reserved.
This content is provided for test preparation purposes only and does not imply an endorsement by Mometrix of any particular political, scientific, or religious point of view.

so marketers can use them to compare their performance from years past. Here are the formulas for **gross margin percentage, the net profit percentage, the operating expense percentage, and the returns and allowances percentage.**

$$\text{Gross margin percentage} = \frac{\text{gross margin}}{\text{net sales}}$$

$$\text{Net profit percentage} = \frac{\text{net profit}}{\text{net sales}}$$

$$\text{Operating expense percentage} = \frac{\text{total expenses}}{\text{net sales}}$$

$$\text{Returns andallowances percentage} = \frac{\text{returns and allowances}}{\text{net sales}}$$

Return on Investment

An effective way to measure a manager's effectiveness is to use a formula designed to figure out the company's return on their investment. This ratio called return on investment is the ratio of net profit to investment. It is important to note that the ROI cannot be found just by finding the ratio of net profit to investment because marketers use this formula to figure out what might have happened if they invested differently.

$$ROI = \frac{net\ profit}{sales} \times \frac{sales}{investment}$$

Markups and Markdowns

Businesses **markup goods** to turn a profit and **markdown goods** to move inventory or outsell competitors. Markups can be computed two different ways, by cost or by selling price.

$$\text{Markup percentage on cost} = \frac{\text{dollar markup}}{\text{cost}}$$

$$\text{Markup percentage on selling price} = \frac{\text{dollar markup}}{\text{selling price}}$$

When a seller knows his cost and markup, the selling price can be found with the following formula:

$$\text{Selling price} = \frac{\text{cost}}{1 - \text{markup}}$$

When a seller wants to see how much money they would make after a markdown, they use the following ratio:

$$\text{Markdown percentage} = \frac{\text{dollar markdown}}{\text{total net sales in dollars}}$$

Discounts

Seasonal discounts are price reductions that are offered for goods or services that are not in their peak season. They are given to reduce inventory or to stimulate business. An example would be a sale on ski equipment that occurs in June. An example of a short-term seasonal discount is happy hour. Bars and restaurants often offer free food or drink specials in the afternoon to get people in

Copyright © Mometrix Media. You have been licensed one copy of this document for personal use only. Any other reproduction or redistribution is strictly prohibited. All rights reserved.
This content is provided for test preparation purposes only and does not imply an endorsement by Mometrix of any particular political, scientific, or religious point of view.

the building in hopes that they will stay. A trade discount is a discount given to companies that help distribute, promote, or perform some sort of function. These discounts are often used in channels controlled by the retailer.

Important Traits in Marketing

Marketing is a very demanding job that requires a diverse set of skills. When you are selling a product, often you are selling yourself. This is why personal skills are so important. To be successful in marketing a person should: be able to communicate their ideas clearly, to be able to get along with any type of person, to be motivated to make money, have good math skills, be creative, and have good problem-solving skills. While this seems like a lot of qualities for one job, marketing is one of the most diverse jobs in the world. However, for people in this field, it is also why it is one of the most satisfying.

Hiring New Employees

When hiring a new employee, there a few important steps that a person must take. First, the business must analyze what needs to be done and write it into a job description. The business must figure out how much the job will cost them. This is more complex than just calculating wages. Most specialized jobs offer benefits, insurance, vacations, etc. It will also cost money to train the employee. Sometimes it is better to hire from within the company. This offers the benefit of already knowing the employee and their abilities. The company processes the applications and chooses candidates for interviews. After the interview process, an employee is offered the job. Employers need to make sure that their employees are properly trained to carry out their specific tasks in the most efficient way. This starts with on-the-job training in which the employee explains the job and shows them how to do it. The employer should then provide feedback as to how the employee is performing. Employers also provide performance appraisals that give employees information and feedback about their job performance. Employers are also expected to give promotions to the workers that show they are ready for more responsibility. They also are responsible for terminating employees who do not perform or behave satisfactorily.

Decision-Making Process

Much like life, the most successful businesses tend to make rational, informed decisions. They don't guess or make impulsive decisions. They do this by taking an issue through a five-step process.

1. **The problem** --This has to be the first step, but is also the easiest. If you don't know your problem, you can't find a solution.
2. **The alternatives** -- Think the problem through and figure out all the possible options that you have. Even if an alternative is undesirable, it needs to be included.
3. **Determine the pros and cons** -- List all the good things and bad things about your alternatives. It is important that you look at them in the context of your businesses or own objectives.
4. **Make the best decision possible** -- Rank your alternatives from most desirable to least desirable. Choose the best alternative and compare it to the second-best. Ask yourself if the difference is something that you can live with.
5. **Evaluate your decision** -- Ask yourself if you would make the same decision again.

Copyright © Mometrix Media. You have been licensed one copy of this document for personal use only. Any other reproduction or redistribution is strictly prohibited. All rights reserved.
This content is provided for test preparation purposes only and does not imply an endorsement by Mometrix of any particular political, scientific, or religious point of view.

Consumer Rights

A consumer has six basic rights:

1. **The right to be informed** -- Consumers have the right to be provided with information to make safe choices and to be protected against misleading or false advertising or other malicious business practices.
2. **The right to choose** -- Consumers should be protected from monopolistic practices and be able to choose from a variety of products in the market.
3. **The right to safety** -- Consumers should be informed and protected against hazardous products.
4. **The right to be heard** -- Consumers should have their input and concerns are taken into consideration in the making of laws regarding business.
5. **The right to have problems corrected** -- Consumers have the right to have problems remedied in a timely and fair manner.
6. **The right to consumer education** -- Consumers have the right to be educated about products, the market system, and how businesses work.

Consumer Responsibilities

Not all responsibility in business can be placed on the company. There are six basic responsibilities that every consumer is expected to be held accountable to in the capitalist system.

1. **The responsibility to be informed** -- Consumers should read and understand the information provided to them by businesses. In the United States, it is necessary to put warning labels on everything because of consumer negligence.
2. **The responsibility to choose carefully** -- Consumers should use their purchasing power to hold companies responsible for ethical behavior.
3. **The responsibility to use products safely** -- Consumers should use products the way they are intended and not use them in a way that is different from what they are designed for.
4. **The responsibility to speak out** -- Consumers should not be a passive voice in the market. With the advent of the Internet, there are infinite ways to inform people of unsatisfactory business practices.
5. **The responsibility to seek remedy** -- Consumers have a responsibility to inform company's when their products are defective or not performing to standard.
6. **The responsibility to learn consumer skills** -- It is important that consumers get and stay informed about the products that they are interested in purchasing.

Marketing Research Ethics

When marketing research is obtained and used in the correct way, it can be a benefit to both the business and the consumer. However, when it is obtained in an inappropriate manner, it can be annoying and harmful to the consumer. Some companies rig or manipulate their test data so that their product will look superior to a competitor. Consumer's biggest concern is what business does with the personal information that they have provided them. With the advent of the Internet, identity theft has become a legitimate problem. Sensitive data such as social security and bank account numbers are vulnerable to hackers. Companies have an obligation to keep this information safe.

Outside Partners

Companies do not always have adversarial relationships with other companies. In **supply chain management**, companies seek to strengthen relationships between companies that they work with at each level of the supply chain. They know that if any of these companies are inefficient or

Copyright © Mometrix Media. You have been licensed one copy of this document for personal use only. Any other reproduction or redistribution is strictly prohibited. All rights reserved.
This content is provided for test preparation purposes only and does not imply an endorsement by Mometrix of any particular political, scientific, or religious point of view.

unproductive, it will hurt their business. As a result, companies interact in order to increase communication and efficiency and pass their savings on to the consumer. Companies also know that they need to form **strategic alliances** in order to increase effectiveness. This helps companies expand into new markets, save on overall costs, and implement new ideas.

Demographics

The study of demographics is one of the most important aspects of marketing because it helps categorize its customer base. Demographics is the study of the human population in terms of age, gender, race, religion, income, education level, and several other parameters. It is a vital part of the marketing industry because the better they understand the diversity of people, the easier it is for them to customize their products to make them more appealing to their consumers. For instance, companies have modified their products to aim them more at teenagers because they have more influence on purchases than ever before. By catering to specific demographics, a company increases its chances of profits and customer loyalty.

Engel's Law

Ernst Engel was a sociologist that studied the spending habits of people. He noted that as people's incomes rose, the percentage of their income they spent on different things changed. As incomes rise, people spend a smaller percentage of their income on food and clothing, but other things such as housing, electricity, travel, and transportation remain constant. Better said, as you make more money, the purchases you make reflect the rise in income. Companies watch these things to try to anticipate shifts in the economic climate. By preparing for downturns and booms ahead of time, they can protect the long-term economic health of their company.

Cultural Values

The beliefs and values of a person influence the types of products that they buy. For instance, a married, conservative person is less likely to purchase products that conflict with family values than a single person with less strict values. A person's core beliefs are values that are passed on from parents and community members to children. These values tend to stay with a person for life. Secondary beliefs and values are more likely to change than primary beliefs. An example of a primary belief is that people should go to college. A secondary belief is that people should go to college right after high school, or that they should attend a state university. Marketers pay attention to shifts in secondary products to predict consumer purchasing habits

Marketing Research

Marketing research is a vital aspect of marketing. There are four types of research: exploratory, descriptive, causal, and observational research. The purpose of exploratory research is to gather preliminary information that can be used to define problems and find their solutions. Descriptive research attempts to describe problems, identify markets, and analyze the potential of new markets. Causal research aims to test hypotheses about cause-and-effect relationships. For instance, how might consumers react if the cost of a product was raised 10 percent? Observational research is the gathering of primary data by observing people in various situations. As information has evolved, the way we research it has as well. Ethnographic research is a new form of research that uses customer interviews with intensive observations to understand how customers interact with their products. Mechanical research uses machines such as checkout scanners or people meters (used by Neilsen to track television viewing habits) to understand customer behavior. Survey research uses surveys to gather primary data. Experimental research is research that is gathered by putting people in hypothetical situations.

Copyright © Mometrix Media. You have been licensed one copy of this document for personal use only. Any other reproduction or redistribution is strictly prohibited. All rights reserved.
This content is provided for test preparation purposes only and does not imply an endorsement by Mometrix of any particular political, scientific, or religious point of view.

Businesses need information to grow, evolve, and stay ahead of their customers. One of the hard parts of gathering information is deciding what is relevant to the business and what is not. Companies use internal databases to stockpile information and make it readily available to its workers. What information companies are allowed to keep about their customers has become a growing concern to customers as identity theft has risen. This information has become controversial with the advent of the Internet, which makes all this information vulnerable to hackers. When determining whether marketing research will be useful, it is important to understand how it was obtained. Data can be divided into two categories: primary and secondary data. Primary data is information that is collected with a specific question in mind that researchers want to find out. Secondary data is information gathered that already existed prior to being used by a company. It may reinforce primary data gathered or run contrary to it.

A sample is a small, usually diverse part of a population that is used by marketers to simulate the whole population. When sampling it is important to ask three questions: who is to be surveyed, how many people are to be surveyed, and how the people in the sample should be chosen. The purpose of sampling is to give a company a somewhat accurate representation of how the population at large would think and react to a situation or a product. Sampling is one of the most popular forms of gathering marketing information. Collecting information is the easy part of marketing; figuring out what to do with it is the hard part. Many companies store their information on a company intranet. This gives easy to find information such as documents, purchase history, contact information, and other information about a customer. For instance, say a manager wanted to identify the best time to have a sale. They could use the intranet to analyze the lowest point in the sales cycle. They could have a sale then to stimulate business. When companies share this information with clients and other companies, it is referred to as the extranet. They may use this information to update contact information, check orders, or compare data. These systems enable people to quickly analyze data and increase efficiency.

Global Marketing and E-Commerce

Globalization

Globalization can be defined as the integration of economic, cultural, political, religious, and social systems reaching the whole world and practically all human beings. There are several definitions, many of which mention the increasing connectivity of economies and ways of life across the world. While some observers of globalization stress convergence of patterns of production and consumption and a resulting homogenization of culture, others stress that globalization has the potential to take many diverse forms. In economics, globalization is the convergence of prices, products, wages, rates of interest and profits towards developed country norms. Globalization of the economy depends on the role of human migration, international trade, movement of capital, and integration of financial markets. The International Monetary Fund notes the growing economic interdependence of countries worldwide through increasing volume and variety of cross-border transactions, free international capital flows, and more rapid and widespread diffusion of technology. Theodore Levitt is usually credited with globalization's first use in an economic context.

Copyright © Mometrix Media. You have been licensed one copy of this document for personal use only. Any other reproduction or redistribution is strictly prohibited. All rights reserved.
This content is provided for test preparation purposes only and does not imply an endorsement by Mometrix of any particular political, scientific, or religious point of view.

Globalization has had an effect on international cultural exchanges, and technical legal aspects of trade.

- Greater international cultural exchange
- Spreading of multiculturalism, and better individual access to cultural diversity. However, the imported culture can easily supplant the local culture, causing reduction in diversity through hybridization or even assimilation. The most prominent form of this is Westernization, but Sinicization of cultures has taken place over most of Asia for many centuries.
- Greater international travel and tourism
- Greater immigration, including illegal immigration
- Spread of local consumer products (e.g. food) to other countries (often adapted to their culture)
- World-wide fads and pop culture such as Pokémon, Sudoku, Numa Numa, Origami, Idol series, YouTube, Facebook, and MySpace.
- World-wide sporting events such as FIFA World Cup and the Olympic Games.
- Formation or development of a set of universal values

Technical/Legal

- Development of a global telecommunications infrastructure and greater transborder data flow, using such technologies as the Internet, communication satellites, submarine fiber optic cable, and wireless telephones
- Increase in the number of standards applied globally; e.g. copyright laws, patents and world trade agreements.
- The push by many advocates for an international criminal court and international justice movements.

Globalization has various aspects which affect the world in several different ways such as:

- Industrial (alias trans nationalization) - emergence of worldwide production markets and broader access to a range of foreign products for consumers and companies
- Financial - emergence of worldwide financial markets and better access to external financing for corporate, national and subnational borrowers
- Economic - realization of a global common market, based on the freedom of exchange of goods and capital.
- Political - political globalization is the creation of a world government which regulates the relationships among nations and guarantees the rights arising from social and economic globalization.
- Informational - increase in information flows between geographically remote locations
- Cultural - growth of cross-cultural contacts; advent of new categories of consciousness and identities such as Globalism - which embodies cultural diffusion, the desire to consume and enjoy foreign products and ideas, adopt new technology and practices, and participate in a "world culture"
- Ecological- the advent of global environmental challenges that cannot be solved without international cooperation, such as climate change, cross-boundary water and air pollution, over-fishing of the ocean, and the spread of invasive species. Many factories are built in developing countries where they can pollute freely.
- Social - the achievement of free circulation by people of all nations
- Transportation - fewer and fewer European cars on European roads each year (the same can also be said about American cars on American roads).

Copyright © Mometrix Media. You have been licensed one copy of this document for personal use only. Any other reproduction or redistribution is strictly prohibited. All rights reserved.
This content is provided for test preparation purposes only and does not imply an endorsement by Mometrix of any particular political, scientific, or religious point of view.

International Trade Risks

Economic Risks

- Risk of insolvency of the buyer
- Risk of protracted default - the failure of the buyer to pay the amount due within six months after the due date
- Risk of non-acceptance
- Surrendering economic sovereignty

Political Risks

- Risk of cancellation or non-renewal of export or import licenses
- War risks
- Risk of expropriation or confiscation of the importer's company
- Risk of the imposition of an import ban after the shipment of the goods
- Transfer risk - imposition of exchange controls by the importer's country or foreign currency shortages
- Surrendering political sovereignty

Absolute Advantage

A country has an absolute advantage over another in producing a good, if it can produce that good using fewer resources than another country.

The benefits to nations from trading are the same as to individuals: trade permits specialization, which allows resources to be used more productively.

Measuring Globalization

Looking specifically at economic globalization, it can be measured in different ways. These center around the four main economic flows that characterize globalization:

- Goods and services, e.g. exports plus imports as a proportion of national income or per capita of population
- Labor/people, e.g. net migration rates; inward or outward migration flows, weighted by population
- Capital, e.g. inward or outward direct investment as a proportion of national income or per head of population
- Technology, e.g. international research & development flows; proportion of populations (and rates of change thereof) using particular inventions (especially 'factor-neutral' technological advances such as the telephone, motorcar, broadband)

Regulation of International Trade

Traditionally trade was regulated through bilateral treaties between two nations. For centuries under the belief in Mercantilism most nations had high tariffs and many restrictions on international trade. In the 19th century, especially in Britain, a belief in free trade became paramount and this view has dominated thinking among western nations for most of the time since then which led to the general decline of Great Britain. In the years since the Second World War, controversial multilateral treaties like the GATT and World Trade Organization have attempted to create a globally regulated trade structure. These trade agreements have often resulted in protest and discontent with claims of unfair trade that is not mutually beneficial.

Copyright © Mometrix Media. You have been licensed one copy of this document for personal use only. Any other reproduction or redistribution is strictly prohibited. All rights reserved.
This content is provided for test preparation purposes only and does not imply an endorsement by Mometrix of any particular political, scientific, or religious point of view.

Free trade is usually most strongly supported by the most economically powerful nations, though they often engage in selective protectionism for those industries which are strategically important such as the protective tariffs applied to agriculture by the United States and Europe. The Netherlands and the United Kingdom were both strong advocates of free trade when they were economically dominant, today the United States, the United Kingdom, Australia and Japan are its greatest proponents. However, many other countries (such as India, China and Russia) are increasingly becoming advocates of free trade as they become more economically powerful themselves. As tariff levels fall there is also an increasing willingness to negotiate non tariff measures, including foreign direct investment, procurement and trade facilitation. The latter looks at the transaction cost associated with meeting trade and customs procedures.

Traditionally agricultural interests are usually in favor of free trade while manufacturing sectors often support protectionism. This has changed somewhat in recent years, however. In fact, agricultural lobbies, particularly in the United States, Europe and Japan, are chiefly responsible for particular rules in the major international trade treaties which allow for more protectionist measures in agriculture than for most other goods and services.

During recessions there is often strong domestic pressure to increase tariffs to protect domestic industries. This occurred around the world during the Great Depression leading to a collapse in world trade that may have deepened the depression.

The regulation of international trade is done through the World Trade Organization at the global level, and through several other regional arrangements such as MERCOSUR in South America, NAFTA between the United States, Canada and Mexico, and the European Union between 27 independent states. The 2005 Buenos Aires talks on the planned establishment of the Free Trade Area of the Americas (FTAA) failed largely due to opposition from the populations of Latin American nations. Similar agreements such as the MAI (Multilateral Agreement on Investment) have also failed in recent years.

The Ricardian Model

The Ricardian model focuses on comparative advantage and is perhaps the most important concept in international trade theory. In a Ricardian model, countries specialize in producing what they produce best. Unlike other models, the Ricardian framework predicts that countries will fully specialize instead of producing a broad array of goods. Also, the Ricardian model does not directly consider factor endowments, such as the relative amounts of labor and capital within a country.

International Agreements

Since World War II, barriers to international trade have been considerably lowered through international agreements - General Agreement on Tariffs and Trade (GATT). Particular initiatives carried out as a result of GATT and the World Trade Organization (WTO), for which GATT is the foundation, have included:

Promotion of Free Trade:

- Reduction or elimination of tariffs; construction of free trade zones with small or no tariffs
- Reduced transportation costs, especially from development of containerization for ocean shipping.
- Reduction or elimination of capital controls
- Reduction, elimination, or harmonization of subsidies for local businesses

Copyright © Mometrix Media. You have been licensed one copy of this document for personal use only. Any other reproduction or redistribution is strictly prohibited. All rights reserved.
This content is provided for test preparation purposes only and does not imply an endorsement by Mometrix of any particular political, scientific, or religious point of view.

Restriction of Free Trade:

- Harmonization of intellectual property laws across the majority of states, with more restrictions.
- Supranational recognition of intellectual property restrictions (e.g. patents granted by China would be recognized in the United States)

Domestic vs. Global Marketing

A company marketing only within its national boundaries only has to consider domestic competition. Even if that competition includes companies from foreign markets, it still only has to focus on the competition that exists in its home market. Products and services are developed for customers in the home market without thought of how the product or service could be used in other markets. All marketing decisions are made at headquarters. The biggest obstacle these marketers face is being blindsided by emerging global marketers. Because domestic marketers do not generally focus on the changes in the global marketplace, they may not be aware of a potential competitor who is a market leader on three continents until they simultaneously open 20 stores in the Northeastern US These marketers can be considered ethnocentric as they are most concerned with how they are perceived in their home country.

Some of the reasons for the shift from domestic marketing to global marketing include:

- **Saturation of Domestic Markets** - For a company to keep growing, it must increase sales. Industrialized nations have, in many product and service categories, saturated their domestic markets and have turned to other countries for new marketing opportunities. Companies in some developing economies have found profitability by exporting products that are too expensive for locals but are considered inexpensive in wealthier countries.
- **Worldwide Competition** - One of the product categories in which global competition has been easy to track is in US automotive sales. Three decades ago, there were only the big three: General Motors, Ford, and Chrysler. Now, Toyota, Honda, and Volkswagen are among the most popular manufacturers. Companies are on a global playing field whether they had planned to be global marketers or not.
- **e-Commerce** - With the proliferation of the Internet and e-commerce (electronic commerce), if a business is online, it is a global business. With more people becoming Internet users daily, this market is constantly growing. Customers can come from anywhere. According to the book, "Global Marketing Management," business-to-business (B2B) e-commerce is larger, growing faster, and has fewer geographical distribution obstacles than even business-to-consumer (B2C) e-commerce. With e-commerce, a brick and mortar storefront is unnecessary.

Global Laws

Expanding a manufacturing industry to a global reach can cause many companies to get ahead of the legal issues facing overseas business. Countries can vary in legal expectations and even social rules that strongly impact the success of a product or plant facility within a country. Going global is no simple stretch. Whether your company is pursuing global marketing and supply soon or years down the road, a team must put together of experienced public relations, sales, and marketing staff to do some on-site investigating about the laws and legal issues your company will have to comply with in order to market a product correctly and legally in another country. Launching a marketing campaign unprepared and uninformed is one of the worst decisions an industry corporation can make. One wrong move can kill any chance of business there now or even ever again, and can create a collective overseas view of your company that isn't easily changed.

Copyright © Mometrix Media. You have been licensed one copy of this document for personal use only. Any other reproduction or redistribution is strictly prohibited. All rights reserved.
This content is provided for test preparation purposes only and does not imply an endorsement by Mometrix of any particular political, scientific, or religious point of view.

International Trade Terms

A **tariff** is a tax on imports by a government to encourage its citizens to buy goods made in their country.

A **quota** is the exact number of products that is allowed to be imported into a country.

An **embargo** is when a country prohibits doing business with certain countries until they meet certain demands.

Exchange controls prohibit inflation by capping the amount of foreign exchange and the exchange rate with certain countries.

Sometimes companies face **non-tariff barriers**, which are usually cultural differences between countries that prevent another business from exporting there.

Economic Environment

When deciding whether to do business in a country, a business will study two major economic factors: their **industrial structure** and their **income distribution**. There are four types of industrial structures:

- Subsistence economies exist in countries where the majority of the people are farmers. These are the poorest areas of the world.
- Raw material exporting economies exist in countries that have abundant natural resources but have high amounts of poverty.
- Industrializing economies are the economies of the world that import raw materials and have a large level of manufacturing business.
- Industrial economies are in countries with well-developed economies and a high level of specialization.

The way that income is distributed in a country gives a business insight as to whom they should market their products to.

Political Environment

In international marketing, it does not matter how large a potential market is if a country's government makes it too difficult to conduct business there. Before a business enters a country, they need to understand the countries attitude towards international companies. Some countries welcome foreign investment, others set quotas or unreasonable demands. **Government bureaucracy** is another factor. Officials in many countries commonly demand bribes for things to get done. The **political stability** of a country can keep a business out. There is a reason why there are not many businesses in Iraq. Businesses also need to understand a country's **monetary regulations**. Artificial exchange rates or investment rules can make certain countries unappealing for investment.

International Marketing

International marketing can provide many benefits that are not available in national markets. However, it also comes with a whole new set of problems that are unique to its market. There are three main challenges associated with working in foreign markets.

Communication is the first barrier. Americans take for granted that everybody should speak English, but the need to know other languages is greater than it has ever been. There are several

Copyright © Mometrix Media. You have been licensed one copy of this document for personal use only. Any other reproduction or redistribution is strictly prohibited. All rights reserved.
This content is provided for test preparation purposes only and does not imply an endorsement by Mometrix of any particular political, scientific, or religious point of view.

amusing stories of American companies whose English slogans translated into something completely different in another language.

A country's traditions and customs can be a problem with your business. Budweiser and Absolut do not sell well in places like the Middle East where alcohol is forbidden. It is also important to know the business customs of the area that you are doing business in. For instance, bribes are taboo in some cultures, but are embraced in others.

Other cultures can also have different buying habits that should influence a business's decision to enter a foreign market. Sometimes there are items in certain products that foreigners look for that Americans don't. It is important to understand these differences.

There are three ways a company sells its products internationally: **exporting, joint venturing, and direct investment**. Exporting is the easiest way to enter a market. To export all a company has to do is sell its goods to a foreign distributor. Joint venturing is when a company joins forces with a foreign country in order to share costs and learn about the market. It is different from exporting because the company is actually joining with the foreign company to sell the product. Direct investment is the riskiest way to enter a foreign market, but also the most highly profitable. When a company directly invests in an international market, they build and maintain assembly or manufacturing plants and a foreign workforce.

Global Marketing Programs

Companies have to decide how they are going to adapt their marketing mix for each foreign market that they enter. Companies that do little to change their marketing mix use a **structured marketing mix**. This is effective in countries that have similar cultures such as the United States, Canada, Britain, and Australia. An **adapted marketing mix** is an international marketing strategy where companies adjust their strategies to gear them towards a target market. This strategy is initially more expensive due to the adjustments, but the hopes are that it will make the company more profitable in the long run.

Global Market Strategies

There are several strategies companies can choose from when adapting their products to the global market that generally depend on the level of product adaptation. **Straight product extension** means to market a product in a foreign market without any change. **Product adaptation** means to adapt a product to meet the specifications of a foreign market. **Product invention** is when a company creates a completely new product for sale in a foreign market. This usually happens with large food companies that want to operate in places where the people do not eat the same things that Americans eat.

How to Be an Effective Global Marketer Within Cultural Bounds

This research has important implications for brand and global marketing efforts by consumer-oriented companies. After all, notions about cultural differences are often the basis for international marketing communications as well as global brand management strategies. The perceived importance of cultural issues has been increasing, fueled by new technologies that allow marketers to reach consumers across country boundaries. Marketers are spending increasing amounts of time and effort trying to understand subtle cultural differences.

But for a message to be effective, marketers must understand not only how to tailor a message to a particular culture but when such cultural-values-based messages are most effective. For example, this research suggests that marketing communications that hinge on culture-specific values might

Copyright © Mometrix Media. You have been licensed one copy of this document for personal use only. Any other reproduction or redistribution is strictly prohibited. All rights reserved.
This content is provided for test preparation purposes only and does not imply an endorsement by Mometrix of any particular political, scientific, or religious point of view.

work best when advertisements draw brief, focused attention (e.g., online banner ads, roadside billboards).

Additionally, this notion that culture sometimes guides consumer judgments and behaviors and at other times does not could be helpful in understanding conflicting findings in previous research. For example, although numerous studies have found cultural differences matter enormously to consumers, in other studies such differences sometimes fail to appear. Such failures tend to offer uninteresting findings and often remain unpublished.

Researchers also may want to consider the distinction between personal and cultural knowledge. When will personal knowledge override socio-cultural norms? Answers to such questions will further illuminate the psychology of consumers across cultural contexts and shed insight on what types of global marketing efforts may be most effective.

General cultural knowledge includes implicit theories about the world we live in that are largely shared by the members of our society. But in addition to this shared set of ideas, we also have personal knowledge that can conflict with accepted, culturally derived practices. For example, a boy growing up in China may generally accept the importance of his relationships with others, and therefore seek to keep harmony with family members. But more personal knowledge—such as being exposed to pictures of American cultural icons like Green Day or Madonna—may lead him to sometimes wear clothes that his parents don't like. In other words, when pressured to form a quick judgment, we generally rely on cultural norms as a "default." But when making a thoughtful deliberation, we're more likely to engage in an internal debate, and waver.

E-Commerce

Electronic commerce, commonly known as e-commerce or eCommerce, consists of the buying and selling of products or services over electronic systems such as the Internet and other computer networks. The amount of trade conducted electronically has grown dramatically since the wide introduction of the Internet. A wide variety of commerce is conducted in this way, including things such as electronic funds transfer, supply chain management, e-marketing, online marketing, online transaction processing, electronic data interchange (EDI), automated inventory management systems, and automated data collection systems. Modern electronic commerce typically uses the World Wide Web at least at some point in the transaction's lifecycle, although it can encompass a wider range of technologies such as e-mail as well.

A small percentage of electronic commerce is conducted entirely electronically for "virtual" items such as access to premium content on a website, but most electronic commerce eventually involves physical items and their transportation in at least some way. E-commerce or electronic commerce is generally considered to be the sales aspect of e-business.

Technical and Organizational Aspects of Internet Business

Sufficient work done in market research and analysis: E-commerce is not exempt from good business planning and the fundamental laws of supply and demand. Business failure is as much a reality in e-commerce as in any other form of business.

A good management team armed with information technology strategy: A company's IT strategy should be a part of the business re-design process.

Providing an easy and secured way for customers to effect transactions: Credit cards are the most popular means of sending payments on the internet, accounting for 90% of online purchases. Most

Copyright © Mometrix Media. You have been licensed one copy of this document for personal use only. Any other reproduction or redistribution is strictly prohibited. All rights reserved.
This content is provided for test preparation purposes only and does not imply an endorsement by Mometrix of any particular political, scientific, or religious point of view.

merchants today process credit card transactions on site through arrangements made with commercial banks or credit cards companies.

Providing reliability and security: Parallel servers, hardware redundancy, fail-safe technology, information encryption, and firewalls can enhance this requirement.

Providing a 360-degree view of the customer relationship, defined as ensuring that all employees, suppliers, and partners have a complete view, and the same view, of the customer. However, customers may not appreciate the big brother experience.

Constructing a commercially sound business model.

Engineering an electronic value chain in which one focuses on a "limited" number of core competencies -- the opposite of a one-stop shop. Operating on or near the cutting-edge of technology and staying there as technology changes.

Setting up an organization of alertness and agility to respond quickly to any changes in the economic, social and physical environment.

Providing an attractive website. The tasteful use of color, graphics, animation, photographs, fonts, and white-space percentage may aid success in this respect.

Streamlining business processes, possibly through re-engineering and information technologies.

Providing complete understanding of the products or services offered, which not only includes complete product information, but also sound advisors and selectors.

Naturally, the e-commerce vendor must also perform such mundane tasks as being truthful about its product and its availability, shipping reliably, and handling complaints promptly and effectively. A unique property of the Internet environment is that individual customers have access to far more information about the seller than they would find in a brick-and-mortar situation.

Disadvantages

There are also many disadvantages of e-commerce. One of the main ones is fraud. This is where your details (name, bank card number, age, national insurance number) are entered into what look to be a safe site but really it is not. These details can then be used to steal money from you and can be used to buy things on line that you are completely unaware of until it is too late. If this information is leaked into the wrong hands, people are able to steal your identity, and commit more fraud crimes under your name. Some other problems with e commerce some are:

- **Failure to understand customers (why they buy and how they buy)**. Even a product with a sound value proposition can fail if producers and retailers do not understand customer habits, expectations, and motivations. E-commerce could potentially mitigate this potential problem with proactive and focused marketing research, just as traditional retailers may do.
- **Failure to consider the competitive situation**. One may have the will to construct a viable book e-tailing business model, but lack the capability to compete with Amazon.
- **Inability to predict environmental reaction**. What will competitors do? Will they introduce competitive brands or competitive web sites? Will they supplement their service offerings? Will they try to sabotage a competitor's site? Will price wars break out? What will the government do? Research into competitors, industries and markets may mitigate some consequences here, just as in non-electronic commerce.

Copyright © Mometrix Media. You have been licensed one copy of this document for personal use only. Any other reproduction or redistribution is strictly prohibited. All rights reserved.
This content is provided for test preparation purposes only and does not imply an endorsement by Mometrix of any particular political, scientific, or religious point of view.

- **Over-estimation of resource competence.** Can staff, hardware, software, and processes handle the proposed strategy? Have e-tailer's failed to develop employee and management skills? These issues may call for thorough resource planning and employee training.

Website

A website is a collection of Web pages, images, videos or other digital assets that is hosted on one or several Web server(s), usually accessible via the Internet, cell phone or a LAN. A Web page is a document, typically written in HTML that is almost always accessible via HTTP, a protocol that transfers information from the Web server to display in the user's Web browser. All publicly accessible websites are seen collectively as constituting the "World Wide Web".

The pages of websites can usually be accessed from a common root URL called the homepage, and usually reside on the same physical server. The URLs of the pages organize them into a hierarchy, although the hyperlinks between them control how the reader perceives the overall structure and how the traffic flows between the different parts of the sites.

Some websites require a subscription to access some or all of their content. Examples of subscription sites include many business sites, parts of many news sites, academic journal sites, gaming sites, message boards, Web-based e-mail, services, social networking website, and sites providing real-time stock market data.

Static pages don't change content and layout with every request unless a human (web master/programmer) manually updates the page. **Dynamic pages** adapt their content and/or appearance depending on end-user's input/interaction or changes in the computing environment (user, time, database modifications, etc.) Content can be changed on the client side (end-user's computer) by using client-side scripting languages (JavaScript, JScript, Actionscript, etc.) to alter DOM elements (DHTML). Dynamic content is often compiled on the server utilizing server-side scripting languages (Perl, PHP, ASP, JSP, ColdFusion, etc.). Both approaches are usually used in complex applications.

Turning a website into an income source is a common practice for web-developers and website owners. There are several methods for creating a website business which fall into two broad categories. A website is a useful way to expand on traditional forms of business.

Online Information Businesses

Some websites offer no products at all but provide free information with income coming from clicks the visitors make on advertisements. There is a wide range of monetizing used on such sites and the sites themselves are actively traded and bought and sold as going concerns. Guides have been published which explain how to create such a business.

Online Retail

While most business websites serve as a shop window for brick and mortar businesses it is increasingly the case that some websites are businesses in their own right. These websites are fully self-contained businesses entities offering, for example, immediate downloads of retail software on payment of the product's price via their shopping cart.

Online Services Businesses

It offers a lot of services in every field, such as, tourism, economic, politic, social welfare. Business web sites can be divided into four categories: Business to consumer, business-to-business, consumer to consumer, and consumer to business. Business to business (B2B) is an e-marketplaces where businesses sell directly to other businesses. They can be auction sites like ebay.com, but are

Copyright © Mometrix Media. You have been licensed one copy of this document for personal use only. Any other reproduction or redistribution is strictly prohibited. All rights reserved.
This content is provided for test preparation purposes only and does not imply an endorsement by Mometrix of any particular political, scientific, or religious point of view.

also places where companies can learn and purchase products to better run their companies, like sun.com.

Business to consumer (B2C) websites are the most popular types of business websites. These sites are where companies sell to the final consumer. Almost every company has a website where a customer can research and/or purchase goods online. These sites accounted for over $112 billion dollars in 2005. Consumer to consumer web sites (C2C) are similar to the want ads in the local newspaper except on a global scale. Consumer to Business (C2B) websites are sites where consumers enter a market and search for a business that they want to do business with. Priceline.com would be an example.

Web Design

Web design is a process of conceptualization, planning, modeling, and execution of electronic media delivery via Internet in the form of Markup language suitable for interpretation by Web browser and display as Graphical user interface (GUI).

The intent of web design is to create a web site -- a collection of electronic files that reside on a web server/servers and present content and interactive features/interfaces to the end user in form of Web pages once requested. Such elements as text, bit-mapped images (GIFs, JPEGs, PNGs), forms can be placed on the page using HTML/XHTML/XML tags. Displaying more complex media (vector graphics, animations, videos, sounds) requires plug-ins such as Flash, QuickTime, Java run-time environment, etc. Plug-ins are also embedded into web page by using HTML/XHTML tags.

Improvements in browsers' compliance with W3C standards prompted a widespread acceptance and usage of XHTML/XML in conjunction with Cascading Style Sheets (CSS) to position and manipulate web page elements and objects. Latest standards and proposals aim at leading to browsers' ability to deliver a wide variety of media and accessibility options to the client possibly without employing plug-ins.

Suitability of Products

Certain products or services appear more suitable for online sales; others remain more suitable for offline sales. While credit cards are currently the most popular means of paying for online goods and services, alternative online payments will account for 26% of e-commerce volume by 2009. Many successful purely virtual companies deal with digital products, (including information storage, retrieval, and modification), music, movies, office supplies, education, communication, software, photography, and financial transactions. Examples of this type of company include: Google, eBay and Paypal. Other successful marketers use Drop shipping or Affiliate marketing techniques to facilitate transactions of tangible goods without maintaining real inventory. Examples include numerous sellers on eBay. Products less suitable for e-commerce include products that have a low value-to-weight ratio, products that have a smell, taste, or touch component, products that need trial fittings — most notably clothing — and products where color integrity appears important. Nonetheless, Tesco.com has had success delivering groceries in the UK, albeit that many of its goods are of a generic quality, and clothing sold through the internet is big business in the US Also, the recycling program Cheapcycle sells goods over the internet, but avoids the low value-to-weight ratio problem by creating different groups for various regions, so that shipping costs remain low.

Non-Digital Products

Virtual marketers can sell some non-digital products and services successfully. Such products generally have a high value-to-weight ratio, they may involve embarrassing purchases, they may

Copyright © Mometrix Media. You have been licensed one copy of this document for personal use only. Any other reproduction or redistribution is strictly prohibited. All rights reserved.
This content is provided for test preparation purposes only and does not imply an endorsement by Mometrix of any particular political, scientific, or religious point of view.

typically go to people in remote locations, and they may have shut-ins as their typical purchasers. Items which can fit through a standard letterbox — such as music CDs, DVDs and books — are particularly suitable for a virtual marketer. Products such as spare parts, both for consumer items like washing machines and for industrial equipment like centrifugal pumps, also seem good candidates for selling online. Retailers often need to order spare parts specially, since they typically do not stock them at consumer outlets -- in such cases, e-commerce solutions in spares do not compete with retail stores, only with other ordering systems. A factor for success in this niche can consist of providing customers with exact, reliable information about which part number their particular version of a product needs, for example by providing parts lists keyed by serial number.

Launching An E-Business

Develop Concept- The first stage in the countdown, of course, is to develop the concept for the new business as clearly as possible. This can take months or come in a furious session at 2:00 am. But it needs to be thorough.

Prepare a Unique Selling Proposition - Once the concept is pretty well worked out, now it needs to be squeezed down to a single sentence or two that summarizes the Unique Selling Proposition (USP), and differentiates it from the many thousands of other products on the Internet today. The USP is the next stage in the launch countdown. Incidentally, don't skip the step of refining your concept down to a USP. If you can write a clear and precise USP, you have a chance for success. If you can't, don't waste your energy, time, and money. A clear USP is an essential component for a prosperous e-business -- any business for that matter.

Obtain a Domain Name - It is easily seen that securing the appropriate domain name for your business is worth much more than the $70 (or less) that it costs from the registration service.

Secure Funding - The next countdown stage in the launch is to secure funding for your project. Sometimes this can forestall going any farther. There are times when a quick entry into the marketplace is an essential part of a marketing plan. But sometimes a more gradual approach is called for, and allows you to retain control of your business AND its profits.

Lay Out a Project Plan - While getting close to launch, at least in terms of countdown, there's an important planning stage before liftoff: calendaring and delegating the execution of the various projects involved.

Construct Website and E-mail Systems - Write website introduction and guidelines for group participation. It's important to carefully qualify participants and manage expectations.

- Design basic webpage templates.
- Prepare site graphics that help tell the story, but minimize download time.
- Devise and test a mock-up of the product.
- Set up a navigation system to allow the site to grow in complexity.
- Install online e-commerce software on an SSL secure server to facilitate online contributions. Of course, a merchant credit card account is necessary to take credit card payments.
- Develop an online subscription system that will simultaneously subscribe participants.
- Work out an online tab-delimited logfile that records information from each subscriber for statistical and contact purposes, and can be downloaded and imported into Microsoft Access for analysis.
- Make available an online system to allow participants to automatically change an e-mail address or discussion group, or to unsubscribe from the service entirely.

Copyright © Mometrix Media. You have been licensed one copy of this document for personal use only. Any other reproduction or redistribution is strictly prohibited. All rights reserved.
This content is provided for test preparation purposes only and does not imply an endorsement by Mometrix of any particular political, scientific, or religious point of view.

- Provide for e-mail lesson distribution.
- Recruit leaders to monitor discussion in each group to ensure quality, and spot problems early.
- Arrange a random number generator so that discussion groups fill evenly with participants.
- Secure volunteer staffing for each discussion group. This involves preparing online application forms and moderator instructions, and taking the time for telephone interviewing and reference checking.
- Complete miscellaneous business functions, such as filing a fictitious business name statement, securing a business license, setting up a bank account, etc.

Execute Marketing Strategies - There are many activities to carry out in this last stage, though some of them can continue after the launch. Many sites don't really have a marketing plan, but without a marketing plan, you can't expect to succeed.

- Announce via in-house participant lists.
- Publicize via in-house newsletter lists.
- Provide news releases to key editors of e-mail newsletters, with a request to review the new site. This has been successful in the past.
- Register with search engines and directories after preparing titles and META description and keyword tags for each webpage.
- Display banner ads.
- Encourage "viral marketing" by deliberately asking subscribers to request that people include a short blurb in their bulletins and newsletters.
- Stimulate "viral marketing" by asking each subscriber to forward a copy of your e-mail newsletter to a friend who might be interested. We strongly discourage people from actually signing up their friends to the study, and make it extremely easy to get off the list in case that happens.

Customer Experience

A successful customer experience can be insured by providing the customer with the following:

- Value: Vendors can achieve this by offering a product or product-line that attracts potential customers at a competitive price, as in non-electronic commerce.
- Service and performance: Offering a responsive, user-friendly purchasing experience, just like a flesh-and-blood retailer, may go some way to achieving these goals.
- Incentive for customers to buy and to return: Sales promotions to this end can involve coupons, special offers, and discounts. Cross-linked websites and advertising affiliate programs can also help.
- Personal attention: Personalized web sites, purchase suggestions, and personalized special offers may go some of the way to substituting for the face-to-face human interaction found at a traditional point of sale.
- Sense of community: Chat rooms, discussion boards, soliciting customer input and loyalty programs can help in this respect.

A business can also affect the customers experience by:

- Owning the customer's total experience: E-tailers foster this by treating any contacts with a customer as part of a total experience, an experience that becomes synonymous with the brand.

Copyright © Mometrix Media. You have been licensed one copy of this document for personal use only. Any other reproduction or redistribution is strictly prohibited. All rights reserved.
This content is provided for test preparation purposes only and does not imply an endorsement by Mometrix of any particular political, scientific, or religious point of view.

- Letting customers help themselves: Provision of a self-serve site, which is easy to use without assistance, can help in this respect.
- All product information should be available
- Cross-sell information
- Advise for product alternatives
- Supplies & accessory selectors.
- Helping customers do their job of consuming: E-tailers and online shopping directories can provide such help through ample comparative information and good search facilities. Provision of component information and safety-and-health comments may assist e-tailers to define the customers' job.

Marketing Web Pages

There are many ways to evaluate the quality of a marketing web page. Some of those include:

Authority

- Is it clear what company is responsible for the contents of the page?
- Is there a link to a page describing the nature of the company, who owns the company, and the types of products the company sells?
- Is there a way of verifying the legitimacy of this company? That is, is there a phone number or postal address to contact for more information? (Simply an email address is not enough.)
- Is there a way of determining the stability of this company?
- Is there a statement that the content of the page has the official approval of the company?
- Is there a statement giving the company's name as copyright holder?

Accuracy

- Has the company provided a link to outside sources such as product reviews or reports filed with the SEC (the Securities and Exchange Commission) which can be used to verify company claims?
- Are the sources for any factual information clearly listed so they can be verified in another source?
- Is the information free of grammatical, spelling, and typographical errors? (These kinds of errors not only indicate a lack of quality control, but can actually produce inaccuracies in information.)

Objectivity

- For any given piece of information, is it clear what the company's motivation is for providing it?
- If there is any advertising on the page, is it clearly differentiated from the informational content?

Currency

- Are there dates on the page to indicate:
  - When the page was written?
  - When the page was first placed on the Web?
  - When the page was last revised?
- Are there any other indications that the material is kept current?

Copyright © Mometrix Media. You have been licensed one copy of this document for personal use only. Any other reproduction or redistribution is strictly prohibited. All rights reserved.
This content is provided for test preparation purposes only and does not imply an endorsement by Mometrix of any particular political, scientific, or religious point of view.

- For financial information, is there an indication it was filed with the SEC and is the filing date listed?
- For material from the company's annual report, is the date of the report listed?

Coverage

- Is there an indication that the page has been completed, and is not still under construction?
- If describing a product, does the page include an adequately detailed description of the product?
- Are all of the company's products described with an adequate level of detail?
- Is the same level of information provided for all sections or divisions of the company?

Internet Marketing Effect on Business

Internet marketing has had a large impact on several industries including music, banking, and flea markets - not to mention the advertising industry itself. In the music industry, many consumers have begun buying and downloading music files (e.g. MP3s) over the Internet instead of simply buying CDs.

More and more banks are offering the ability to perform banking tasks online. Online banking is believed to appeal to customers because it is more convenient than visiting bank branches. Currently, over 150 million US adults now bank online. Online banking is now the fastest-growing Internet activity. The increasing speed of Internet connections is the main reason for the fast-growth.

Internet auctions have gained popularity. Unique items that could previously be found at flea markets are being sold on eBay instead. eBay has also affected the prices in the industry. Buyers and sellers often look at prices on the website before going to flea markets and the eBay price often becomes what the item is sold for. More and more flea market sellers are putting their items up for sale online and running their business out of their homes.

The effect on the ad industry itself has been profound. In just a few years, online advertising has grown to be worth tens of billions of dollars annually. As Advertisers increase and shift more of their budgets online, it is now overtaking radio in terms of market share. The cost to acquire a customer is lower with internet marketing than with traditional marketing however costs are rising as more companies take traditional budgets and push it to internet marketing avenues. Search engine marketing for example, which is part of internet marketing continues to grow at tremendous rates. Email marketing also grows. Web analytics is a growing aspect of internet marketing, as there is more accountability than in the history of advertising.

Security Concerns

For both companies and consumers that participate in online business, security concerns are very important. Many consumers are hesitant to buy items over the Internet because they do not trust that their personal information will remain private. Recently, some companies that do business online have been caught giving away or selling information about their customers. Several of these companies have guarantees on their websites, claiming customer information will be private. By selling customer information, these companies are breaking their own, publicized policy. Some companies that buy customer information offer the option for individuals to have their information removed from the database (known as opting out). However, many customers are unaware that their information is being shared and are unable to stop the transfer of their information between companies.

Copyright © Mometrix Media. You have been licensed one copy of this document for personal use only. Any other reproduction or redistribution is strictly prohibited. All rights reserved.
This content is provided for test preparation purposes only and does not imply an endorsement by Mometrix of any particular political, scientific, or religious point of view.

Security concerns are of great importance and online companies have been working hard to create solutions. Encryption is one of the main methods for dealing with privacy and security concerns on the Internet. Encryption is defined as the conversion of data into a form called a cipher. This cipher cannot be easily intercepted unless an individual is authorized by the program or company that completed the encryption. In general, the stronger the cipher, the better protected the data is. However, the stronger the cipher, the more expensive encryption becomes.

The W3C

The World Wide Web Consortium (W3C) is the main international standards organization for the World Wide Web (W3). It is arranged as a consortium where member organizations maintain full-time staff for the purpose of working together in the development of standards for the W3. As of March 2007, the W3C had 441 members. It is always open for new organizations to join. W3C also engages in education and outreach, develops software and serves as an open forum for discussion about the Web. The Consortium is headed by Sir Tim Berners-Lee, the primary author of the original URL (Uniform Resource Locator), HTTP (HyperText Transfer Protocol) and HTML (HyperText Markup Language) specifications, the principal technologies that form the basis of the World Wide Web.

ICANN

ICANN is responsible for the global coordination of the Internet's system of unique identifiers. These include domain names (like .org, .museum and country codes like .UK), as well as the addresses used in a variety of Internet protocols. Computers use these identifiers to reach each other over the Internet. Careful management of these resources is vital to the Internet's operation, so ICANN's global stakeholders meet regularly to develop policies that ensure the Internet's ongoing security and stability.

ISOC

The Internet Society is a non-profit, non-governmental, international, professional membership organization. Its more than 100 organization members and over 20,000 individual members in over 180 nations worldwide represent a veritable who's who of the Internet community. The work of the Internet Society focuses on four "pillars:" standards, public policy, education and training, and membership.

Chapter Quiz

Ready to see how well you retained what you just read? Scan the QR code to go directly to the chapter quiz interface for this study guide. If you're using a computer, simply visit the online resources page at **mometrix.com/resources719/gacemarketed** and click the Chapter Quizzes link.

Copyright © Mometrix Media. You have been licensed one copy of this document for personal use only. Any other reproduction or redistribution is strictly prohibited. All rights reserved.
This content is provided for test preparation purposes only and does not imply an endorsement by Mometrix of any particular political, scientific, or religious point of view.

Professional Development and Marketing Education Programs

Trends in Employment

The particular trends in the job market will always be unique to the part of the country in which a business teacher is working, so there is no substitute for staying aware of the employment situation by monitoring the local news and classified ads. That being said, a general trend in the United States over the past few decades has been the loss of manufacturing jobs, coupled with a rise in the demand for technology workers. The service industries in the United States have also seen a sharp rise in employment in recent years. Students can be assured that careers in computer technology will continue to be lucrative and easy to acquire. Students should also be prepared, however, to move to a different location in order to find the career they desire.

Ethical Behavior

One of the most important missions of the modern business education teacher is to show students what constitutes ethical behavior in the workplace. Put simply, ethical behavior is just good business sense; customers that are lost by unethical behavior are a much bigger concern to a company than any short-term profits that may be gained from the behavior. Companies work hard to earn reputations for ethical behavior because they know it will help them in the market. To this end, they discourage lying to customers, employee theft, and misuse of company time. If a business teacher can instill a good sense of ethics in his or her students, then he or she has given them perhaps the most valuable tool for success in the contemporary workplace.

In order to ensure that all employees understand and can abide by the basic principles of business ethics, the managers of a business should set out a concrete code of ethics for their company. In doing so, they should consider the general principles that will lead to fair business practice in their industry, and then confer with any similar organizations. The managers should then write out a specific code of conduct for employees, using examples from the business itself and making sure to align the code with company policy. Some businesses may find it necessary or advantageous to provide employees with specific training in ethics. Finally, the managers of a business should recognize that ethical decisions are not always easy to make, and therefore they should resolve to continually monitor adherence to the company code, and update the code if necessary. Although every business will have a unique set of issues that are relevant to its operations, there are certain topics that are generally applicable to business, and should therefore be covered in any company code of ethics. These include the company policy for handling checks and cash from customers, as well as the forbidding of any preferential pricing for personal friends. Employees should know whether they can accept gifts from suppliers and business associates, as well as how they should deal with shoplifters or damaged merchandise. A company code of ethics usually includes provisions for making accurate advertising promises, handling problems with employee performance, the accounting procedures that will be used for cash sales, and how to deal with the return of purchased merchandise.

Review Video: Ethical and Professional Standards
Visit mometrix.com/academy and enter code: 391843

Copyright © Mometrix Media. You have been licensed one copy of this document for personal use only. Any other reproduction or redistribution is strictly prohibited. All rights reserved.
This content is provided for test preparation purposes only and does not imply an endorsement by Mometrix of any particular political, scientific, or religious point of view.

Promoting Business Education

Teachers should be familiar with some ways of promoting their classes to the local community, so that they can develop helpful relationships with local businesses. One good way to do this is by interacting with the community advisory councils from local businesses and municipal groups. These are committees whose only purpose is to discover ways in which the business can create positive connections with their community. Obviously, a great way for them to do this is by setting up relationships with local schools, and so they can become a wonderful resource for business teachers. Through partnerships with community advisory councils, business teachers can set up mentoring, job-shadowing, or internship programs, organize class trips, or simply acquire useful information about contemporary business practices.

In an effort to promote their programs and to establish relationships with local businesses, business teachers should avail themselves of every possible resource. One good way to access the outside community is to create a business class newsletter. This kind of document can be created with any basic desktop publishing program, and sent home with students or through the mail to local businesses. Often, the parents of business students are leaders in the business community themselves, and will be glad to help out if the class' needs are made clear. Business teachers may also find it helpful to advertise their requests for community involvement in the school newspaper, the school bulletin, or the newsletter for the local parent-teacher association

Most business classes currently have a broad array of technology available to them. Teachers should anticipate having several computers (if not one for every student), a printer, a scanner, a television with VCR and DVD player, and a projector. Typically, all of the computers will have broadband access to the internet, so students can receive up-to-the-minute information. Students will probably also have access to graphing calculators, which can be used to demonstrate economic concepts as well as to calculate accounting data. Some teachers may want to make use of the telephones that most classrooms are equipped with in order to help their students with proper telephone etiquette.

Simulations

In the past, business classes have relied mainly on case studies to give students some experience looking at real-world applications of business concepts. Unfortunately, business case studies have some drawbacks: they don't allow students to experience events as they happen, they don't allow students to make business decisions themselves, and they don't allow students to test out what might have happened if different decisions had been made. It is a great aid to study, then, that computer simulations have been created. Business simulation software enables students to act out any number of scenarios, immediately see the results of their decisions, and adjust all kinds of variables to see their effects on business. Many teachers have discovered that this is an excellent way to show students how business concepts apply to real economic exchange.

Teaching Ethical Behavior

Unfortunately, making ethical decisions in the business world is often quite difficult. Business teachers should recognize this fact, and equip their students with a good decision-making process.

1. The first step in the process should be defining the problem; students may often jump to conclusions about a problem without ever really articulating it to themselves.
2. Next, students should be trained to consider the various alternative solutions to the problem. Making a list on paper is a good way of externalizing choices.

Copyright © Mometrix Media. You have been licensed one copy of this document for personal use only. Any other reproduction or redistribution is strictly prohibited. All rights reserved.
This content is provided for test preparation purposes only and does not imply an endorsement by Mometrix of any particular political, scientific, or religious point of view.

3. After this, students should get in the habit of identifying the consequences of the various proposed solutions. Consequences may be both short-term and long-term; as every businessperson knows, losing a customer in the name of short-term profit is always a bad decision.
4. Finally, students should determine whether they have enough information to make decision, and if not they should have the discipline to acquire the information they need.

Professional Organizations and Literature

In order to take full advantage of the resources available to the modern business teacher, it is important for prospective teachers to familiarize themselves with the appropriate organizations and literature. The National Business Education Association and its affiliate, the National Association for Business Teacher Education, provide a host of online and print publications to serve business instructors. The website for the NBEA also provides an online bookstore that allows business teachers to procure the most recent texts on business and vocational education. There are also a number of other free sources if valuable information on the internet, including the federal government's Department of Education homepage.

Current Research

Many teachers find it useful to include in their curriculum any modern research and topics that can help enliven their subject matter for students. There are always new studies of business behavior being published in magazines, journals, newspapers, and on the internet, and it is wise for students not only to have access to this information, but to have learned the proper way to interpret it. Business teachers should strive to inculcate the same sort of skills in regards to research as they do in their consumer education program; that is, students should be trained to determine the quality of research, the source of that research, the potential interest of the source in presenting information of a certain type, and the usefulness of the research to the student.

Vocational Education

Vocational education is the training of individuals to perform certain jobs. Often, large communities will have separate schools whose sole purpose is to cultivate workplace skills. These schools may work in conjunction with local industries to tailor the students' education to the anticipated job market. Vocational classes and schools may also offer cooperative training opportunities, in which students gain first-hand experience in their field of interest. As industrial work becomes more and more specialized, companies are requiring extensive vocational training and on-the-job experience for their employees. Public vocational education is designed to enhance the entire life of the worker; to this end, non-vocational classes are required so that students can earn a secondary degree as they gain work skills and experience.

Competency-Based Instruction

Most vocational classrooms now feature what is known as **competency-based instruction**. Loosely defined, competency-based instruction is a style of teaching in which progress is determined by students' mastery of skills rather than some arbitrary time limit. For example, in a business class, the teacher will ensure that every student is reasonably adept at making a basic budget before moving on. In a teacher-based classroom, a certain number of days would be allotted to each subject, and the teacher would adhere to this schedule whether students learned or not. Research has shown that a more learner-focused style of instruction, like competency-based instruction, ensures that students will retain the most of the curriculum. Teachers using competency-based instruction methods will be required to issue periodic assessments, so that they can gauge whether students have mastered a particular concept or skill.

Copyright © Mometrix Media. You have been licensed one copy of this document for personal use only. Any other reproduction or redistribution is strictly prohibited. All rights reserved.
This content is provided for test preparation purposes only and does not imply an endorsement by Mometrix of any particular political, scientific, or religious point of view.

Computer Technology

There is a wide range of uses for computer technology in business classes. Using computers, students may improve their visual presentations, hone their skills of enquiry, perform any number of business simulations, and gain access to a wealth of information that is pertinent to the course material. For teachers, computers can provide the latest business information, enhance presentation through the use of slide show presentation programs, and serve as a virtual forum for students to access course information and discuss concepts outside of the time and space restrictions of the class. Many teachers develop their own course web pages, on which they provide course outlines, copies of important forms, further discussion of difficult concepts, grades and assignments, and any news pertaining to the course. In deciding when and how to use technology in a business class, teachers should bear in mind a few things.

1. First, they should consider their degree of access to equipment. It is important that there be enough equipment for all students to remain involved throughout the course of the program.
2. Teachers should also consider the amount of time available for the activity; most teachers have found that short, specific activities encourage the best use of time and equipment.
3. It is important that teachers take into account their students' experience with the technology to be used, so that there is no delay and confusion over how to do the work.
4. In this same line, teachers should have a back-up plan in case of technical malfunction.
5. Finally, the teacher should ensure that students will be monitored, and that, particularly when the internet is involved, that all the subject matter will be appropriate to the age group.

Multicultural Class

One of the great aspects of teaching in most American classrooms is the diversity of the student population. This diversity can be a great advantage to a class, though it can also be an obstacle if it is not handled properly. Too many teachers take the easy way out and make their instructional methods the same for all students, when it would be to their benefit to modify their methods to best suit the student. Research has found that teachers are most successful when they focus on academic achievement, and allow their students to maintain their cultural differences. The best teachers are also those that attempt to cultivate in their students a fair-minded view of diversity; that is, a pride in their own culture and respect for the cultures of others.

Some Available Resources on Cultural Diversity

There are many resources available for teachers who would like to improve their sensitivity to differences in culture. The Center for Multicultural Education at the University of Washington maintains a comprehensive online library of multi-cultural information at http://depts.washington.edu/centerme/home.htm. Brigham Young University publishes Culturegrams, a series of summary descriptions of various cultural beliefs and practices. Teaching Tolerance is a biannual publication designed especially for teachers, and includes projects and activities that will encourage cultural literacy and appreciation. The International Multicultural Education Association publishes the Mulicultural Messenger, with reviews of multicultural resources and news updates.

Review Video: Multiculturalism/Celebrating All Cultures
Visit mometrix.com/academy and enter code: 708545

Copyright © Mometrix Media. You have been licensed one copy of this document for personal use only. Any other reproduction or redistribution is strictly prohibited. All rights reserved.
This content is provided for test preparation purposes only and does not imply an endorsement by Mometrix of any particular political, scientific, or religious point of view.

Inclusion of Exceptional Children

A great deal of time is spent trying to equip teachers to handle students labeled "exceptional" for one reason or another. Furthermore, Public Law 94-142 mandates that schools must identify those students that require special treatment, whether from being extremely gifted or disabled. Many schools, however, feel that the best way to handle exceptional students is simply to include them in the regular classroom. Advocates of this program assert that specialists can come in to the class and help exceptional students as necessary, and that otherwise these students will benefit from being in contact with students of a wide range of ability. However, many classroom teachers feel overwhelmed when they are asked to instruct a very wide range of students.

Learning Disabilities

Learning disabilities are physiological disorders that may damage a person's ability to store, process, and retrieve information. For the most part, learning disabilities affect reading and language skills. It is important to note that learning disabilities do not indicate that a student has a lower level of intelligence, or is more likely to be emotionally disturbed. Teachers should be aware of their students with learning disabilities, so that they can avoid discriminating against them for their handicaps. The most common learning disability is dyslexia. One reason why learning disabilities can be so frustrating is that they are so specific, so that a student who excels in almost every area of school may be terrible in one particular area.

Enabling Students with Learning Disabilities

There are a few common ways for teachers to minimize the problems their learning-disabled students face in a normal classroom.

- One way is to break complicated tasks down into a series of small steps; often, students with learning disabilities have a difficult time imagining the chain of tasks they will need to perform to accomplish some larger goal.
- Establishing a regular routine is also a good way to keep students involved in class.
- Learning-disabled students may need to learn abstract concepts through drawing, movement, or conversation.
- Finally, teachers can help remove some of the anxiety associated with having a learning disability by assuring their students that it is alright to make mistakes, as long as the best effort is given.

Signs to Help Recognize Learning Disabilities in High School Students

Some students may struggle for years without ever realizing that they have a natural learning disability. For this reason, secondary school teachers should be familiar with the signs that a student may be learning disabled.

1. One sign of a disability is spelling the same word several different ways in the same document.
2. A teacher may also become alarmed if a student is unable to answer open-ended questions, or accomplishing basic reading and writing tasks.
3. If students seem to be consistently misreading information, or having a hard time grasping abstract concepts, they may be battling an undiagnosed learning disability.
4. Finally, students with learning disabilities frequently have a hard time focusing on details and working at a fast pace.

Copyright © Mometrix Media. You have been licensed one copy of this document for personal use only. Any other reproduction or redistribution is strictly prohibited. All rights reserved.
This content is provided for test preparation purposes only and does not imply an endorsement by Mometrix of any particular political, scientific, or religious point of view.

Attention Deficit Disorder

Teachers should have little trouble identifying those students who may be suffering from attention deficit disorder, as the behavior of these students will probably be disruptive. Students with ADD usually make careless mistakes in their work and have a hard time sustaining their attention during long lecture periods. They are typically disorganized and are often losing things. They may fidget a great deal with their hands, and just seem to have a great deal of nervous energy. They often talk too much and out of turn. They often have a difficult time working quietly and keeping their hands off of the other students. Many students are so afflicted by attention deficit disorder that they almost seem to be possessed, or driven by some internal motor. Although dealing with students that have attention deficit disorder can be a challenge for teachers, there are a few ways to manage this behavior effectively. It is essential first of all to provide a consistent schedule and routine for students, so that they will not have idle time in which they are not sure what they need to be doing. Students with ADD may need help keeping themselves organized. As a teacher, one should always allow kids with ADD to take frequent movement breaks, so that they can work out some of the nervous energy that may drive them to distraction. It is also a good idea for teachers to maintain good communication with parents, so that both can determine the best strategies for dealing with a particular student.

Apraxia, Dysgraphia, Dyslexia, Dyssemia, Auditory Discrimination, and Visual Perception

There are a few common learning disabilities that teachers are likely to encounter. **Apraxia** is the inability to plan motor activity; that is, the inability to move correctly to accomplish a particular task. **Dysgraphia** is difficulty in writing, and difficulty with spelling. **Dyslexia** is difficulty with language that extends beyond just reading. **Dyssemia** is any difficulty an individual may have distinguishing social cues and signals. Problems with **auditory discrimination** mean that a student has a hard time telling the differences between sounds and their sequence. Problems with **visual perception** are those in which a student has trouble identifying and assigning meaning to the things that he or she sees.

Gifted Students

The Education Consolidation and Improvement Act of 1981

Not all exceptional children are designated as such because they are disabled in some way. Many students are considered exceptional because they are more intellectually advanced than their peers. Gifted students may be able to think faster and to solve more complex problems than their peers. They may be able to think creatively and empathetically, and to have profound insights. According to the **Education Consolidation and Improvement Act of 1981**, gifted children are those that surpass their peers in reasoning, leadership, artistic, and academic fields. These students, according to the government, are entitled to special treatment from the school so that they can fully develop their abilities.

Three Basic Types of Programs for Gifted Children

There are three basic types of programs designed to serve gifted children.

1. **Enrichment programs** are those that extend the regular classroom work, either by providing more topics of study or giving a deeper treatment of the material covered in the normal class. Enrichment seems to work best when it capitalizes on the interests of the student.
2. **Acceleration programs** are those in which the student moves ahead to content that normally he or she would receive later in life. This may involve grade skipping or early entrance to school.

Copyright © Mometrix Media. You have been licensed one copy of this document for personal use only. Any other reproduction or redistribution is strictly prohibited. All rights reserved.
This content is provided for test preparation purposes only and does not imply an endorsement by Mometrix of any particular political, scientific, or religious point of view.

3. **Affective programs** are those that are designed to address the social and emotional needs of gifted students. These students may have greater trouble assimilating into social groups because of their intellectual differences.

Some Teaching Strategies for Teaching Gifted Students

Teachers may find that helping gifted students work to their potential is just as difficult if not more than helping their disabled students achieve.

1. One way to help gifted children succeed is to give them some independence, and allow them to determine enrichment materials.
2. It is also a good idea to partner gifted children with one another, so they can work on social development while not sacrificing academic difficulty.
3. Gifted children should be challenged; sometimes it may be good to let them struggle with advanced subject matter rather than continually gliding through less complex material.
4. Gifted students should not be required to spend too much time going over material they have already learned.
5. Finally, gifted students should be given the chance to develop their critical thinking skills through independent study.

Gender Issues

Gender Differences in the Classroom

Teachers need to be aware that not all discrimination in the classroom is based on race or ethnicity. Too often, teachers make assumptions about their students based on gender. Although research has shown that there are some differences between the learning styles of males and females, every child should receive the same chances to grow and develop in the classroom. Often, discrimination can be totally unconscious, the result of cultural assumptions about the interests, strengths, and weaknesses of boys and girls. This is harmful if it inhibits children from pursuing the fulfillment of their potential. The result of gender discrimination can be low self-esteem, low achievement, and even open conflict.

Gender Discrimination

There are a number of ways, both intentional and unintentional, that teachers may discriminate against students because of their gender. Research has shown that teachers tend to give boys more attention and approval than girls. There seems to be a broad cultural assumption that boys are better suited to mathematics and science, while girls are better at reading and the arts. Teachers often expect boys to be more assertive and active, and girls to be docile and passive. Boys are more frequently asked to assume leadership positions in the classroom. Boys are also more likely to be punished harshly for breaking the rules. In general, girls are criticized more for deficiencies in skill, while boys are more frequently reprimanded for bad behavior. There are a few easy ways that every teacher can make his or her classroom a more equitable environment for students of both genders. The most important thing is to be conscious of discrimination, and make a point to avoid treating students differently. Specifically, teachers should make sure to assign leadership roles to both boys and girls, and to discourage students from breaking up into groups that are segregated by gender. Teachers should encourage their students to participate in those activities that are considered atypical for their gender; that is, boys can be encouraged to pursue the arts, while girls can be pushed to excel in science and math. It is always a good idea to reinforce instances of intergender cooperation as they occur in the class.

Copyright © Mometrix Media. You have been licensed one copy of this document for personal use only. Any other reproduction or redistribution is strictly prohibited. All rights reserved.
This content is provided for test preparation purposes only and does not imply an endorsement by Mometrix of any particular political, scientific, or religious point of view.

PERSONAL CRISIS INTERVENTION

Some students may be having personal problems during the school year that prevent them from working to their potential. When this is the case, teachers have an obligation to intervene and do whatever thy can to help the student. One of the most important things a teacher can do is to provide an example of a stable and protective adult. If the student is struggling with a parent's divorce or with an abusive parent, it is essential for there to be a steady nurturing presence in their lives. In other situations, it may be important for a teacher to work with parents to help the student through a personal crisis. School administrators and counselors should always be available to help teachers who feel overwhelmed by a situation.

Review Video: Crisis Management and Prevention
Visit mometrix.com/academy and enter code: 351872

BENJAMIN BLOOM

Benjamin Bloom and his team of researchers redefined education by declaring that it is not simply the acquisition of knowledge, but the development of three distinct spheres of knowledge-based skills. These spheres are the cognitive, affective, and psychomotor, and they are known collectively as Bloom's taxonomy. The cognitive sphere is the ability to make a sequential reasoning, and depends on the individual's knowledge and comprehension of a given topic. The affective sphere has to do with the way the individual reacts emotionally, and their ability to imagine other emotional states. The psychomotor sphere has to do with the ability to physically manipulate a tool or instrument.

Review Video: Bloom's Taxonomy
Visit mometrix.com/academy and enter code: 755020

SIX LEVELS OF BLOOM'S TAXONOMY

According to Bloom, the development of every sphere of knowledge (that is, the cognitive, affective, or psychomotor) passes through six successive levels.

1. At the first level, **knowledge**, one can recite facts or concepts from memory.
2. The next level is **comprehension**, in which one can demonstrate an understanding of facts through organization and comparison.
3. After comprehension comes **application**, in which the individual can use the acquired knowledge to solve new problems.
4. One then acquires the ability to **analyze** the new information, breaking it down into parts and identifying causes or motives.
5. After analysis comes **synthesis**, in which one can compile information in a different way, and propose alternatives to some of its parts.
6. Finally, one should be able to **evaluate** the new knowledge, developing opinions about it that can be supported with reasonable arguments.

INTELLIGENCE AND ABILITIES

Too often teachers recognize intelligence solely in terms of verbal and mathematical ability. Recent research has shown that there a number of different ways to be intelligent. with these various ways of expressing knowledge so that they can best work with each student. Instead of focusing on reading ability alone, teachers should try to identify creativity, innovation, group maintenance, visualization skill, strength and dexterity, reasoning skills, problem-solving skills, curiosity, and persistence. These are all forms of expressing intelligence. By becoming attuned to their students' various strengths and weaknesses, teachers can determine the best way to present their material.

Copyright © Mometrix Media. You have been licensed one copy of this document for personal use only. Any other reproduction or redistribution is strictly prohibited. All rights reserved.
This content is provided for test preparation purposes only and does not imply an endorsement by Mometrix of any particular political, scientific, or religious point of view.

The renowned Harvard psychologist Howard Gardner determined after long research that there are eight major forms of intelligence. They are logical-mathematical (ability to reason deductively and inductively, or to see rational patterns), linguistic (ability to read and write easily, and to appreciate subtle differences in language), musical (ability to discern pitch and rhythm), spatial (ability to create visual-spatial representations of the world), bodily-kinesthetic (ability to use the body to solve problems, make things, and convey ideas), interpersonal (ability to work effectively with others and empathize with them), intrapersonal (ability to work effectively by one's self), and naturalist (ability to distinguish among and use effectively the various features of the environment). Gardner is currently exploring a ninth intelligence: existential (the capacity to reflect on questions of life, death and ultimate realities).

Socratic Method

The Socratic method of instruction is patterned after the pedagogical style of Socrates, the ancient Greek philosopher. The Socratic method consists of a free-form conversation in which the teacher explores the ideas of the student by asking him or her a series of questions. In order to be effective, a Socratic dialogue must have the full participation of students. Teachers should also be comfortable with some long silences in class, as one of the results of an effective conversation is that it forces students to stop and think. Likewise, there must eb some flexibility on a teacher's behalf if a Socratic session is to be productive; the improvisatory nature of the conversation means that the subject matter may differ wildly from what the teacher had anticipated.

Cooperative Education Programs

Cooperative education is a method of providing students with academic instruction and practical, hands-on experience at the same time. As the job market has become more competitive, employers have increasingly valued on-the-job experience, so cooperative education gives students the chance to earn valuable training while not sacrificing their education in other areas. Research has shown that cooperative education increases motivation and clarifies career choices for students. For employers, cooperative education helps create a trained workforce and gives business some control over school curricula. However, observers have noted that cooperative education programs are still stigmatized as "non-academic" by some, and may isolate students from the academic community at large.

Experiential Education

Experiential education is simply the process of engaging students in real-life scenarios as a means of educating them. In business education, this might mean encouraging students to take on internships or part-time jobs so that they can gain first-hand experience of the business world. This notion of education as "learning by doing" has been around forever, but it has been seized upon by vocational educators as a means of making their subject matter vivid to students. In an effective instance of experiential education, students will be forced to describe and analyze their experiences when they return to the classroom. Many educators have noted the positive changes that occur when students are required to take full responsibility for their education; concepts that may be seen as boring when they appear in a textbook can become fascinating to students engaged in experiential education.

FBLA-PBL

Future Business Leaders of America- Phi Beta Lambda is a non-profit education association that works to prepare students for careers in business. The Association is divided into four parts: high school students; middle-school students; postsecondary students; and business people, teachers, and parents who support the mission of the group. FBLA was founded in 1940 and added Phi Beta Lambda as an independent division in 1958. The organization is funded by membership dues,

Copyright © Mometrix Media. You have been licensed one copy of this document for personal use only. Any other reproduction or redistribution is strictly prohibited. All rights reserved.
This content is provided for test preparation purposes only and does not imply an endorsement by Mometrix of any particular political, scientific, or religious point of view.

corporate contributions, conference fees, and grants. Two of the most important FBLA-PBL meetings are the Institute for Leaders, a four-day seminar at the state and local level that aims to educate students about entrepreneurship and communication, and the National Fall Leadership Conference, an annual gathering of educators and business leaders.

DECA

DECA (formally known as both Delta Epsilon Chi and/or Distributive Educations Clubs of America) is an organization aimed at promoting marketing skills in students. DECA works specifically to aid the development of marketing in areas like hospitality, finance, sales, business administration, and entrepreneurship. To this end, it provides students with technical training, academic help, and conferences on employability skills and human relations. More broadly, DECA strives to build self-esteem in students by involving them in community service and giving them leadership experience. DECA publishes a number of journals and newsletters, holds frequent conferences around the country, hosts competitive events, and provides classroom resources to teachers and students.

Junior Achievement Program

Junior Achievement is a combination of teachers, parents, and volunteers that seek to educate children about free enterprise, economics, and business. Junior Achievement runs programs for children all they away from elementary school through high school, in the hopes of preparing students for their future participation in the business world. At the high school level, Junior Achievement focuses on four areas: economics, personal finance, business and entrepreneurship, and work preparation. JA also offers a number of scholarships for students who have completed JA programs and plan on studying business or economics in college. JA is a non-profit organization funded by the contributions of corporations and individuals.

Business Professionals of America

The Business Professionals of America is an organization devoted to helping high school students successfully enter the business community. It was created after the passing of the 1963 law expanding the role of vocational education in American schools. The BPA conducts a number of programs and conferences aimed at advancing business education. The Work place Skills Assessment Program is held all over the country, and gives students a chance to see how they measure up to other people in the job market. The BPA also offers a number of scholarships and leadership awards to students who distinguish themselves. Every year, the BPA holds a National Leadership Conference to set goals for the year and discuss how best to promote the organization's agenda.

Vocational Education Act

The Vocational Education Act of 1963, also called the Carl D. Perkins Act of 1963, broadened the government's conception of vocational education. It established some procedures to provide part-time employment to students, and established a federal advisory council on vocational education. It also set aside some federal money for the construction of local vocational schools. This act also established some work-study programs enabling students to get real-life experience while earning some school credit. Some amendments were made to this act in 1968, including some direct support for cooperative education and a renewed emphasis on postsecondary education. The amendments also included new provisions for funding an expanded vocational curriculum.

The Carl D. Perkins Act of 1984 was issued in the hopes of improving the basic skills of the labor force and preparing students for the job market by enhancing vocational education. Specifically, the Perkins Act sought to establish equal opportunities for adults in vocational education, and to aid in the introduction of new technologies in vocational instruction. In order to meet its objectives, the

Copyright © Mometrix Media. You have been licensed one copy of this document for personal use only. Any other reproduction or redistribution is strictly prohibited. All rights reserved.
This content is provided for test preparation purposes only and does not imply an endorsement by Mometrix of any particular political, scientific, or religious point of view.

Perkins Act set aside money for research into vocational education, as well as money to ensure access to vocational studies for people with disabilities, adults in need of retraining, single parents, and ex-convicts. This act was enhanced in 1990 with the issuing of the Perkins Vocational and Applied Technology Act. This act sought to integrate academic and vocational studies, as well as to fund better technology in vocational classrooms and better cooperation between the business and education communities.

Business Education Objective

Business education has a host of applications for students. Although it is typically assumed to be only relevant for people who are planning to make or sell goods or services for a living, the skills that are essential to business are also used by charities, governments, and farmers, just to name a few. Students may reconsider their future plans after learning a bit about business, especially if they live in an area with seemingly narrow career choices. Business studies will acclimate students to the set of standards they will be held to in their future life as a contributing member of the economy. Moreover, the skills in manipulating numbers and creating and analyzing various graphs and charts will serve students well in many different endeavors.

Advisory Council

A school's advisory council can help a great deal in fostering a positive environment for business classes. First, business teachers can use the advisory council as a sounding board for new ideas regarding curricula. The school advisory council may also have connections to the local business community that can be helpful for business teachers. By communicating well with the advisory council, business teachers can ensure that their equipment needs are known. An advisory council can also officiate any disputes that may arise between members of a business department, business teachers and the administration, and business teachers and their students.

Developing Business Programs

In order to put together an appropriate business education program, a teacher must conduct a needs assessment and determine what material needs to be covered, what changes need to be made in students, and what the costs will be of achieving those changes.The first step in conducting a needs assessment is performing a gap analysis; in other words, comparing the performance of the school's business department with the standard set by other schools. In order to do this effectively, the department head has to be aware of the technologies that the school already has, those that they will need, and the other strengths and weaknesses of the school. This may result in the purchase of new equipment, some new training for teachers, and perhaps a new philosophy for the department as a whole.

Needs Assessment

In order to construct an appropriate needs assessment, a business education department head needs to first conduct a gap analysis. After this is done, though, he or she needs to identify priorities for the department and rank them in importance. Sometimes a cost-benefit analysis is helpful in figuring out which are the most important actions that the department can take. Next, teachers will try to identify whatever problems may be keeping the department from reaching its potential. Possible problems might include under-trained staff or a failure to make department goals clear. Finally, the effective needs assessment will identify solutions to these problems, as well as any chance for improvement in other areas. The completed needs assessment provides a basis on which the whole department can work in the future.

Copyright © Mometrix Media. You have been licensed one copy of this document for personal use only. Any other reproduction or redistribution is strictly prohibited. All rights reserved.
This content is provided for test preparation purposes only and does not imply an endorsement by Mometrix of any particular political, scientific, or religious point of view.

TEACHING PLANS

A teacher cannot be effective without properly planning every aspect of class. Good plans give a teacher confidence, security, and a definite direction in class. Teachers that are successful planners typically follow four steps when they plan an activity.

1. First, the have a total understanding of the activity: what it will involve, what it is designed to teach, what potential problems it might have.
2. Next, the teacher imagines its implementation in the classroom, and makes whatever modifications to the environment are necessary.
3. Then, the teacher evaluates the strengths and weaknesses of his or her class, and alters the activity to suit them.
4. Finally, an effective teacher will create a mental image of the finished activity, and imagine exactly how it will be accomplished.

LONG-RANGE PLANS

For teachers, long-range plans are those that stretch out over a grading period, a semester, or a school year. They typically are closely related to state curriculum standards. Usually, a teacher will start a long-range plan by studying a calendar to determine exactly how many instructional hours will be available. Next, the teacher should consider which activities are most appropriate for which time of year. Many teacher use long-range plans to decide how they will try to develop a certain theme throughout the school year. These long-range plans will be frequently referred to when teachers are developing their weekly and daily lesson plans. Long-range plans serve as a sort of point of orientation for the rest of the planning process.

WEEKLY SCHEDULES

Every teacher needs to compose a weekly schedule in order to ensure that progress is maintained. Most teachers use their long-range plans to determine the amount of progress they need to make from week to week. In making weekly plans, teachers should consider which activities are appropriate for classes at the beginning of the day, and which are more appropriate for those after lunch and later. Next, teachers should consider how much direct instructional time will be necessary to give students the abilities to complete any assignments. Many beginning teachers run their weekly plans by more experienced colleagues to make sure that they are viable. The weekly schedule serves as the basic framework for the daily lesson plan.

DAILY LESSON PLANS

Effective teaching always includes composing clear, detailed, and well-considered daily lesson plans. Many schools place such a high value on daily plans that they require teachers to show their plans to the principal every week. A good daily lesson plan should include the specific content and activities that will be covered in each class period. It will also detail whatever procedures, assignments, student groupings, and materials will be necessary to meet the day's objectives. The composition of a lesson plan is a good chance for a teacher to consider whether his or her plan has an appropriate balance, and whether they are right for a particular class. In other words, plans should be made with the results of recent assessment in mind. Lesson plans are essential to maintaining an organized class and making sure that all of the goals of the syllabus are attained. Just as businesses create detailed budgets to ensure that there is a clear path to their objectives, so

Copyright © Mometrix Media. You have been licensed one copy of this document for personal use only. Any other reproduction or redistribution is strictly prohibited. All rights reserved.
This content is provided for test preparation purposes only and does not imply an endorsement by Mometrix of any particular political, scientific, or religious point of view.

must teachers plan every class in advance to ensure success. When drawing up lesson plans, a teacher should consider several things.

1. First, he or she must have a clear idea of what content is to be covered.
2. Second, he or she should know the time and resources available, as well as the ability level of the students.
3. Third, the teacher should have an idea of what teaching method is most appropriate to deliver that particular lesson.
4. Finally, the teacher should make sure that the lesson has a clear introduction, and an end that brings the material together and gives the student an idea of what they need to remember.

Review Video: Creating Effective Lesson Plans
Visit mometrix.com/academy and enter code: 100377

Maximizing Instruction Time

Too many teachers allow time to be wasted in class and cheat their students out of valuable instructional time. There are a few basic ways to remedy this problem. For one thing, teachers can minimize the amount of time students are given to socialize at the beginning or end of class. Next, teachers can try to make transitions between activities as smooth as possible by having the necessary materials ready at the beginning of class. Many teachers try to avoid giving students too much seatwork that could just as easily be completed out of class. Also, teachers should have a clear policy on restroom breaks, so that their time is not wasted by constant requests to be excused.

Managing Time as a Teacher

Teachers are always being pulled in several different directions, and sometimes they may feel that the responsibilities they have outside the classroom are making it difficult for them to meet their teaching goals. There are a few good ways to avoid this problem. First, teacher should list and prioritize their responsibilities, so that they do not get caught up in performing insignificant tasks. If necessary, teachers should avoid being drawn into committee and volunteer work organized by the school administration. Teachers should always have quiet space in which they can concentrate. Also, managing time effectively means abandoning perfectionism and procrastination. Setting firm time limits for open-ended tasks is a good way to avoid spending too much time on things less important than teaching.

First Day Preparation

The first day of the new school year is a nerve-wracking event for any teacher, much less a first-year professional. In order to make the first day a success, a teacher should arrive early and make sure that everything is ready for the arrival of students. Most teachers write their names on the board, and post a schedule so that students will know what to expect. Some teachers find it helpful to have an activity laid out for students when they come in, so that they will be immediately drawn into the flow of the class. Finally, and most importantly perhaps, teachers should just relax: if they have planned properly, the first day of school should be an exciting and hopeful day.

Effective Ways of Handling Students on the First Day of School

A teacher always wants to make the right first impression at the beginning of every school year. It is a good idea to greet students individually as they come in, and start the year with some ice-breaking activity. The first day of school is also the right time to acquaint the students with the class rules and goals, as well as to give them a brief idea of your background and expectations. Some teachers use the first day of school to develop a contract with students. If all of this is accomplished

Copyright © Mometrix Media. You have been licensed one copy of this document for personal use only. Any other reproduction or redistribution is strictly prohibited. All rights reserved.
This content is provided for test preparation purposes only and does not imply an endorsement by Mometrix of any particular political, scientific, or religious point of view.

with time left in the period, it may be a good idea to review some of the previous year's material with students, or to outline in brief the topics the course will cover. Some teachers use the first day to try to stir up some enthusiasm for the subject matter by previewing some exciting topics or activities.

First Weeks of School

The first few weeks can make or break a school year, so it is crucial to maintain effective control over activities. A good teacher will make sure to be firm and consistent in enforcing the rules; if students get the impression early in the year that they can get away with disobedience, they will bedevil their teacher for the rest of the course. Frequent assessment should be a feature of the first few weeks, so that the teacher can get a sense of what skills students already possess, and what they need to improve upon. The first few weeks are the time to drill into students the routines of the class, as well as the things that they will need to bring to class each day. In order to make the first few weeks of class a positive foundation for the rest of the year, students should be closely supervised as much as possible.

Syllabi

A syllabus is essential for effectively organizing and administrating a business class. Preparing a clear and detailed syllabus before the start of the school year allows teachers to be sure that all of the essential areas will be covered, that there will be enough variety among assignments to hold the interest of the class, and to make sure that all the students will understand the program and the expectations. A proper syllabus should include a defined aim for the course, clear assessment objectives, an outline of the assessment structure (that is, how students will be examined), the content of the curriculum, and a grading scale. The grading scale should include a sufficient description of the quality of work that merits each letter grade.

An Effective Syllabus and Assessessment Objectives

An effective syllabus will adequately describe the assessment objectives for the class. The assessment objectives are the skills that the class will be trying to develop in the student. In business education classes, there are considered to be four basic assessment objectives.

1. The first is knowledge and understanding, meaning that the student should be able to recall the basic facts and concepts of the course.
2. The second objective is application, the ability of the student to take the facts and concepts he or she has learned and apply them to the appropriate situations.
3. The third objective is analysis, the ability of the student to select, order, and interpret information, whether in the form of text, chart, or number.
4. Finally, students should be assessed on their ability to evaluate material; that is, to develop and justify arguments based on the content of the course.

General Structure

Although there is no one way to order the material of a business course, some ways seem to make more sense than others. For instance, most teachers will want to begin the course with an overview of the general themes of the course, so that students will have an idea of the structure of the course and will be prepared for its various transitions. Most teachers cover the nature of business activity, the types of businesses, and the objectives of various businesses early in the year. From there, it makes sense to move on to organizational structure and then to close studies of the various divisions within a large business: accounting, marketing, and so on. From there, the class may want to move to a larger view of business within the context of the whole economy, and to a consideration of macroeconomic trends.

Copyright © Mometrix Media. You have been licensed one copy of this document for personal use only. Any other reproduction or redistribution is strictly prohibited. All rights reserved.
This content is provided for test preparation purposes only and does not imply an endorsement by Mometrix of any particular political, scientific, or religious point of view.

Differentiation

In business classes that consist of students with varying abilities, it is crucial that a teacher practice differentiation: that is, distinguishing between students and adjusting the class material to engage all of them. This of course is a great responsibility for a teacher: more time must be spent planning, and teachers must guard against settling for lessons that appeal strictly to the middle level of the class. Besides differentiating between students, teachers must also differentiate between classes. Some classes may have a different "character" than others, depending on the time of day when they are held and their composition. Differentiation is especially important in business classes because they are frequently available to all students, regardless of aptitude.

Student and Teacher-Centered

An effective business class will have a mixture of student-centered and teacher-centered instruction. It is important for students to acquire a base of knowledge before they try to apply it, and teacher-centered instructional methods will tend to be more appropriate for this. Although the lecture is the traditional form of teacher-centered instruction, teachers may also use textbooks, newspapers, the internet, or CD-ROMs to accomplish this goal. After this, it is desirable to move on to activities in which the students are required to do something with the knowledge they have acquired. Group discussions, individual problem-solving exercises, and case studies are all student-centered instruction methods that force students to analyze and evaluate situations based on what they have learned.

Business Worksheets

Worksheets are a typical way to underscore key points in a reading assignment and ensure that students understand the basic material covered in a business class. Traditional worksheets may require students to fill in a blank, answer a multiple-choice question, or provide a short written answer. When designing worksheets, teachers should consider whether the language used is likely to be understood by all the members of the class. Also, teachers should try to vary the difficulty of the questions, so that there will be some way to discern the differentiation among the students. It is also important that the teacher have a clear idea of what material is to be covered by the worksheet, and makes sure that the worksheet fully and fairly covers the material.

Assignments

Business teachers will typically assign students a task or series of tasks to solidify and assess learning. Class assignments encourage students to manipulate and analyze course material. When making assignments, teachers should make sure to have a clear idea of what knowledge they are seeking to reinforce. Assignments should have varying degrees of difficulty, such that the least able students can attempt everything and the most able students will feel challenged. If research is required to complete the assignment, the teacher should have established the means for the students to perform this research. Finally, teachers should always grade every particular part of an assignment separately, so that students will have a better idea of what is expected of them, and also in what areas they need to improve.

Investigative Assignments

Teachers should encourage students to apply their knowledge by performing investigative assignments involving research. Investigations are especially useful in reinforcing difficult concepts: students can try to apply their knowledge of a subject to a real-life example, record their findings, and hopefully enhance their overall understanding of the concept. For example, a teacher might have students investigate the marketing mix of a familiar product. For a short assignment, students might isolate one aspect of marketing for a major product (say, price control), and discuss

Copyright © Mometrix Media. You have been licensed one copy of this document for personal use only. Any other reproduction or redistribution is strictly prohibited. All rights reserved.
This content is provided for test preparation purposes only and does not imply an endorsement by Mometrix of any particular political, scientific, or religious point of view.

how it is adjusted to meet market demands. A longer assignment might require students to investigate all the aspects of the product's marketing mix, and describe how the business adjusts them to achieve its goals. A teacher should keep a few things in mind when developing an investigative assignment for his or her class.

- First, it is better to assign several short tasks than one long task; students are more likely to become confused and flustered by long and unclear assignments.
- Also, the teacher should leave some of the questions open-ended, so that students can distinguish themselves by their enthusiasm and understanding.
- Teachers might consider whether a particular investigation would be better carries out by a group or by an individual. Some investigations are more beneficial when students have a chance to talk amongst themselves, whereas in others it may be essential that a student handle every element him or herself.
- Teachers should make clear requirements about the way the investigation should be presented; it is wise to vary the format throughout the course, so that students gain experience giving speeches, writing reports, and creating visual presentations.

Case Studies

Business teachers can effectively use case studies to solidify conceptual knowledge that has been taught in a particular unit. In a case study, the teacher provides specific information, and students are required to analyze and evaluate the information. For example, students might be presented with a business plan and asked to describe its strengths and weaknesses. When developing case studies, a business teacher should make sure that the information is comprehensible to all the members of the class, and that no untaught concepts are required to perform an adequate analysis. It is also important to limit the amount of information given: too much data may confuse students and detract from the power of the exercise. Finally, teachers should ensure that there are some areas of the assignment that require creative thought, rather than simply recitation of the course material.

Role Plays

In a role play, students are required to assume the roles of the various parties in a debate or discussion. This kind of instruction is especially useful for subjects in which it is important that students understand and empathize with the parties concerned; in a discussion of industrial layoffs, for instance, it might be helpful for students to see the pressures acting on both the management and the laborers. It is very important that students are well prepared for their roles, and that the subject of the role play is appropriate for the age group and the progress that has been made in the course. Lastly, teachers should take great care to emphasize that students are merely acting out roles, and that any disagreements should not be personal.

Class Discussion

Class discussion is an effective teaching method when going over difficult concepts or covering material on which there are varying viewpoints. Sometimes, teachers might want to organize discussion by giving an agenda or a list of questions to be collectively answered, while other times teachers may want to allow the conversation to flow where it will. One of the main concerns in a large class is that some students will dominate discussion, while others will remain silent. Teachers may want to make participation mandatory to remedy this, or they may want to divide the class up into smaller discussion groups. Teachers may also find class discussion more profitable if they plan ahead by providing students with a list of the topics to be discussed before the day of the discussion.

Copyright © Mometrix Media. You have been licensed one copy of this document for personal use only. Any other reproduction or redistribution is strictly prohibited. All rights reserved.
This content is provided for test preparation purposes only and does not imply an endorsement by Mometrix of any particular political, scientific, or religious point of view.

Group Work

Group work may be an effective way of encouraging students to master difficult material, because it forces them to describe the material to one another and agree on concepts. Group work also helps develop social skills and the ability to debate objectively and fairly. Teachers may want to select the groups themselves, to ensure that there is the desired distribution of males and females, of high and low ability students, and so that any disruptive students will not be grouped together. It is essential that groups be held responsible for presenting their work either to the teacher or to the rest of the class, so that time is not wasted. Also, teachers will want to set a series of small goals for groups rather than one large one, so that students are continually required to demonstrate progress in their work.

Presenting Information

It is important that students in a business class work to develop their skill at synthesizing and presenting information to an audience, as this will be necessary in the business world. Teachers may want to assign group presentations at first, if he or she feels students will be extremely uncomfortable speaking in front of the class. It is essential to provide a clear list of what is expected in the presentation. If multimedia equipment, such as televisions or video projectors, is necessary, the teacher should ensure that these are available to students. Students should probably be required to produce a handout accompanying their worksheet, in order to encourage an organized presentation as well as to aid the audience. Evaluation of presentations must be detailed and precise, so that students will know where they need to improve.

Games and Simulations

Games and simulations are an excellent way for students to model complicated business processes and thereby better understand some difficult concepts. Moreover, they are a fun way to conclude a unit while still ensuring that students have mastered the material. There are plenty of games available that deal with running a simulated business. Differentiation is key when assigning games to a class; teachers want to avoid creating unfair teams or creating situations in which some students will be embarrassed. On the other hand, game situations are more likely to encourage cooperation among students of different ability, as they strive to win a contest. As with other activities, it is essential that directions are clear and exact, so that controversy and confusion can be avoided.

Assessments

Even students with special needs must be regularly assessed, so that teacher's can determine their progress and also determine how best to serve them. According to the present system, students with special needs will be subject to all the normal state assessments, although some allowances may be made for them. These allowances may include untimed exams, or isolation during examinations for students with attention-deficit disorder. Students with severe cognitive disabilities may be assessed against their level of previous achievement, rather than at their grade level. Teachers may also discover that some students are better able to perform during oral examinations, or that students may respond positively to indirect questioning.

Formative Assessments

Formative assessment is the testing carried out by the teacher during the course of the school term. Its aim is to ensure that students understand the material, as well as to diagnose any gaps in their understanding. It should provide a clear view of the varying ability levels of the members of the class, and it should indicate some ways in which the teacher needs to improve his or her instruction. Formative assessment should often result in a different means of presenting

Copyright © Mometrix Media. You have been licensed one copy of this document for personal use only. Any other reproduction or redistribution is strictly prohibited. All rights reserved.
This content is provided for test preparation purposes only and does not imply an endorsement by Mometrix of any particular political, scientific, or religious point of view.

information, or more time spent with troublesome material. It is a good idea to include self-assessment and peer-assessment, so that students can indicate how they feel about their progress in the course and alert the teacher to any problems in morale.

SUMMATIVE ASSESSMENT

Summative assessment is carried out less frequently by the teacher; it is appropriate for checking knowledge at the end of a unit of study or at the end of the course. Whereas formative assessment is an assessment for learning, in that it helps the teacher to make positive adjustments to the course, summative assessment is an assessment of learning. It is likely that the means of summative assessment will be affected by the performance of students on formative assessments. It is important that summative assessments provide a comprehensive evaluation of students' mastery of the material, such that every area of knowledge is questioned and every skill is tested. Also, summative assessment should include questions of varying difficulty, so that students can distinguish themselves.

Review Video: Formative and Summative Assessments
Visit mometrix.com/academy and enter code: 804991

ORAL QUESTIONING

One easy way for teachers to conduct a formative assessment in class is to briefly quiz students on the material covered. Indeed, whether it is to be done for a grade or not, it is generally useful to recapitulate the previous day's lesson at the beginning of class. Oftentimes, this can be best accomplished by allowing students to articulate the material, and to critique one another's understanding. Some probing questions from the teacher can ensure that the recent material is understood in the context of the material that has already been learned. It is not always necessary to formally grade students on their participation or performance in an informal question-and-answer session; the main thing is to develop an idea of the students' progress.

WRITTEN COMMENTS

Perhaps the most important kind of formative assessment a teacher can provide is helpful written comments on student papers. This is the place for teachers to clarify the strengths and weaknesses of the student's work, as well as to generally assess the student's progress in the class. Moreover, this is the perfect venue in which to differentiate between students; in order to keep all of the students motivated, teachers must set different standards for them, and indicate these standards in their comments. Comments should always be positive and supportive, but not at the expense of being constructive: simply assigning a letter grade is inadequate. The important thing when commenting on student work is to indicate areas for improvement without alienating or embarrassing the student.

SELF-ASSESSMENT AND PEER ASSESSMENT

It is always a good idea to incorporate some self-assessment and peer assessment into a business class, so that students will be encouraged to think about their own progress relative to the progress of the class, as well as to stay focused on the goals of the course. Interestingly, students are usually much harder on themselves in their evaluations that they are on their fellow students. In order for self-assessment to be successful, the teacher must have clearly outlined the learning objectives of each activity. Furthermore, the teacher must have provided adequate constructive criticism, so that

Copyright © Mometrix Media. You have been licensed one copy of this document for personal use only. Any other reproduction or redistribution is strictly prohibited. All rights reserved.
This content is provided for test preparation purposes only and does not imply an endorsement by Mometrix of any particular political, scientific, or religious point of view.

students will have a clear idea of where they stand. Sometimes, it may be useful to design a specific assessment checklist so that students will not resort to vague praise or criticism.

Review Video: Learning Objectives
Visit mometrix.com/academy and enter code: 528458

Role of Department Head

The head of a business department occupies an important mediating role between teachers and school administrators. Along with the school's principals, he or she will be responsible for developing the aims of the school and crafting policy that fits the curriculum. As the head of the business department, he or she will be charged with making sure that all of the business teachers understand and employ the school policy, and that the business department cooperates with other departments to achieve school-wide goals. The department head is responsible for making sure that the staff is properly trained, and that all necessary technology is provided by the school. The department head will also be required to handle disputes between business teachers and their students, as well as any conflicts between teachers themselves.

Equipment Needs

A business department will typically require a few technological items in order to give students proper exposure to the methods currently employed in the business community. Obviously, a business department will need to have computer access, do that students can perform business simulations and get current information of economic and business topics. Most classrooms will need to be equipped with a video projector, so that students can practice creating and delivering slide show presentations. It may be useful for every room to have a television with VCR and DVD player, so that instructors can take advantage of the many visual resources available for business education.

Staffing

Assembling the proper staff for a business department can be a challenging task for the school administration and the department head. In order to adequately determine how many teachers will be required, the school officials will need to predict how many students are likely to register for business classes. Officials will then take this number and, based on the number of students they allow in a single class, determine the number of teachers required. Schools will often try to hire teachers with differing areas of expertise; for instance, a school may hire one teacher with a background in economics and another with a background in business law. If the department is large enough, the school may need to hire a secretary to help the department head and act as a liaison between the department and the main office.

Preparing a Budget

Typically, the budget for a business department is developed by the head of the business department in consultation with the business teachers and the school administration. This collaborative process usually starts with the business leader making a list of the equipment and supplies that he or she feels will be necessary for the upcoming school year. Then, he or she shares the list with the faculty and encourages them to make suggestions and to prioritize the requests. Then, the department head presents the budget proposal to the school administration, who will decide which of the department requests can be fulfilled. Sometimes, the administration will provide a limit to spending to the department head before the creation of a budget proposal.

Copyright © Mometrix Media. You have been licensed one copy of this document for personal use only. Any other reproduction or redistribution is strictly prohibited. All rights reserved.
This content is provided for test preparation purposes only and does not imply an endorsement by Mometrix of any particular political, scientific, or religious point of view.

Classroom Management

There are a few things that a beginning teacher needs to do in order to be properly prepared for the start of the school year. It is always a good idea to familiarize yourself with the school layout, and to introduce yourself to as many of your colleagues as possible. Also, you should meet the staff: secretaries, custodians, and counselors. These people can help make your transition successful. It is also a good idea to read the school policy manual and the state curriculum standards. A beginning teacher should become familiar with the school's philosophy and goals by reading whatever promotional literature is available. Finally, a beginning teacher should have a detailed schedule for his or her first day on the job.

Review Video: Classroom Management - Rhythms of Teaching
Visit mometrix.com/academy and enter code: 809399

Arranging the Classroom

The physical arrangement of a classroom will be best when it suits the style of the teacher. If most classes are going to be lectures, then it makes sense to arrange all the desks in rows facing the front of the room. If students are going to spend a lot of time working in small groups, then it is better to group desks together. Large group discussions are best held in a room in which desks have been arranged so that they face one another. It is also important for a teacher to create a generally welcoming environment in their classroom, by posting picture, laying some rugs, or setting out some plants. The point of arranging your classroom is to make it the place most conducive to meeting your goals, so you should avoid things that will be distracting or unpleasant to some students.

Creating a Positive Environment

In order for teachers to engage the minds of their students at the highest level, they have to first make sure that certain lesser needs are taken care of. Lighting, for instance, is important for creating a good classroom environment. Some kids may prefer bright light to dim light, so it is a good idea to include areas that receive different amounts of light. It is not a bad idea for there to be some open space in one section of the classroom, so that kids can move around a bit if they get restless. Many teachers have some softer furniture in their classrooms, so that students can get comfortable and focus on their work. Last but not least, teachers should try to determine what temperature is most popular in the classroom, and encourage students to bring whatever clothing they will need to be comfortable at that temperature.

Rules of Conduct

Just as a business posts its internal rules for employees, so do teachers need to post a set of basic rules for students to follow when they are in class. The most important and all-encompassing of these rules is simply to treat others the way you would like to be treated. Students should also be told to respect the property and personal space of their teacher and fellow students, and to keep their hands off of one another. Students should never laugh at one another. Students should be responsible for their own learning, and work together to create an environment in which they can be successful. This includes being on time for class each day, and handing in all assignments on time.

Review Video: Student Behavior Management Approaches
Visit mometrix.com/academy and enter code: 843846

Copyright © Mometrix Media. You have been licensed one copy of this document for personal use only. Any other reproduction or redistribution is strictly prohibited. All rights reserved.
This content is provided for test preparation purposes only and does not imply an endorsement by Mometrix of any particular political, scientific, or religious point of view.

Managing Paperwork

Most beginning teachers are overwhelmed at first by the amount of record-keeping and procedural paperwork they are required to fill out every day. The barrage of paper coming at a teacher can include attendance reports, lesson plans, lunch counts, report cards, homework, class reports, etc. There are a few good way to avoid being bogged down by paperwork. First, teachers can minimize their grading by having students grade one another for small assignments. Students can even be encouraged to make up their own worksheets. Many teachers try to use a lot of small quizzes to assess their students, so that they do not get caught up in grading large assignments. Teachers can even administer oral exams to their students, and thereby remove the need for paper altogether.

Grading Papers

Grading papers can be one of the more time-consuming tasks for any teacher. There are a few ways to alleviate the burden of grading.

1. One method that many teachers use is marking incorrect answers with an "O," so that when the student corrects the answer the teacher can just add a "K" to indicate approval.
2. Most teachers use one chart to keep track of all the student grades, so that they can keep them well-organized.
3. Students can often be enlisted to grade one another on short or insignificant assignments, and this may even be an effective learning strategy in some cases.
4. Finally, many teachers use a variety of different ink colors to tell themselves whether a paper is late, or on-time, or to tell themselves how much of it has been graded.

Relationship with Parents

Teachers too rarely make use of students' parents, or run into problems later in they year as a result of not communicating properly with them. It is important to start off every school year by sending a letter home with your students. This note should generally welcome the student to your class, and also give out your contact information. Also, this is a great chance to make any requests for equipment or help that you might have. Some teachers ask parents to send them a list of their child's strengths and weaknesses. It is always a good idea to inform parents at the beginning of the year about your policies on homework, grading, and assessment. Also, an early note is a good chance to mention whatever supplies the students will need for class.

Career Advice and Counseling

One of the common tasks of a business teacher is to provide students with career advice and counseling. Because of a business teacher's area of expertise, students have a right to expect that teachers will be able to dispense valuable information about careers. In order to do so, a business teacher must stay apprised of changes in the job market, and must be knowledgeable on the responsibilities and functions of various professions. This is not to say that a business teacher must be an expert on every career; on the contrary, one of the most valuable functions a teacher may perform is directing students to online or text resources on a certain profession, or setting up a meeting between a student and a member of the community currently working in the student's area of interest.

Job-Shadowing

Job-shadowing is one of the many ways that students can gain some experience in the workplace. In job-shadowing, a student simply follows along with a worker in the field in which they are interested as that worker goes through a normal day. Through shadowing a real worker, students can learn first-hand what skills they will need to hold a certain job and what exactly a job entails. Sometimes, students may discover that they are not as interested in a particular job as they

Copyright © Mometrix Media. You have been licensed one copy of this document for personal use only. Any other reproduction or redistribution is strictly prohibited. All rights reserved.
This content is provided for test preparation purposes only and does not imply an endorsement by Mometrix of any particular political, scientific, or religious point of view.

originally thought. For instance, a research study showed that students that originally were interested in fire-fighting often changed their minds once they realized the real, day-to-day life it would involve. One of the limitations of job-shadowing is that students only observe; they do not actually practice any job skills.

Copyright © Mometrix Media. You have been licensed one copy of this document for personal use only. Any other reproduction or redistribution is strictly prohibited. All rights reserved.
This content is provided for test preparation purposes only and does not imply an endorsement by Mometrix of any particular political, scientific, or religious point of view.

Pricing, Promotion, Selling, and Product and Service Management

MARKETING MIX

The marketing mix is the specific combination of tools used by a marketing program to promote a certain product to its market. The marketing mix includes the product mix, the distribution mix, the communications mix, and the service mix.

- The **product mix** is the composition, design, and packaging of particular products.
- The **distribution mix** is the method of storing and transporting goods to the place where they are sold.
- The **communications mix** is the sum total of advertising, sales, promotional and market research activities.
- The **service mix** is the activities that follow a purchase and strive to ensure customer satisfaction.

Marketing executives must try to find the balance in their marketing mix that creates the most profitable scenario for their product.

TOTAL MARKETING CONCEPT

Marketing did not assume its prominence in American business until the middle of the twentieth century. At this point, in order to succeed in a more competitive market it became imperative to tailor every aspect of the business to meet the needs and wants of the customer. Product development, marketing research, product servicing, and business forecasting all became part of the marketing department's mission. This idea, that a business must organize itself such that the marketing department has the resources and power to attract customers, is called the total marketing concept, and it is standard practice in business today. Now, marketing activities account for one third to one fourth of the workforce, and include such diverse areas as transportation, communications, retailing, and warehousing.

MARKET SEGMENTATION

When marketing executives attempt to remove the threat of competition by marketing their product to an exclusive portion of the population, they are practicing what is known as **market segmentation**. For instance, a shoe company that specializes in high-quality sandals does not compete with sneaker manufacturers. Market segmentation is particularly successful when businesses tend to sell their product to an intermediate buyer, who collects a number of these diverse lines and sells them to the general public. This can be a dangerous strategy to pursue, though: any shocks to the larger market can devastate a business that only trades in a limited portion of that market, and has no other product lines to fall back on.

COPYRIGHTS, TRADEMARKS, AND PATENTS

Copyrights are the government's means of granting an exclusive right to an individual to produce or sell some product during a certain period of time. Copyrights only protect the particular form in which something is produced; they do not protect any concepts, facts, or processes which may be a part of the product's creation. A **trademark** is a name or symbol placed on a product that identifies it and forbids other companies from copying it. A corporate logo is an example of a trademark. A **patent** is a right granted by the government to certain individuals to be the sole producers and distributors of some good or service that the individual has invented. The system of patenting

Copyright © Mometrix Media. You have been licensed one copy of this document for personal use only. Any other reproduction or redistribution is strictly prohibited. All rights reserved.
This content is provided for test preparation purposes only and does not imply an endorsement by Mometrix of any particular political, scientific, or religious point of view.

encourages innovation by guaranteeing the exclusive right to the profits created by some new invention.

Customers

Although most people think of private citizens when they envision the American consumer, there are actually a number of other kinds of customers that marketing executives must consider when they plan their strategies. Industrial buyers are those that purchase goods with the intent to resell them, either as is or in an altered form. Most complex products, books for instance, are the result of many industrial sales. Commercial buyers are those that don't alter goods before resale. They include hotels, offices, banks, schools, hospitals, and theaters. The things that they buy may be used in production or resold without any change. The government, perhaps surprisingly to some, is the largest consumer in the United States. They buy everything from office supplies to nuclear warheads.

There are three main ways in which marketing executives try to determine what consumers want.

1. First, they may study the consumer. This can involve surveys or questionnaires, all with the aim of discovering how consumers will respond to a new product or advertisement.
2. Another way of assessing the market is by determining what products would improve the lives of consumers, and then marketing these products. Some companies even go so far as to "manufacture" previously unknown needs among people, and then fulfill those needs.
3. The last approach to market research is to try the product out in a test market; that is, sell it in a limited area in order to gauge whether it is worth the risk of larger scale manufacture and marketing.

Intermediate Purchasers

Typically, intermediate purchasers (those who buy things in order to resell them) are more systematic in making their purchases than final customers. They usually buy things according to a rigid set of rules and are unlikely to be susceptible to flashy marketing. The people that make purchases for intermediate buyers, known as purchasing agents, value stability in the supply source. They frequently buy in bulk, and appreciate a discount for large purchases or for consistent purchases over a long period of time. The purchasing agent typically works with supply sources to ensure that the product is best suited to his or her business; price, while important, is not always the determining factor in intermediate purchases.

Motivation

Marketers who wish to sell their products to the general public are aware that private buyers are often much less systematic in their purchasing than professional buyers. They may be more easily influenced by emotion. Generally, marketers consider several sources of motivation in consumers. First, the consumer may be moved by the satisfaction of the senses if they enjoy the way a product feels, tastes, looks, smells, or sounds. They may be afraid of what will happen to them if they do not make the purchase (bike helmets, for instance). They may be moved to buy a product that represents the accomplishment of a worthwhile goal, or they may seek to satisfy their curiosity with a particular product. Buyers may also buy something simply because they believe it will change the way they feel about themselves, and the way others view them.

Selling

Personal selling is when an individual salesperson tries to persuade a customer to purchase a product in a face-to-face encounter. One good thing about personal selling is that it can be tailored to the audience. The two main types of personal selling are retail and industrial sales. Retail sales

Copyright © Mometrix Media. You have been licensed one copy of this document for personal use only. Any other reproduction or redistribution is strictly prohibited. All rights reserved.
This content is provided for test preparation purposes only and does not imply an endorsement by Mometrix of any particular political, scientific, or religious point of view.

are those made to the final consumer, taking place mainly in retail stores. In this case, the salesperson may do little more than facilitate the transaction. Retail selling can also include door-to-door sales. A more lucrative form of selling is industrial sales, in which products are sold to another business. This might include selling office equipment to a law firm, or tube socks to a department store.

There are several typical steps to a sale.

1. First, potential customers are scouted out, or prospected, by the salesman. Many firms conduct extensive research to identify prospective customers.
2. Next, the salesperson approaches the potential customer and indicates an interest to show them the product.
3. A presentation or demonstration will hopefully follow, in which the product is shown to its best advantage. The salesperson will then handle any objections to the product, and answer any questions.
4. Closing the sale is the negotiation of price and payment plan.
5. Finally, the salesperson will conduct what is known as a follow-up: processing the order, delivering or installing the product, and ensuring that the customer is satisfied with his or her purchase.

Marketing Phases

The typical marketing process has two distinct phases. First, marketing executives research the market in an attempt to determine exactly what goods and services customers are looking to buy. This may include looking at the past performance of the company or similar companies, conducting surveys or focus groups, or working in product development to anticipate future trends in the market. Next, the company attempts to provide the product to the public at the appropriate time, place, and price. This is much easier said than done: it takes a great deal of research and attention to the market to successfully serve the customer. Advocates of the new focus on marketing suggest that it creates a business community more attuned to consumer needs; critics, however, sense the same hunger for profits alone beneath the seemingly customer-oriented marketing.

Direct Sales

Direct sales, in which an individual tries to make a sale in a personal encounter with a prospective buyer, is a difficult way to be successful in business. Although there is very little of the old-fashioned door-to-door salesmanship at present, telephone solicitation still constitutes a huge industry. Sales managers probably have the toughest jobs in the area of sales. It is their job to keep the sales force energetic and successful. One of the best ways to do this, obviously, is through careful selection and training of the sales force. A sales manager must also pay close attention to the sales market, so that any changes in the character in the market can be met by changes in sales technique. Lastly, an effective sales manager should keep in mind the company's philosophy and make sure it is understood by the sales force.

Shoplifting and Employee Theft

Shoplifting is defined as any theft of merchandise that is for sale in a retail establishment. Shoplifting is one of the most common crimes, and has a significant effect on retail profits. Usually, store owners have to increase prices in order to offset money lost due to shoplifting. In 2001, researchers declared that shoplifting was costing the United States' retailers $25 million every day. Some of the stolen goods that are considered to have been shoplifted may actually have been stolen by employees. Although most shoplifters are amateurs, there are known to be various rings of

Copyright © Mometrix Media. You have been licensed one copy of this document for personal use only. Any other reproduction or redistribution is strictly prohibited. All rights reserved.
This content is provided for test preparation purposes only and does not imply an endorsement by Mometrix of any particular political, scientific, or religious point of view.

organized shoplifters. Some people even shoplift goods from chain stores in a perverse attempt to criticize the dominance of large retail corporations in American commerce.

Goods Categories

Goods on sale in the marketplace may be considered as belonging to one of four types: seasonal, staple, luxury, or convenience.

1. **Seasonal goods** are those that are only available at particular times during the year. Examples of seasonal goods may include fruits and vegetables, or holiday decorations.
2. **Staple goods** are those that are available year-round and are required by just about everybody in a society. They include things like gasoline, milk, and basic clothing.
3. **Luxury goods** are of the highest quality and price, and are generally not necessary for sustaining life. Many markets of seemingly staple goods may include luxury lines.
4. **Convenience goods** are those that the customer will have to purchase often and without much effort. Newspapers, hygiene products, and candy bars are all examples of convenience goods.

Public Relations/Publicity

One form of promotion that is frequently overlooked is **public relations** (also called **publicity**). Public relations includes any information about the company that is published or aired without being paid for. For instance, magazine and newspaper writers are often invited to visit corporate headquarters or to tour new factories, to try out new products or attend trade shows. The print space or airtime that they then devote to the company and its products is essentially free advertising. Publishers and music companies send free copies of their products to journalists, in the hopes of getting reviewed. Many publicists insist that even negative publicity can be beneficial, if it serves to remind the public of the company.

Promotional Mix

Marketing executives are always trying to find the appropriate **promotional mix** for their product: that is, the combination of promotional techniques that is right for their product. In doing so, marketers must consider the amount of money available for promotion, the nature of the market, and the nature of the product. The amount of money that a company has for advertising and other sales promotions depends on a number of factors. Typically, a small company will spend a greater percentage of each sales dollar on promotion, though the larger company may spend more altogether. New products will require more promotion. Many companies base promotion funds on the success of the product, and some allocate a specific amount of promotional money for every unit that is produced. The best way to determine promotion allocation is to make specific goals and plan precisely to reach those goals.

Retail and Wholesale Trade

Retail trade is that section of the economy that sells goods and services directly to the ultimate consumer. There are over a million retail companies in the United States, offering a wide variety of durable and non-durable merchandise. The United States Census Bureau classifies these businesses by their main product line, so a department store that sells much more clothing than home furnishings will have all its home furnishing sales reported under "clothing." The retail trade has in recent years accounted for approximately one-fifth of all non-farm jobs in America, and most economic analysts expect it will maintain or exceed this proportion in the future. They do say, though, that retail jobs may require an increasing amount of education as products diversify and businesses become more specialized.

Copyright © Mometrix Media. You have been licensed one copy of this document for personal use only. Any other reproduction or redistribution is strictly prohibited. All rights reserved.
This content is provided for test preparation purposes only and does not imply an endorsement by Mometrix of any particular political, scientific, or religious point of view.

Wholesale trade is that part of business in which goods are purchased, and then modified before they are resold. Wholesalers do not sell to the ultimate consumer, although many wholesalers have retail operations that do work directly with consumers. Some of the industries in which wholesalers are important are automobiles, plumbing supplies, electrical supplies, and raw farm produce. Perhaps the most important function of wholesalers is to provide producers with an expanded market in which to sell their products. Many small producers do not have the resources to offer their product to a market outside of their geographic area, but by selling to wholesalers they can make their product available to many more consumers.

Physical Distribution Management

Physical distribution is simply the transfer of goods from the producer to the user. For a long time, this was a neglected area of business. However, since physical distribution costs are a major part of most manufacturing budgets these days, it has become important for managers to discover the most efficient way to move their product. Today, the two main goals of a physical distribution manager are to maximize the level of customer service and minimize the total cost to the company. For instance, storage costs may be lower if less inventory is held, though that might cause an increase in transportation and processing costs. Physical distribution managers have to keep in mind the entire history of the product, from production to warehousing to processing to delivery, when they work to create the most efficient system.

Inventory Control

Manufacturers must constantly struggle to maintain the proper amount of inventory; it can be just as bad to have too much stock and pay high storage costs, as it is to run out of stock prematurely and lose sales. Therefore, managers must try to determine when inventory must be replenished, and how much should be ordered at a time. There are great opportunities to save money by practicing sound inventory management, eliminating waste, and controlling spending on transportation, storage, and distribution to the market. Inventory managers must ensure that a company has all the materials they need to continue production, but that they do not get stuck with large reserves of some material that has become obsolete. They must also ensure that materials will not deteriorate over time.

Periodic, Physical, and Perpetual Inventory, Floor Stock, and Back Stock

Inventory managers use a variety of systems to effectively maintain their stock. The goal of any inventory manager is to ensure that there is enough of a product in stock to meet any sudden demands for it, but that there is not so much around that the company incurs unnecessary costs. **Periodic inventory** is the system inventory managers use to determine the value of merchandise at periodic intervals by taking a physical count of stock. **Perpetual inventory** is another way of assessing the value of inventory, this time by using computers to calculate sales, returns, and receipts. **Physical inventory** is simply the name inventory managers have given to the process of physically counting the items in stock in a certain area at a certain time. **Floor stock** is inventory that is visible and accessible to consumers, and **back stock** is stored out of customer sight in a warehouse.

Inventory managers have a number of options concerning how best to move their goods. Last-in, first-out (LIFO) is a method of managing inventory in which the most recently acquired items are the first to be sold. This method is supposed to create the lowest ending inventory in a period of rising prices. It is also credited with creating lower taxable income, lower gross profit, and a higher cost of goods sold. First-in, first-out, on the other hand, is the method of managing inventory wherein the items that have been around the longest are the first ones to be sold. In periods

Copyright © Mometrix Media. You have been licensed one copy of this document for personal use only. Any other reproduction or redistribution is strictly prohibited. All rights reserved.
This content is provided for test preparation purposes only and does not imply an endorsement by Mometrix of any particular political, scientific, or religious point of view.

characterized by rising prices, this method of managing inventory is said to create a higher ending inventory, lower cost of goods sold, higher gross profit, and a higher taxable income.

Purchasing

Every large company employs people to oversee the purchase of products and materials. These people are generally referred to as purchasing agents, though in retail business they are called buyers, and in the military they are said to be engaged in procurement. Careful purchasing may seem somewhat slow, but if it is done in accordance with a sound system it can save a business a great deal of money. In most companies, the purchasing process begins when an employee fills out a requisition form, be it for raw materials like lumber or steel, or merely for office supplies. At this point, purchasing agents work to discover the most efficient quantity and quality of that good available, and the most economic way to acquire it.

It is crucial that a purchasing agent have the proper specifications for the desired item. When specifications are clear, the purchasing agent can consider options objectively, without having to weigh competing bids from various dealers. More attention can be spent on deriving the best value from the purchase. Of course, the purchasing agent has other things to consider, as well. There is always a cost associated with storing goods. Taxes, any interest the money used for inventory might be accruing, and the chance that the inventory will become obsolete must also be considered. The purchasing agent will also determine the various qualities of service and speed of delivery offered by different vendors. Some industrial buyers allow vendors to bid for their business, whereas retail buyers may visit trade shows to determine their best value. There is always a great deal of money to be made on seemingly insignificant purchasing decisions.

Transportation

Deregulation is the removal of any controls over markets that have been imposed by governments. Deregulation is often designed to make it easier for businesses to enter the market. In the transportation industry, this can be achieved by allowing several companies to operate on one rail line, or by introducing severe penalties for any businesses found to be fixing prices. The immediate benefit of deregulating transport is that more lines become available to consumers, and prices are generally much lower as transport businesses must compete more vigorously for the market. Unfortunately, deregulation can also result in many transport companies operating well below full capacity, thus adding to both pollution and traffic congestion problems.

Transportation of goods has been one of the most direct influences on the American economy throughout its history. Innovations like the steam engine and the highway system immediately resulted in better transportation costs for all businesses. Companies that specialize in the transport of goods are called commercial transportation companies. They can be either common or contract carriers. Common carriers are certified and overseen by the federal government if they ship goods over state boundaries and by state governments if they operate within a single state. Common carriers are obliged to serve the general public, and to provide reasonable speed and rates to all businesses without preference. Contract carriers are also regulated by the government, but they perform more specialized jobs for certain businesses, and they are allowed to negotiate their rates with the business itself.

Railroad Freight

Railroads were at one time the dominant means of transporting goods in the United States. They now face intense competition from other modes of transport, but still represent a considerable portion of business shipping. There are certain terms associated with railroad freight. In-transit privilege refers to the right of shippers to have goods left in a certain location for a period of time,

Copyright © Mometrix Media. You have been licensed one copy of this document for personal use only. Any other reproduction or redistribution is strictly prohibited. All rights reserved.
This content is provided for test preparation purposes only and does not imply an endorsement by Mometrix of any particular political, scientific, or religious point of view.

so that they can be modified, and then carried on to their final destination. Diversion of transit refers to the right of the shipper to have goods sent to a different location while they are in transit. Carload rates (that is, the cost of shipping per railroad car) is the most common rates of rail shipment; businesses use cheaper commodity rates when they are consistently shipping the same material to the same place; the rest of rail cargo moves at either class rates, which are rates determined by certain weight and content criteria, and exception rates, the rates that apply to everything else.

Coordinated Systems

Often, competing modes of transport work together to maximize their various advantages. Some of the more common combinations are "piggyback," the combination of trucks and trains; "birdyback," the combination of trucks and planes; and "fishyback," the combination of boats and trucks. Combined methods of transport are more popular since the advent of containerization, in which materials are stored in large, standard-sized containers that can easily be transferred from one type of transport to another. Containerization not only reduces handling time and expense, but, because the containers can be sealed and locked, reduces theft during transportation as well.

Trucking

As carriers of freight, trucks are generally more reliable and faster than railroads. Trucks are especially efficient at traversing short distances. For this reason, trucks have taken over from railroads as the preeminent means of moving goods. Although there are only a few rail carriers, there are many different and specialized trucking companies. One advantage of trucks is that they can easily combine goods from several different companies in one load. However, trucks tend to be more susceptible to bad weather than trains, and they are more often beset by labor problems. Trucks cannot hold as much as trains, and in fact have their load capacities regulated by the government. Trucking companies have also been hard-hit by rapid increases in the price of gasoline. For these reasons and others, the price of having goods shipped by truck has risen considerably in recent decades.

Watercarriers

Before the explosion of rail transport, the inland and coastal waterways were once the dominant means of goods transportation. Since then, other methods have risen which are faster and more flexible, but water transport is still a substantial business in America. Shippers of heavy, nonperishable goods like iron ore, grain, and steel often find that transport by barge is most efficient. The primary handicap of water transport is that it can easily be interrupted by ice or fog. For this reason, much water shipping is planned around the changing seasons. There has also been a movement to try to extend the shipping season on the frigid northern lakes and rivers by developing large "icebreaker" vessels to make waterways navigable.

Pipelines

Pipelines have some obvious advantages and disadvantages as a means of transporting goods. They are excellently suited for carrying liquids, and are a main source of transport for petroleum and natural gas. They are also quite inexpensive to use, much less so than trucks or trains. Because of this, there have been efforts to ship other goods via pipeline: coal, wood, and ore can be suspended in water, creating a mixture called slurry, and sent through pipelines. Certain pipelines in the United States have been curtailed because the government deemed they would be too destructive to the railroad business. Obviously, one of the main disadvantages of shipping by pipeline is inflexibility; it is quite expensive to divert a pipeline to more than a couple of destinations. Also, pipelines tend to require a great deal of water.

Copyright © Mometrix Media. You have been licensed one copy of this document for personal use only. Any other reproduction or redistribution is strictly prohibited. All rights reserved.
This content is provided for test preparation purposes only and does not imply an endorsement by Mometrix of any particular political, scientific, or religious point of view.

Airlines

Air transport generally is the most expensive means of shipping goods. However, shipping by air may lower costs for a firm in other areas, if it allows them to hold a lower inventory, close some warehouses, and decrease the amount of product deterioration. There may also be less need for extensive packaging for air transport, as there tend to be fewer stops and transfers. Not every product is suited to air transport, but businesses that deal in expensive, low-weight goods tend to benefit from shipping by air. Also, highly perishable products like flowers and fruit are often best shipped by air. For a long period, American electronic firms have shipped tiny parts overseas to be quickly put together and sent back; the high number of electronic parts that can be sent at a low weight makes them a viable candidate for air transport.

Storage of Goods

Businesses tend to run into problems with the storage of goods when the demand for a product is inconsistent with the supply. This may be caused by seasonal unavailability of a product, like agricultural products. In order to try to avoid great fluctuations in price, companies may elect to store excess products until demand rises again. In these cases, the managers must consider whether holding products off the market for a while will allow them to be sold at a higher cost, and thereby make back the money spent on storage. Storing excess goods may be especially smart if they are likely to be in great demand at peak periods. It may also be necessary for managers to determine the correct locations to store goods, so that they can be available immediately.

Warehouse

A warehouse is a building used for storing goods at some point between factory and consumer. Most warehouses used to be in the center of cities, making parking and therefore delivery difficult. Businesses eventually determined that is more efficient to have automated warehouses in the suburbs. The main job of the warehouse is to receive, disassemble, store, transfer, and reassemble goods for delivery. Businesses can make a great deal of money by streamlining the ways they organize inventory in the warehouse and minimize the need for human labor. Warehouses may be either public or private, depending on whether they are leased or owned by the firm. The greatest storage needs are typically at the production end; as the product nears its final destination, the consumer, it usually requires less storage space because it is fully assembled.

Forms of Advertising

Advertising takes two main forms: image advertising and retail advertising.

- **Image advertising** is also known as brand advertising. Large corporations that are selling an image along with their product produce this. Companies such as McDonald's, Coca-Cola, and Nike are examples of companies that use their name to convince you to buy their product. Usually their advertisements are not persuading you to go out and buy their product; they are designed to make you loyal to their brand.
- **Retail advertising** makes up all other types of advertising. This type tells you where to buy the products from the image advertisements. Retail advertising tends to be more low-budget because most businesses have fixed advertising budgets. Usually these advertisements are designed to get you to go down to the store and purchase the product.

Advertising is the practice of trying to call public attention to a business' products, services, plans, or philosophies by paying to communicate through the media. The most common venues for advertising are the Internet, television, radio, print media, direct mailings, billboards, or public displays. Advertising is most prevalent in those nations with a free market economy and little censorship. In these places, market power is based on consumer preference, and so businesses

Copyright © Mometrix Media. You have been licensed one copy of this document for personal use only. Any other reproduction or redistribution is strictly prohibited. All rights reserved.
This content is provided for test preparation purposes only and does not imply an endorsement by Mometrix of any particular political, scientific, or religious point of view.

must compete vigorously for the consumer's attention. Advertising also has the side effect of financing most of the media outlets in which it runs: most radio and television networks, for instance, are almost entirely paid for by advertising. For this reason, the government must keep a strict eye on the relation between business and the media, to make sure that any information presented as objective is not unduly influenced by business.

Online Advertising

Online advertising is among the most popular forms of advertising today. Ads placed on web pages, search engines, and social media and mobile platforms can reach vast audiences. There are a number of benefits to online advertising, including low cost per person reached, high measurability of effectiveness, ease of targeting specific markets or groups, and speed of deployment and change. Compared to other advertising avenues, Internet ads are fairly cheap. Advertisers can choose to pay per view, thousand views, click, or engagement. It is easy for the advertiser to see how many times the ad has loaded within a visitor's view, and if the ad resulted in a sale. There are, however, several drawbacks to online advertising. Security and privacy concerns are high on list, and fraud on the advertiser is easy to commit. Additionally, many users use ad-blocking software to avoid seeing the ads altogether.

Newspaper Advertising

Newspaper advertising remains one of the more popular means of advertising, particularly for local businesses. Those who advertise in newspapers appreciate the flexibility, meaning that they can adjust their ads daily if they so choose. They also know they will have a good idea who is seeing the ad, and they expect that being advertised in the newspaper will confer some kind of prestige in their company. It is very easy for local distributors of a nationally-known product to coordinate their newspaper ads with the television and magazine ads of the national company. Of course, newspaper ads have an extremely short life span; they need to be re-run every day to have any kind of longevity. Also, they are usually read hastily, and sometimes photos do not show up well in them.

Radio Advertising

Radio advertising is immediately available for broadcast, and can be developed for a relatively low cost, so it is a good option for business that are trying to promote a series of events or a special sale. Radio stations typically have a good idea of their audience, so companies will be able to air their commercials on the stations that contain the most of their target audience. There are some drawbacks to radio advertising, however. For one thing, it is easy to miss or to only hear part of, which may prevent the company name from getting across. Radio ads also are very temporary things, and unless they are part of a larger, consistent campaign, they may be quickly forgotten by the general public.

Magazine Advertising

Many larger companies do a great deal of advertising in magazines. They appreciate the ability to select their audience by advertising only in certain publications. Magazine ads also tend to look glamorous, and expensive photography will look much better in this format than in a newspaper. Magazine ads also have a longer life than newspaper ads, and therefore have a greater chance of lodging in the public imagination. On the other hand, magazine ads are relatively inflexible; a campaign that is discovered to be ineffective cannot be removed from the pages of a magazine in which it has already been published. Also, depending on the prestige and readership of the magazine, advertising can be quite expensive.

Copyright © Mometrix Media. You have been licensed one copy of this document for personal use only. Any other reproduction or redistribution is strictly prohibited. All rights reserved.
This content is provided for test preparation purposes only and does not imply an endorsement by Mometrix of any particular political, scientific, or religious point of view.

Outdoor Advertising

Although some communities are trying to diminish the amount of advertising that can be displayed outdoors, many companies still use billboards and other outdoor signs to alert the public about their products and services. Outdoor advertising is an excellent way to quickly communicate simple ideas, and is especially useful for promoting products or services that can be purchased nearby. Since they are a quick way to communicate, outdoor ads are often used for repeating a company slogan. There are some disadvantages to advertising out of doors, however. Besides public distaste for this kind of advertising, there is also concern that the brevity of the message will make it forgettable to too many viewers.

Television Advertising

Television advertising is perhaps the most successful form of promotion, because it allows the company to develop a narrative around their product and guarantees them a large audience. Television ads run repeatedly, so they allow companies to drill their message into the audience. It is also quite easy to take ads on and off the air, so companies can make quick adjustments to their campaigns. There is also a certain prestige that goes with advertising on television. Some of the disadvantages of advertising on television are the fleetingness of the presentation, and the high cost compared to other forms of promotion. There is also evidence that the public more reflexively distrusts television advertising than other forms, and that many viewers do not watch advertisements at all.

Direct Mail Advertising

Direct mail advertising is when a company sends brochures or leaflets directly to the homes of potential customers. It is easy to be quite selective when using direct mail because businesses know exactly who will be seeing their ads. There is also a great deal of flexibility in this form of promotion, as businesses can remake their ads as often as they please. Direct mail ads can be created and sent in a very brief period of time. Furthermore, direct mail is a great venue of businesses to go into detail about their products or services. Of course, direct mail is only as effective as the company's mailing list. Other disadvantages of direct mail are general public distrust of so-called "junk" mail, and the rather high cost of direct mail per customer.

Advertising Agency

With the advent of enormous advertising campaigns, it became impractical for businesses to handle their own advertising, and so this work has been assigned to advertising agencies, which are hired to create and develop particular campaigns. Agencies typically have a creative department that will come up with the theme of the campaign; produce the artwork, jingles, or ad copy; hire the people necessary to accomplish the job; and direct the development of the campaign. Agencies also frequently have a media services group that decides where to run advertisements that will best reach the target audience. The account management department of the advertising agency acts as a liaison between the agency and their client, ensuring satisfaction with the campaign.

Determining Price

Pricing is one of the most important factors in marketing. If a product is too expensive, consumers won't buy it. If it is too cheap, it will affect profit margins. The price is a delicate balance between these two factors. All the costs that go into making a product is called its **overhead**. This is labor, supplies, insurance, shipping, etc. When a product sells enough to offset these costs, this is called the equilibrium price or break-even point. All sales after this become profit. Sometimes a product is deliberately priced high or low in order to send a message to the consumer about it. A very high price can suggest its superiority to other products or that by owning it, that consumer is a wealthy individual. A low price can inform a consumer that a product may not be of very high quality.

Copyright © Mometrix Media. You have been licensed one copy of this document for personal use only. Any other reproduction or redistribution is strictly prohibited. All rights reserved.
This content is provided for test preparation purposes only and does not imply an endorsement by Mometrix of any particular political, scientific, or religious point of view.

Companies use three general approaches to set prices. The most common method is **cost-plus pricing**. This is a general markup to the cost of the product. **Value-based pricing** sets the price based on what the buyer believes is the fair market value instead of what the seller wants to move the good for. This is an effective pricing method in the US because their consumers often seek the best combination of value and quality. **Competition-based pricing** sets the prices based on what the competitors in a market are charging for a similar product. Smaller companies who follow the leaders in a market or use their prices to undercut them use this. Price is the amount of money a company charges for a product or service. How much a company charges for their product or service is one of the most important decisions that they make. Charge too much and people will not purchase the product. Charge too little and you won't be able to turn a profit. Most pricing is fixed, meaning that everybody pays the same amount for the good. Other companies use dynamic pricing, which means that the price varies depending on individual customers and buying situations. For instance, a loyal customer or one that is buying large amounts of the product may pay less than a new customer.

Internal Factors Related to a Company's Pricing Decisions

A company doesn't just choose a magic number when it sets its price. Several internal and external factors are taken into account before the price is set. A company first decides what its objectives are. They then settle on a marketing mix strategy. This is how all their different products will work together in the market. It factors in costs related to developing the product or service. If the costs to create the product or service are high then the price of the goods are high. Some other organizational factors that influence the price are: the price of workers and who sets the prices.

External Factors Related to a Company's Pricing Decisions

There are two main external factors that influence a company's price: the market and demand of the product. Several factors in the market influence price. They could be the number of competitors in a market, a company's share in a market, and what the public perceives the value of the product. Better said, if the public is willing to pay more for a product, a company will raise their prices accordingly. The demand of a product influences the level of a price through the law of supply and demand. If there is a large demand for a product, the price will rise. If there is little demand, a company will drop its prices in order to create demand. This relationship is known as the **demand curve**.

Inventory and Inventory Control

Inventory is the amount of stock a company has on hand at one time. This includes: raw materials, finished goods, and supplies. Inventory control refers to how to balance the amount of materials on hand with what to purchase in the future in a way that keeps costs down while ensuring that the company has enough of the product to meet customer demand. Production forecasting refers to predicting how much of a product must be produced to meet future demand. This is tricky because the company must take into account several different factors such as: economic swings, supply and demand, and the time of year. There are three basic inventory control methods: Just-in-time planning, manufacturing resource planning, and materials requirement planning.

- The **Just-in-time (JIT) system** means that companies hold just enough materials to keep fully stocked. New materials arrive precisely when they are needed. This system is popular with electronics companies.

Copyright © Mometrix Media. You have been licensed one copy of this document for personal use only. Any other reproduction or redistribution is strictly prohibited. All rights reserved.
This content is provided for test preparation purposes only and does not imply an endorsement by Mometrix of any particular political, scientific, or religious point of view.

- **Materials requirement planning (MRP)** is where finished products are analyzed (usually by computer) to determine what materials are needed to produce them. This is meant to prevent stockpiling of products.
- **Manufacturing resource planning (MRPII)** is the same thing as MRP except that it includes input from all aspects of a company including marketing and advertising.

Wholesalers

There are three different types of wholesalers: *Merchant wholesalers, agents, and brokers.*

- **Merchant wholesalers** account for 50 percent of wholesaling. They sometimes offer services to their customers, assisting them in the buying process.
- A **broker** assumes a different role than a merchant wholesaler. They use their various contacts to bring buyers and sellers together and help them conduct business. They may negotiate prices or set the terms between two companies.
- An **agent** has a more permanent relationship to a buyer and seller. They look out for the best interests of their clients in developing a deal. They don't carry inventory, or get involved in financing.

Marketing Decisions That Wholesalers Have to Make

Wholesalers have the same marketing mix decisions to make that other businesses have to make. They have to decide what their target markets are going to be. A wholesaler's market options are fairly limited especially in rural areas. Only large retailers can buy the large quantities that wholesalers sell. They also need to decide how much service they are going to provide. They need to decide if they are going to just sell products or if they are going to offer financing, promotion, advice, etc.

Brokers and Agents

There are several different types of brokers and agents to serve the various needs of retailers.

- A **broker** brings buyers and sellers together and negotiates prices and terms. They don't assume any risk or provide any financing.
- **Agents** are a more permanent form of brokers.
- **Manufacturer's agents** are usually hired by small businesses that can't hire their own sales force or large businesses that are opening new territories.
- **Purchasing agents** make purchases for buyers and assist them in the process of getting products to retail stores.
- **Selling agents** have contractual authority over how to sell a manufacturer's total output. They have influence over prices, terms, and conditions of sale.

Societal Product Classification

An enlightened marketer will try to design products that will make the consumer happy in the short and long term. All products can be placed into one of four categories according to their consumer benefits.

- **Deficient products** are unappealing and do not provide any benefits.
- **Pleasing products** such as fast food, beer, and cigars give immediate satisfaction but cause long-term harm.

Copyright © Mometrix Media. You have been licensed one copy of this document for personal use only. Any other reproduction or redistribution is strictly prohibited. All rights reserved.
This content is provided for test preparation purposes only and does not imply an endorsement by Mometrix of any particular political, scientific, or religious point of view.

- **Salutary products** are products that benefits consumers but are often unappealing or an afterthought to consumers.
- **Desirable products** like healthy food or a gym membership are examples of products that provide are beneficial to consumers and are appealing purchases.

New Product Pricing Strategies

As a product or service passes through its product life cycle, the strategy used to price it changes with it. Companies use two general strategies for setting prices: **market-skimming pricing and market-penetration pricing**.

- **Market-skimming pricing** sets an initial high price for people willing to pay more to have it first. This creates demand while maximizing profitability. After its initial release, the price is dropped so more consumers may purchase the item.
- **Market-penetration pricing** is the opposite. Companies set an initial low price to get people to buy their products or to recoup their investment. Once they have gained a significant part of the market, they usually raise their prices gradually.

Product Mix Pricing Strategies

When a product is marketed as part of a mix, the way it is priced is influenced by several factors.

- **Product line pricing** takes into account the prices of other products in the line. The quality of the product in relation to other in the mix usually determines the price. For instance, a television company is not going to sell its 4K TV's for less than their traditional models.
- **Optional-product pricing** is the practice of selling accessories and options in conjunction with the main product. For instance, Apple makes a large profit with its IPhone series, but it also makes money off of docks, chargers, software, music, and other products designed to enhance the iPhone.
- **Captive-product pricing** is the name of deciding how much to charge for products that must be purchased for use with other products. Things such as razor blades, accessories, and CD's are examples of captive-product pricing.
- **By-product pricing** sets a price for poor selling products and are used to sell other products in the mix.
- **Product bundle pricing** moves inventory by combining several products together and discounting them.

Price Adjustment Strategies

There are a few different strategies for adjusting prices of products.

- Discounted pricing offers the chance for the buyer to save money. Psychological pricing uses the price to make a statement about the product.
- Segmented pricing sells the product for more than one price, but the price is based on something besides costs.
- Promotional pricing reduces a price in order to increase awareness of it.
- Geographical pricing changes the price based on where it is sold.

Discounts

There are many different methods people use to discount their products. **A quantity discount** reduces the price according to the volume of goods a consumer buys. *A* **cash discount** is offered to people that pay their bills on time or early. **A seasonal discount** is offered to people that buy goods out of season so retailers can move or change their inventories. **A functional discount** is offered to

Copyright © Mometrix Media. You have been licensed one copy of this document for personal use only. Any other reproduction or redistribution is strictly prohibited. All rights reserved.
This content is provided for test preparation purposes only and does not imply an endorsement by Mometrix of any particular political, scientific, or religious point of view.

companies that assist in the conducting of a business. This is also known as a form of bartering, the exchange of goods and services without money changing hands.

Inventory and Inventory Control

Inventory is the amount of stock a company has on hand at one time. This includes: raw materials, finished goods, and supplies. Inventory control refers to how to balance the amount of materials on hand with what to purchase in the future in a way that keeps costs down while ensuring that the company has enough of the product to meet customer demand. Production forecasting refers to predicting how much of a product must be produced to meet future demand. This is tricky because the company must take into account several different factors such as: economic swings, supply and demand, and the time of year. There are three basic inventory control methods: Just-in-time planning, manufacturing resource planning, and materials requirement planning.

- The **Just-in-time (JIT) system** means that companies hold just enough materials to keep fully stocked. New materials arrive precisely when they are needed. This system is popular with electronics companies.
- **Materials requirement planning (MRP)** is where finished products are analyzed (usually by computer) to determine what materials are needed to produce them. This is meant to prevent stockpiling of products.
- **Manufacturing resource planning (MRPII)** is the same thing as MRP except that it includes input from all aspects of a company including marketing and advertising.

Price, Packaging, and Promotion

The price of a product has a tremendous effect on consumers. Some people will buy something because it says "sale" on it regardless of whether they need it or not. Other people buy only high-end merchandise as a sign of status. With products, a low price signals value but can also suggest poor quality. A high price suggests exclusivity but may also scare consumers away. Some consumers will buy a product because of the way it is packaged. A successful product usually has its logo on the package to show what it is. If the package is not attractive to the consumer, they may think that the product is of poor quality. Promotions are paid advertisements that give people information about a product. This is what makes people want to go out and buy a product. A good promotion delivers a clear, concise message to the consumer.

Customer Motivations

One of the most important aspects of marketing is to find out what motives people to buy a product. When this is known, they can change their product to fit these motivations. There are three types of motives for people who are purchasing a product.

- **Rational motives** are when consumers have motivation to think rationally about what they want to purchase. Rational motives include: comparing price, value, and quality of two or more products.
- **Emotional motives** are what drive us to make impulse buys. This is when you purchase a product despite the fact it runs counter to rational economic choices. Impulse buys compel the buyer to purchase a product despite the fact that they can't afford it, don't need it, or do not have room for it.
- **Patronage motives** are what influence a consumer to be loyal to certain brands or products. There are rational and irrational motives as to why a person may only drink Coke or drive Hondas. Companies spend large amounts of their advertising budgets to try to get people loyal to their brands.

Copyright © Mometrix Media. You have been licensed one copy of this document for personal use only. Any other reproduction or redistribution is strictly prohibited. All rights reserved.
This content is provided for test preparation purposes only and does not imply an endorsement by Mometrix of any particular political, scientific, or religious point of view.

RETAILING

While shopping has evolved tremendously with increased technology and innovative methods, the traditional retail store will always be the most popular way people shop. **Retailing** is everything associated with selling goods and services for non-business use. **Retailers** are the people that make these sales. Types of retail stores include: convenience, specialty, discount, department, supermarkets, and off-price retails. The stores vary in terms of service, price, product lines, and value. **Non - store retailing** has become popular as businesses look for ways to pass savings on to consumers. Companies that sell through catalogs, the Internet, television, or the phone eliminate the retailer and their fees. The tradeoff to the consumer is the loss of a level of service and a reliable connection to the product in case it malfunctions.

SALESPEOPLE

It is very difficult to have one definition for **salesperson** because they do so many jobs. One of the oldest professions in the world, they are usually the final representative of a business that a customer deals with before deciding whether or not to make a purchase. Being a salesperson requires persuasive and interpersonal skills, and the ability to think quickly. They also perform many other functions such as: taking orders, prospecting, communicating, servicing customers, and gathering information. Salespeople provide a link to a company and represent it to customers.

Sales force management is the task of managing all aspects of a sales operation and the people that work for it. This is done by one or many levels of management depending on the size of the company and its goals. Management decides which sales force strategies they will use to sell their products. They decide how to recruit, train, evaluate, compensate, and manage the salespeople in a company. Being in management usually requires several years of work experience and often an advanced degree.

Depending on what it is, there are several ways that a company can decide how to sell its product. If a company only sells one product or service, they use a **territorial sales force structure**. This means that they assign their salespeople a certain territory and they are accountable for sales in that area. If a company has many complex products, then they use a **product sales force structure**. This means that each salesperson sells only a portion of their product lines. **Customer sales force structure** is a strategy in which certain salespeople focus on selling a small amount of products to a small number of customers in order to enhance communication and the sales experience for the consumer.

Inside salespeople work inside the company and have interested customers visit them or contact them on the phone or email. **Outside salespeople** travel to visit or service clients. Inside and outside salespeople work together to reduce the many demands of their jobs. For instance, **technical support** and **telemarketing** are two growing types of inside sales jobs that provide leads and technical information to customers and salespeople, helping the salespeople focus more on selling products. **Team selling** is a sales strategy that uses a group of people from different departments in a business to service large clients that have immediate, diverse, or complex needs.

There are seven steps in the selling process: Prospecting, pre-approach, approach, presentation and demonstration, handling objections, closing, and follow-up.

- **Prospecting** is identifying potential customers.
- **Pre-approach** is when a salesperson learns as much as they can about a prospective customer.
- **Approach** is the salesperson's first meeting with the customer.

Copyright © Mometrix Media. You have been licensed one copy of this document for personal use only. Any other reproduction or redistribution is strictly prohibited. All rights reserved.
This content is provided for test preparation purposes only and does not imply an endorsement by Mometrix of any particular political, scientific, or religious point of view.

- The **demonstration** and **presentation** is the pitch of the salesperson to the consumer.
- **Handling objections** are the clarifications a salesperson makes to the customer.
- The **closing** is when the salesperson asks the customer to place an order.
- The **follow-up** is when the sales person contacts the buyer after the sale to ensure customer satisfaction.

Copyright © Mometrix Media. You have been licensed one copy of this document for personal use only. Any other reproduction or redistribution is strictly prohibited. All rights reserved.
This content is provided for test preparation purposes only and does not imply an endorsement by Mometrix of any particular political, scientific, or religious point of view.

GACE Practice Test

Want to take this practice test in an online interactive format?
Check out the online resources page, which includes interactive practice questions and much more: **mometrix.com/resources719/gacemarketed**

1. Business firms and _______ are the two primary kinds of organizations that use marketing as a method of communication.

a. brick-and-mortar firms
b. strategic business units
c. nonprofit organizations
d. advertising agencies

2. A person who creates a marketing campaign for a new dishwasher would most likely be part of which level in General Electric's corporate structure?

a. Business unit
b. Functional
c. Corporate
d. Financial

3. Which of the following ensures that a direct mail sweepstakes includes the phrase "No purchase is necessary to enter"?

a. Telephone Consumer Protection Act
b. Better Business Bureau
c. National Do Not Call Registry
d. Deceptive Mail Prevention and Enforcement Act

4. The Federal Dilution Act was passed in order to:

a. enable a firm to register multiple trademarks for a single product.
b. allow someone to secure a trademark before actually using it.
c. protect US trademarks from being used in foreign countries.
d. prevent the use of a trademark on a noncompeting product.

5. Which of the following is the primary function of a product manager?

a. Prepare product materials for sales representatives
b. Plan and control long-range plans for specific products
c. Manage and oversee the training of field representatives
d. Allocate resources to various members of the supply chain

Copyright © Mometrix Media. You have been licensed one copy of this document for personal use only. Any other reproduction or redistribution is strictly prohibited. All rights reserved.
This content is provided for test preparation purposes only and does not imply an endorsement by Mometrix of any particular political, scientific, or religious point of view.

6. Which of the following is not a benefit of the product manager system?

a. Product managers strongly advocate for the products that are their assigned responsibility.
b. Product managers take responsibility for profits and losses related to a product's performance.
c. Product managers bypass bureaucracy to work with people inside and outside the firm if it benefits the product.
d. Product managers maintain direct authority over numerous groups and firm functions to meet product sales goals.

7. What is the term for marketing efforts that are intended to produce and promote environmentally sensitive products?

a. Environmental marketing
b. Green marketing
c. Clean marketing
d. Responsible marketing

8. McDonald's has developed Ronald McDonald Houses, which enable families of chronically and terminally ill children to stay together. This is an example of:

a. social responsibility.
b. profit responsibility.
c. cause marketing.
d. sustainable development.

9. Illegal trespassing, fraud, misrepresentation, and wiretapping are examples of:

a. Internet piracy.
b. unethical marketing.
c. corporate espionage.
d. corruption perceptions.

10. Which of the following is a form of business self-regulation and is an alternative to federal and state regulations?

a. Code of Business Practices
b. Robinson-Patman Act
c. Better Business Bureau
d. Consumer Reports

11. How does effective marketing benefit society?

a. It utilizes technology, increases product support, and decreases consumer waste.
b. It eliminates unnecessary products, increases customer value, and improves sales.
c. It decreases competition, improves customer service, and increases product choices.
d. It increases competition, improves product quality, and lowers product prices.

12. Which of the following would most likely occur if a natural disaster caused a mass shortage of corn?

a. The demand curve for corn cereal would shift to the right.
b. The demand curve for corn cereal would shift to the left.
c. The supply curve for corn cereal would shift to the right.
d. The supply curve for corn cereal would shift to the left.

Copyright © Mometrix Media. You have been licensed one copy of this document for personal use only. Any other reproduction or redistribution is strictly prohibited. All rights reserved.
This content is provided for test preparation purposes only and does not imply an endorsement by Mometrix of any particular political, scientific, or religious point of view.

13. Which of the following is an example of a product with elastic demand?

a. Milk
b. Air travel
c. Electricity
d. Medication

14. Which of the following BEST defines the business cycle?

a. A period of inflation and deflation that affects a nation's economic growth
b. A predictable fluctuation in a nation's economy that affects investments
c. A period of recovery and recession that affects inflation, growth, and employment
d. An unpredictable fluctuation in a nation's economy that affects the cost of living

15. What is the MOST important pricing strategy for a successful business?

a. Prices cover costs and profits
b. Prices match those of competitors
c. Prices include a specific profit margin
d. Prices fluctuate with supply and demand

16. The number of hours it takes workers to assemble a Corolla in a Toyota factory is a measure of:

a. productivity.
b. distribution.
c. labor costs.
d. revenue.

17. Use the graph below to answer the question that follows:

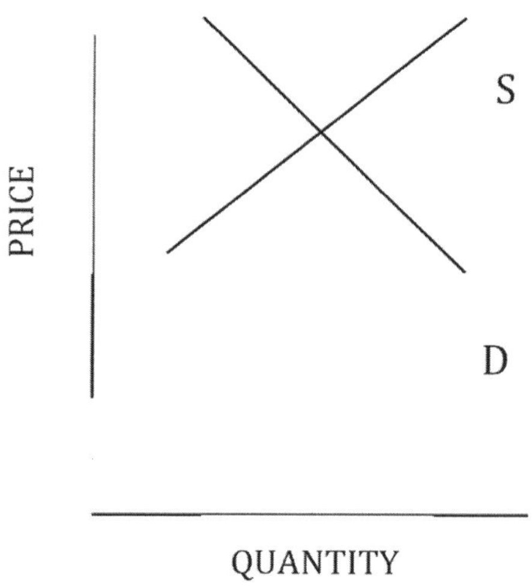

What occurs at the intersection of the demand curve (D) and the supply curve (S)?

a. Suppliers produce more than enough goods to meet consumer demands.
b. Suppliers sell their products at a loss, and consumers get the products that they demand.
c. Suppliers produce only enough items to meet consumer demands due to a lack of sales profits.
d. Suppliers sell all of the items that they produce, and consumers get all of the items that they demand.

Copyright © Mometrix Media. You have been licensed one copy of this document for personal use only. Any other reproduction or redistribution is strictly prohibited. All rights reserved.
This content is provided for test preparation purposes only and does not imply an endorsement by Mometrix of any particular political, scientific, or religious point of view.

18. A nation that allows private businesses and individuals to operate and compete with minimal government regulation is a:

a. political economy.
b. commercial economy.
c. free enterprise economy.
d. merchant capitalist economy.

19. Which of the following is a function of markets in a free enterprise economy?

a. Monitoring the legal rights of businesses
b. Bringing buyers and sellers together
c. Providing opportunities for entrepreneurship
d. Regulating supply and demand

20. A nation's economy is described as healthy when it has all of the following EXCEPT:

a. sustained growth.
b. steady investment.
c. high employment.
d. stable prices.

21. How would a furniture manufacturer most likely utilize the Consumer Confidence Index?

a. To plan a new marketing strategy
b. To decide how to advertise their products
c. To determine the color of sofas to produce
d. To plan how many sofas to produce

22. Which of the following is the primary disadvantage of a sole proprietorship?

a. Both business and personal assets are at risk because of unlimited liability.
b. The business is difficult to dissolve because of its complicated structure.
c. Initial set up is too difficult and expensive for most small business owners.
d. Employee benefits cannot be deducted or adjusted from business income.

23. What is the key difference between a marketing plan and a business plan?

a. Marketing plans include details about a firm's research and development activities.
b. Business plans include details about a firm's operations and manufacturing activities.
c. Marketing plans include details about a firm's marketing program and market-product focus.
d. Business plans include details about a firm's implementation plans and strategic focus.

24. Jessie Matthews has decided to start a small business. What should she do next?

a. Rent office space and lease equipment
b. Write a business plan and investigate financing
c. Interview and hire an office manager and support staff
d. Develop a marketing plan and create an advertising campaign

Copyright © Mometrix Media. You have been licensed one copy of this document for personal use only. Any other reproduction or redistribution is strictly prohibited. All rights reserved.
This content is provided for test preparation purposes only and does not imply an endorsement by Mometrix of any particular political, scientific, or religious point of view.

25. For an entrepreneur just starting a small business, what are the two primary types of financing available?

a. Equity and venture capital financing
b. Personal loans and stock offerings
c. Debt and commercial financing
d. Equity and debt financing

26. Sorting prospective customers into similar groups based on common needs is called market:

a. penetration.
b. development.
c. classification.
d. segmentation.

27. The identification of a target market allows a marketer to:

a. concentrate a marketing program towards the needs of a specific group of potential customers.
b. determine the specific product demanded by a wide variety of potential long-term consumers.
c. reduce the amount of time involved in developing a marketing plan and advertising campaign.
d. focus on customer value and satisfaction by establishing a balance of price, quality, and service.

28. Use the equation below to answer the question that follows.

Firm's Sales ÷ Total Market Sales = X

Which of the following completes the equation (meaning, what does *X* stand for)?

a. Unit volume
b. Profit margin
c. Market share
d. Market revenue

29. L.L. Bean's motto is "Guaranteed. You Have Our Word." What is the retailer's most likely marketing goal?

a. Social responsibility
b. Customer satisfaction
c. Employee welfare
d. Market share

30. All of the following occur in the planning phase of the strategic marketing process EXCEPT:

a. identifying industry trends.
b. developing the budget.
c. setting product goals.
d. obtaining resources.

Copyright © Mometrix Media. You have been licensed one copy of this document for personal use only. Any other reproduction or redistribution is strictly prohibited. All rights reserved.
This content is provided for test preparation purposes only and does not imply an endorsement by Mometrix of any particular political, scientific, or religious point of view.

31. The overall objective of marketing research is to:

a. improve marketing objectives and streamline results.
b. distinguish between relevant and irrelevant data.
c. improve marketing decisions and reduce risk.
d. analyze demand and predict sales revenue.

32. The first step in the marketing research process is to:

a. collect information.
b. define the problem.
c. develop a research plan.
d. specify research constraints.

33. Which of the following is an advantage of using secondary data in marketing research?

a. Time and money are saved.
b. Personal reactions can be observed.
c. Current information can be gathered.
d. Data is specific for one product or service.

34. A marketing manager will most likely use a marketing information system (MIS) to:

a. manipulate data for stockholders.
b. show product features to sales staff.
c. make product improvements.
d. determine supplier costs.

35. A firm's marketing department has total control of the:

a. market share.
b. derived demand.
c. customer value.
d. marketing mix.

36. All of the following are primary marketing reasons for the failure of new products EXCEPT:

a. insignificant point of difference.
b. insignificant idea generation.
c. poor product quality.
d. poor timing.

37. Concept tests and weighted point systems separate good product ideas from bad ones in the _______ stage of the new product process.

a. market testing
b. business analysis
c. idea generation
d. screening and evaluation

Copyright © Mometrix Media. You have been licensed one copy of this document for personal use only. Any other reproduction or redistribution is strictly prohibited. All rights reserved.
This content is provided for test preparation purposes only and does not imply an endorsement by Mometrix of any particular political, scientific, or religious point of view.

38. According to the US Federal Trade Commission, a product can be advertised as "new" up to _______ months after it enters regular distribution.

a. three
b. six
c. nine
d. twelve

39. Use the table below to answer the question that follows.

Amount of Price Competition	Moderate: Firms compete over a range of prices
Amount of Product Differentiation	Moderate: Firms differentiate products from competitors
Amount of Product Advertising	Extensive: Firm's goal is to differentiate its product from competing products

Which type of competitive market is summarized in the table?

a. Pure monopoly
b. Oligopoly
c. Monopolistic competition
d. Pure competition

40. Use the table below to answer the question that follows.

Sony PSP handheld game system	$169.99
Nintendo DS handheld game system	$119.99

What type of pricing did Nintendo most likely use when it introduced its game system?

a. Skimming pricing
b. Penetration pricing
c. Prestige pricing
d. Bundle pricing

41. Which of the following is an external factor that affects pricing decisions made by a company's managers?

a. Competition
b. Labor costs
c. Price elasticity
d. Pricing objectives

42. Which of the following firms has the MOST extensive product mix?

a. IBM
b. Procter & Gamble
c. Kawasaki
d. Barnes & Noble

Copyright © Mometrix Media. You have been licensed one copy of this document for personal use only. Any other reproduction or redistribution is strictly prohibited. All rights reserved.
This content is provided for test preparation purposes only and does not imply an endorsement by Mometrix of any particular political, scientific, or religious point of view.

43. Use the diagram below to answer the question that follows.

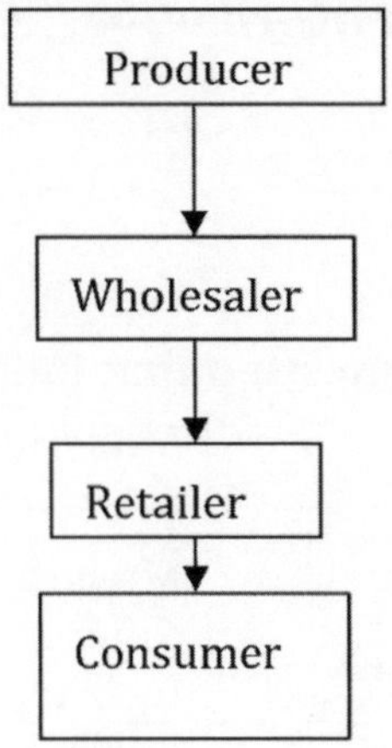

Which of the following firms would most likely use the marketing channel structure shown in the diagram?

a. Chevrolet
b. Wal-Mart
c. Frito-Lay
d. Land's End

44. For which of the following reasons would a firm be most likely to eliminate wholesalers and buy directly from producers?

a. Damaged products are a regular problem.
b. Retail sales of the product are sporadic.
c. A product is in the early stage of its life cycle.
d. Freshness of the product is essential to quality.

45. Which of the following is a disadvantage of sales promotions in the promotional mix?

a. They have a small return on high investments.
b. They lose effectiveness when held continuously.
c. They require costly database management.
d. They lack flexibility when used in print media.

46. Which of the following is most likely responsible for a decline in the success of direct marketing?

a. Concerns about privacy
b. Inconsistent sales messages
c. Difficulties with feedback
d. High absolute costs

47. In what stage of a product's life cycle does reminder advertising occur?

a. Introduction stage
b. Growth stage
c. Maturity stage
d. Declining stage

Copyright © Mometrix Media. You have been licensed one copy of this document for personal use only. Any other reproduction or redistribution is strictly prohibited. All rights reserved.
This content is provided for test preparation purposes only and does not imply an endorsement by Mometrix of any particular political, scientific, or religious point of view.

48. Use the diagram below to answer the question that follows.

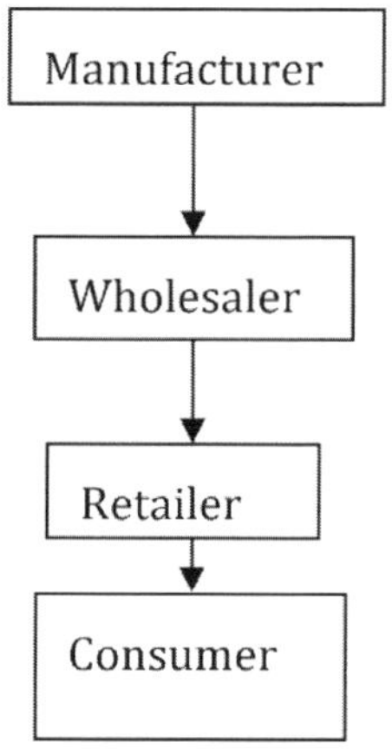

If the flow of promotion and demand stimulation is from the manufacturer through wholesaling and then retailers to meet the consumers where they are as illustrated in the diagram, what type of channel strategy is most likely in place?

a. Direct selling strategy
b. Push strategy
c. Pull strategy
d. Value-added reselling strategy?

49. The "Got Milk?" campaign from America's dairy farmers and milk processors is an example of:

a. competitive institutional advertising.
b. public relations.
c. pioneering institutional advertising.
d. sales promotion.

50. An advertiser who wants the same target audience to view a commercial more than once is MOST concerned about:

a. reach.
b. frequency.
c. ratings.
d. expenditures.

51. Which medium would be the MOST beneficial for an advertiser that wants to convey detailed information about a product to a very narrow target audience?

a. Radio
b. Newspapers
c. Magazines
d. Television

52. Which of the following lists the stages of the personal selling process in the correct order?

a. Pre-approach, prospecting, approach, presentation, follow-up, close
b. Prospecting, follow-up, pre-approach, approach, presentation, close
c. Prospecting, pre-approach, approach, presentation, close, follow-up
d. Pre-approach, approach, prospecting, presentation, close, follow-up

Copyright © Mometrix Media. You have been licensed one copy of this document for personal use only. Any other reproduction or redistribution is strictly prohibited. All rights reserved.
This content is provided for test preparation purposes only and does not imply an endorsement by Mometrix of any particular political, scientific, or religious point of view.

53. Which of the following methods of handling an objection during a sales presentation is appropriate when the prospect's objection is based on false information?

a. Ignore the objection
b. Use the objection as a reason for buying
c. Deny the objection
d. Postpone the objection and return to it later

54. The Uniform Commercial Code is a set of laws that:

a. standardize the tax rate for goods sold over the Internet.
b. monitor advertising and marketing claims for goods and services.
c. control the sale of exported goods to specific countries.
d. regulate commercial transactions involving the sale of goods.

55. Exxon sells different blends of its gasoline depending on a nation's climate. Which global product and promotion strategy is Exxon's marketing department using?

a. Product extension
b. Product adaptation
c. Product invention
d. Product function

56. Which of the following is MOST directly related to a weaker US dollar?

a. Foreign exports increase
b. US exports increase
c. Foreign exports decrease
d. US exports decrease

57. Which of the following is the riskiest strategy when entering a global market?

a. Franchising
b. Joint venture
c. Direct exporting
d. Contract assembly

58. How would a firm utilize a global marketing strategy?

a. By modifying a product's formula and packaging to meet a foreign country's specifications
b. By employing the same marketing activities in the home country and in foreign countries
c. By varying the name and packaging of one product depending on the country in which it is sold
d. By standardizing marketing activities among similar cultures and modifying them when cultures differ

59. How does a boutique hotel benefit from being mentioned in a travel book such as *Frommer's* or *Fodor's*?

a. Influential reviewers and control over content
b. Extensive reach and minimal cost
c. Low-cost advertising and positive publicity
d. Free publicity and credible information

Copyright © Mometrix Media. You have been licensed one copy of this document for personal use only. Any other reproduction or redistribution is strictly prohibited. All rights reserved.
This content is provided for test preparation purposes only and does not imply an endorsement by Mometrix of any particular political, scientific, or religious point of view.

60. Which of the following methods is most likely being used by a Nike salesperson who gives one sales presentation to a small, local sporting goods store and a slightly different presentation to Dick's Sporting Goods?

a. Consultative selling
b. Adaptive selling
c. Formula selling
d. Suggestive selling

61. The need-satisfaction presentation format is most consistent with the marketing concept because it:

a. encourages salespeople to acknowledge objections by listening to customer concerns.
b. requires salespeople to gather financial information before making a sales approach.
c. emphasizes listening to the needs and interests of customers and solving problems.
d. stresses making sales to large customers and providing excellent customer support.

62. Which of the following should a salesperson do in preparation for a business meeting in Tokyo with a Japanese firm?

a. Learn Asian business etiquette
b. Learn to speak fluent Japanese
c. Study the Asian financial system
d. Study Japanese manufacturing

63. Which of the following would a marketing manager most likely use to determine if a marketing promotion is increasing product sales?

a. Profitability analysis
b. Cost focus strategy
c. Microsales analysis
d. Differentiation strategy

64. A marketing manager would most likely use ROI marketing to:

a. determine the program costs of a coupon promotion.
b. assess the costs of using a territorial sales force structure.
c. determine the profitability of an e-mail campaign.
d. assess the validity of an advertising campaign.

Copyright © Mometrix Media. You have been licensed one copy of this document for personal use only. Any other reproduction or redistribution is strictly prohibited. All rights reserved.
This content is provided for test preparation purposes only and does not imply an endorsement by Mometrix of any particular political, scientific, or religious point of view.

65. Use the information below to answer the question that follows.

Profit and Loss Statement USA Widget Company March 2009	
Sales Revenue	$10,000
Less Cost of Products Sold	$5,500
Gross Profit on Sales	$4,500
Expenses:	
Salaries	$1,750
Advertising	$1,250

What percentage of USA Widget Company's total revenue equals the firm's total expenses?

a. 20%
b. 30%
c. 45%
d. 55%

66. Use the information below to answer the question that follows.

AAA Company	
Cost of goods sold	$36
Markup	$44
Selling Price	$80

What percentage markup on the selling price does AAA Company use?

a. 25%
b. 35%
c. 45%
d. 55%

67. Use the equation below to answer the question that follows.

Cost of goods sold ÷ Average inventory at cost = X

Which of the following completes the equation (meaning, what does *X* stand for)?

a. Stock turn rate
b. Return on investment
c. Markdown rate
d. Selling price

68. Companies that conduct business exclusively through their Websites are known as:

a. Web-and-mortar companies.
b. click-and-mortar companies
c. brick-and-mortar companies.
d. click-only companies.

69. What makes marketspace more valuable to marketers than the traditional marketplace?

a. The chance to attract customers away from competitors
b. The potential for customization of a product or service
c. The ability to offer products and services to niche markets
d. The possibility of lowering distribution expenses

Copyright © Mometrix Media. You have been licensed one copy of this document for personal use only. Any other reproduction or redistribution is strictly prohibited. All rights reserved.
This content is provided for test preparation purposes only and does not imply an endorsement by Mometrix of any particular political, scientific, or religious point of view.

70. What is the term for an online advertisement that pops up between Website screen changes?

a. Banner ads
b. Contextual ads
c. Interstitials
d. Dialog box

71. According to the seven C's of effective Website design, _______ refers to the layout and visual design of the site.

a. context
b. customization
c. communication
d. community

72. All of the following are guidelines employed by firms that successfully use permission marketing EXCEPT:

a. customers only receive information that matches their needs and interests.
b. customers receive rebates and discounts for providing feedback through surveys.
c. customers have the ability to modify the amount or type of information they receive.
d. customers receive assurance that their profile data will not be shared with other firms.

73. Which of the following is a strategy that encourages the forwarding of promotional messages through e-mail?

a. Multichannel marketing
b. Promotional Websites
c. Content sponsorship
d. Viral marketing

74. Which of the following facilitates the communication between a firm and its suppliers, distributors, and advertising agency?

a. Internet
b. Intranet
c. Extranet
d. Web community

75. The greatest benefit that firms gain from using multichannel marketing is an:

a. improved ability to monitor consumer purchasing trends.
b. increase in number of opportunities to promote goods and services.
c. improved ability to develop long-term customer relationships.
d. increase in number of opportunities to personalize services based on customer data.

76. Which of the following would most likely help a marketing education teacher stay informed about technology-based marketing strategies?

a. Subscribe to a marketing magazine or journal
b. Offer marketing services to a nonprofit organization
c. Interview local businesses about their marketing strategies
d. Research the Internet to analyze current marketing techniques

Copyright © Mometrix Media. You have been licensed one copy of this document for personal use only. Any other reproduction or redistribution is strictly prohibited. All rights reserved.
This content is provided for test preparation purposes only and does not imply an endorsement by Mometrix of any particular political, scientific, or religious point of view.

77. What is the first step that a marketing education teacher should take to establish a DECA Chapter at a high school?

a. Advertise the first campus meeting with posters and announcements
b. Determine how many local business owners would be mentors
c. Assess student interest and meet with school administrators
d. Outline campaign and election procedures for chapter officers

78. Which of the following publications would most likely help a marketing education teacher stay abreast of business and marketing trends?

a. *New York Times*
b. *Newsweek*
c. *Entrepreneur*
d. *Forbes*

79. A marketing education teacher should base lesson plans on state curriculum standards in order to:

a. promote academic achievement in both mandatory and elective courses.
b. encourage more federal funding and grants for high school technical programs.
c. guarantee high marks on student achievement tests and college entrance exams.
d. maintain a rigorous course that academically prepares students for college and career.

80. Which of the following would most likely be student requirements in an articulation agreement between the marketing departments of a community college and a high school?

a. At least 10 hours of community service
b. At least 3 semester hours of Marketing
c. A 2.5 GPA and at least a 1500 total score on the SAT
d. A 2.5 GPA and at least 9 semester hours of marketing

81. Which of the following would be the best question for determining the feasibility of an articulation agreement between the marketing departments of a high school and a community college?

a. How do high school and community college instructors assess marketing students at the end of the semester?
b. What are the curriculum guidelines and course objectives in marketing classes at the high school and community college?
c. What types of extracurricular marketing activities are required for students at the high school and community college?
d. Where do marketing students at the high school and community college rank in comparison to marketing students in other states?

82. Which of the following would most likely encourage local businesses to continue supporting a marketing education program?

a. Provide the businesses with the instructional materials used in the marketing classes
b. Ask the businesses to allow students to tour their facilities and interview employees
c. Contact the businesses every semester to discuss job opportunities for marketing students
d. Place the names of the businesses on a display board at school or in school publications

Copyright © Mometrix Media. You have been licensed one copy of this document for personal use only. Any other reproduction or redistribution is strictly prohibited. All rights reserved.
This content is provided for test preparation purposes only and does not imply an endorsement by Mometrix of any particular political, scientific, or religious point of view.

83. All of the following are typical activities performed by members of a marketing education program's advisory committee EXCEPT:

a. reviewing instructional information for technical accuracy.
b. assessing goals and objectives of the marketing curriculum.
c. teaching marketing lessons to students on a regular basis.
d. providing assistance with marketing-related field trips and speakers.

84. Which of the following strategies would most likely be effective for a marketing teacher who wants to get students involved in the local community?

a. Meeting with local charity leaders to discuss how marketing students can help their organization
b. Assigning students a local businessperson to shadow and interview for one day
c. Inviting local businesspeople into the classroom to practice roleplay situations with students
d. Organizing a local job fair to assist marketing students in finding employment

85. Which of the following activities would best facilitate a marketing education instructor's desire to continue learning about various aspects of marketing?

a. Joining a professional marketing organization
b. Working a second job in a marketing firm
c. Helping a charity with their marketing needs
d. Assisting with a marketing advisory group

86. Which of the following must be in a student's training plan before participation in a work-based training program can occur?

a. An agreement between the school and the business regarding student pay
b. Correlations between occupational training objectives and curriculum guidelines
c. An agreement between the school and the business regarding study assignments
d. Correlations between classroom instruction and text-based assignments

87. Which of the following best describes the role of an advisor to a student marketing organization such as DECA?

a. Handles the financial and accounting elements of the organization
b. Contacts local businesses for student employment opportunities
c. Organizes community service and fund raising projects
d. Guides students in managing organization activities

88. A group of students in a marketing class have enjoyed analyzing and compiling consumer information for a project. Which of the following marketing careers would most likely involve similar activities?

a. Data miner
b. Media buyer
c. Industrial salesperson
d. Supply chain manager

Copyright © Mometrix Media. You have been licensed one copy of this document for personal use only. Any other reproduction or redistribution is strictly prohibited. All rights reserved.
This content is provided for test preparation purposes only and does not imply an endorsement by Mometrix of any particular political, scientific, or religious point of view.

89. All of the following are benefits of sales positions EXCEPT:

a. potential for high salary.
b. flexibility in work schedule.
c. opportunities for advancement.
d. chance to develop creative ideas.

90. What should a marketing teacher advise a student to do first in the job search process?

a. Analyze growing sectors in the job market
b. Write a resume and general cover letter
c. Assess personal strengths and weaknesses
d. Prepare for interviews by gathering industry facts

91. The most likely strategy for a marketing teacher to use in preparing students for job interviews is to:

a. write the job training plan.
b. edit the job cover letter.
c. speak with the interviewer.
d. role play the job interview.

92. Which of the following is the primary objective of a work-based learning program?

a. Earn income for college while attending secondary school
b. Prepare students for the transition to college and career
c. Show students how to assess their aptitudes and skills
d. Give on-the-job training that can transfer to college

93. All of the following are the main responsibilities of a student's mentor in a work-based learning program EXCEPT:

a. instruct and critique the student.
b. provide challenges for the student.
c. assist the student with assignments.
d. work with the teacher and employer.

94. What is the primary benefit for marketing students who participate in student organizations such as DECA?

a. Develop good work ethics and social skills
b. Earn extra credit for participating in competitions
c. Gain access to local companies and business leaders
d. Develop leadership skills and help define career interests

95. Which of the following activities would most likely integrate a DECA activity into the marketing curriculum?

a. Students give presentations to local businesspeople about DECA activities.
b. Students invite parents and friends to on-campus DECA fundraisers.
c. Students research DECA programs implemented in other high schools.
d. Students evaluate the DECA Website for employment opportunities.

Copyright © Mometrix Media. You have been licensed one copy of this document for personal use only. Any other reproduction or redistribution is strictly prohibited. All rights reserved.
This content is provided for test preparation purposes only and does not imply an endorsement by Mometrix of any particular political, scientific, or religious point of view.

96. A marketing teacher is developing a unit on retailing and would like to use a performance-based assessment to measure student learning. Which of the following would be the most appropriate way to evaluate the students?

a. Students administer a school-wide survey to assess retail store preferences.
b. Students research the retailing mix utilized by a major retailer.
c. Students develop a retailing strategy for a new store they have created.
d. Students analyze non-store retailing and its impact on standard retailing.

97. Students in a marketing class are responsible for running the school store, but sales at the store have been down for the last two months. Which of the following student activities would model business practices and help resolve the issue?

a. Ask for additional funding from the principal
b. Survey the student body for suggestions
c. Gather marketing students to brainstorm ideas
d. Assign marketing students to monitor inventory

98. Which of the following activities would most likely provide an opportunity for marketing students to integrate language arts concepts with a marketing assignment?

a. Researching ethical issues relevant to marketing
b. Evaluating the effectiveness of a product's Website
c. Designing a billboard and magazine ad for a restaurant chain
d. Writing a press release about a new product on the market

99. A marketing class has completed a unit on personal selling. Which of the following activities would be an appropriate culminating activity for the marketing students?

a. Students give sales presentations to classmates and answer product questions and concerns.
b. Students complete aptitude tests to determine whether they would make good salespeople.
c. Students interview local salespeople about techniques they use in sales presentations.
d. Students outline the six stages of the personal selling process in a spreadsheet.

100. A marketing instructor wants students to be familiar with setting up and using spreadsheets. Which of the following assignments would most likely facilitate the instructor's objective?

a. Analyzing the life cycle stage of a cleaning product
b. Creating a newspaper layout for a computer ad
c. Designing the packaging for an organic cereal
d. Evaluating pricing strategies for a video game platform

Copyright © Mometrix Media. You have been licensed one copy of this document for personal use only. Any other reproduction or redistribution is strictly prohibited. All rights reserved.
This content is provided for test preparation purposes only and does not imply an endorsement by Mometrix of any particular political, scientific, or religious point of view.

Answer Key and Explanations

1. C: The two main types of business organizations are nonprofits and business firms. Organizations that try to serve customers but have no monetary goals are considered nonprofits. Firms that try to serve customers and also earn profits are known as business firms or business corporations. Brick-and-mortars, international firms, e-tailers, retailers, and service providers are all trying to make money and so are all business firms.

2. B: The corporate level is where top management guides the firm's overall strategy. The business unit level is where managers establish the direction of products and markets in order to gain the most profit. The functional level of a firm is where specialists in finance, manufacturing, human resources, and information systems create value and perform a task. A person working on the marketing campaign for a GE dishwasher is performing a function in the marketing department, so choice B is the best answer.

3. D: The *Deceptive Mail Prevention and Enforcement Act* of 1999 was passed to regulate promotion practices, so choice D is correct. The *Telephone Consumer Protection Act* of 1991 involves regulation of telemarketing, while the *National Do Not Call Registry* is a list of consumers who do not wish to receive telephone solicitation. The Better Business Bureau is a voluntary alliance of firms whose goal is to regulate each other's business practices.

4. D: The *Federal Dilution Act* prevents someone from diluting a trademarked name, such as "Cadillac" brushes or "Nike" copy paper, so choice D is correct. Choice A is a distractor. Choice B refers to the 1988 trademark rights around the world.

5. B: Product managers, or brand managers, are the center of the marketing department in most consumer and business product firms. The product manager plans, implements, and controls the annual plans related to products for which he or she is responsible, so choice B is the best answer. Choice A is incorrect because preparing materials for sales representatives would be a job for the sales support staff. Managing field representatives would be a task for a sales force manager, so choice C is wrong. Distributing resources to suppliers is too narrow of a task for the product manager, so choice D is wrong.

6. D: The best answer is choice D because product managers have very little direct authority over anything in an organization except their product. Product managers often use persuasive techniques to gain assistance from different groups in a firm because product managers lack the power to give orders. Choices A, B, and C are all considered benefits of the product manager system.

7. B: Green marketing is the term for marketing with ecological issues in mind, so choice B is correct. Green marketing takes many forms. For example, Hewlett-Packard includes a postage-paid envelope in its boxes of printer cartridges, so consumers can send their old cartridges back to HP for recycling. FedEx and UPS are converting many of their diesel delivery trucks to ones that ones that are more fuel-efficient.

8. A: Ronald McDonald Houses are a way for McDonalds to help the community, so choice A is the best answer. Choice C "cause marketing," is tempting because McDonald's sometimes raises funds to support the Ronald McDonald Houses. However, the question does not mention fundraising, so choice C is wrong. Profit responsibility refers to maximizing profits for stockholders, so choice B is incorrect. Sustainable development occurs when a firm conducts business in a way that is friendly to the environment, which does not relate to Ronald McDonald Houses.

Copyright © Mometrix Media. You have been licensed one copy of this document for personal use only. Any other reproduction or redistribution is strictly prohibited. All rights reserved.
This content is provided for test preparation purposes only and does not imply an endorsement by Mometrix of any particular political, scientific, or religious point of view.

9. C: Corporate espionage is the clandestine collection of proprietary information about a firm's competitors, and trespassing, fraud, and wiretapping are examples of such. Internet piracy refers to downloading music illegally from the Internet, so choice A is incorrect. While the actions listed are unethical, they are not part of a marketing strategy, so choice B is wrong. The term "corruption perceptions" refers to the transparency of international firms and whether business is gained ethically or through bribes and kickbacks. Choice C is the best answer.

10. C: The Better Business Bureau is an agency formed by a voluntary alliance of businesses with the intention of maintaining fair business practices, so C is the best answer. Choice B may have been tempting because the Robinson-Patman Act, also known as the Anti-Price Discrimination Act, is a federal law that makes it illegal for a distributor to sell goods at a lower price to chain stores than small businesses. *Consumer Reports* assists consumers rather than businesses, so choice D is wrong. A code of business practices outlines a firm's goals and standards but does not necessarily regulate business transactions, so choice A is wrong.

11. D: The best answer is choice D because marketing forces firms to compete for business, which in turn forces improvements in quality and lowers product prices. Choice A is incorrect because marketing does not necessarily use technology or relate to consumer waste. Choice B is wrong because improved sales are not necessarily beneficial to society. Choice C is incorrect because competition increases with marketing.

12. D: A shift in the supply curve would occur because one of the primary ingredients in corn cereal would be less available, so choice D is correct. The demand for corn cereal should not be affected by whether or not corn crops have been wiped out, so choice A and choice B are wrong. A shift to the right would suggest that more corn cereal is available because there is more corn, so choice C is wrong.

13. B: Elasticity refers to how responsive a product or service is when price changes. The demand for elastic products changes greatly when price changes. If the cost of air travel declines, people will travel more. If airline prices increase, people will travel less, so choice B is correct. Milk, electricity, and medication are necessary items for most people, so their demand is inelastic. The prices in these industries go up and down, but people still buy essential products.

14. C: The best definition of the business cycle or economic cycle is choice C. During a business cycle a business, industry, or economy expands and contracts. These periods are known as booms and busts and vary in length from a few months to many years. The fluctuations affect durable manufactured goods more than services. Retail prices are less affected than are wholesale prices.

15. A: The costs of running a business must be determined before a price can be set, so choice A is the best choice. If the price of a product or service fails to cover the costs of doing business, then cash flow will decrease and the business may fail. Choice B may be tempting because matching competitor prices is important; however, the competitor's costs may not be the same as yours. Prices should account for a certain profit, so choice C is partially correct. Prices may vary with supply and demand, but the most important aspect of pricing is covering costs and profits.

16. A: Productivity is a way to measure the efficiency of production using a ratio of the output of goods to the input of production costs, such as labor and materials. If workers at a Toyota factory are not assembling cars fast enough, then management needs to evaluate the situation. Perhaps better technology is needed or workers need more training. Choice C is tempting but wrong because labor costs are only one factor of productivity. Toyota's revenue may increase if workers

Copyright © Mometrix Media. You have been licensed one copy of this document for personal use only. Any other reproduction or redistribution is strictly prohibited. All rights reserved.
This content is provided for test preparation purposes only and does not imply an endorsement by Mometrix of any particular political, scientific, or religious point of view.

are more productive, but not necessarily, which means choice D is wrong. Choice B is a distracter not related to the question.

17. D: The intersection of the demand curve and the supply curve is known as equilibrium. When the economy is at equilibrium, the allocation of goods and services is as efficient as it can be. The amount of items supplied to consumers is exactly the amount of items demanded by consumers. Equilibrium is considered a theoretical point because in the real market the price of goods and services fluctuate. Demand and supply also fluctuate, so equilibrium cannot be reached. Therefore, the best answer is choice D.

18. C: Choice A is incorrect because a political economy refers to the social science that studies the relationship between politics and economics. Choice B is a distracter because "commercial economy" is not an economic term. Merchant capitalism was the early stage of modern capitalism that was developed in the 9th century. The best answer is choice C. In a free enterprise system, consumers and businesses decide what to buy rather than having the government making that decision.

19. B: Buying and selling occurs in markets, so choice B is the best answer. The three main types of markets are resource markets, which are used by households, product markets, which are used by businesses, and financial markets, which are used by both households and businesses. Choice A is incorrect because the government monitors the legal rights of buyers and sellers. Although markets may offer entrepreneurial opportunities, that is not their primary function. Choice D is wrong because supply and demand shifts occur in markets but that is not the purpose of markets in a free enterprise system.

20. B: The three factors that create a strong and healthy economy are steady growth, stable prices, and a high rate of employment. Since you are searching for the element that does not lead to a healthy economy, choice B is the best answer. The amount of money invested by businesses and individuals in stocks or real estate has an impact on the economy. However, the meaning of the term "steady investment" is unclear.

21. D: The Consumer Confidence Index is a survey of consumer expectations. The survey tracks the responses of consumers to specific questions and releases the results monthly. Typical questions ask consumers how they feel about their financial situations. Automakers and manufacturers of appliances and furniture carefully watch the survey in order to plan how many goods to produce. Therefore, the best answer is choice D. A furniture manufacturer would be able to determine how many sofas to produce during a given period based on whether consumers thought they would make large purchases.

22. A: Choices B and C are incorrect because a sole proprietorship is the easiest and least expensive form of business ownership to set up and dissolve. Choice D is tempting. Some employee benefits cannot be directly deducted from business income, but they can be partially deducted as an adjustment to income. The best answer is choice A. Sole proprietors are legally responsible for all debts against their business.

23. B: Choice A is wrong because only business plans include R & D information. Choice C is incorrect because both marketing plans and business plans include information about the firm's marketing program and market-product focus. Choice D is wrong because marketing plans provide details about a firm's implementation plans. Choice B is the best answer. Marketing plans do not provide details related to a firm's operations or manufacturing. These details are only found in a company's business plan.

Copyright © Mometrix Media. You have been licensed one copy of this document for personal use only. Any other reproduction or redistribution is strictly prohibited. All rights reserved.
This content is provided for test preparation purposes only and does not imply an endorsement by Mometrix of any particular political, scientific, or religious point of view.

24. B: After making the decision to become an entrepreneur, Jessie needs to write a business plan and then look into the type of financing that is available. Although renting office space occurs in the early stages of entrepreneurship, a business plan needs to be in place first. Employees will be hired after office space is determined and financing has been obtained, so choice C is wrong. The business plan must be written before any marketing and advertising can occur, so choice D is wrong.

25. D: The correct answer is choice D because the two main types of financing are equity financing and debt financing. Financing from a venture capitalist is a type of equity financing, so choice A is wrong. Similarly, commercial financing from a bank is a type of debt financing, which makes choice C wrong. Stock offerings are not a primary type of financing, so choice B is wrong.

26. D: Market segmentation is the term used to describe the process of dividing the market into groups with similar needs. These groups or segments should respond similarly to a marketing action, which is beneficial when marketing a product. Market penetration is a strategy of increasing sales of current products within a market, so choice A is wrong. Market development refers to the strategy of selling existing products in new markets. Choice C is a distracter.

27. A: A target market is one or more specific groups of possible customers. A marketing program will try to gain these specific consumers, so choice A is the best answer. Choice B is tempting, but a target market includes the most likely consumers of a product rather than all consumers. A product will not please everyone, so a target market helps marketers know which customers to attempt to reach. While understanding a target market will benefit marketing and advertising programs, it does not necessarily reduce the amount of time involved, which means choice C is wrong. Knowing the target market does not directly relate to customer value, so choice D is wrong.

28. C: The equation in the diagram illustrates how market share is determined, so choice C is correct. A firm's performance can be compared to the competition by determining market share. Unit volume refers to the quantity of products manufactured and sold, so choice A is wrong. Profit margin is determined by a ratio of net profits divided by sales, so choice B is wrong. Market revenue is not a business term, so choice D is wrong.

29. B: L.L. Bean wants its customers to be completely satisfied based on the firm's unconditional guarantee, so choice B is the best answer. If L.L. Bean advertised that it had reduced its packaging then their goal might be one of social responsibility. Firms that state their commitment to employee opportunities and good working conditions are interested in employee welfare. The retailer's motto does not relate to market share, although market share is of some concern to most firms.

30. D: In the planning phase of the strategic marketing process, a firm identifies trends, develops a budget, and sets product goals. Obtaining resources does not occur until the implementation phase of the strategic marketing process. Therefore, choice D is the correct answer.

31. C: The primary purpose of doing marketing research before releasing a product is to help managers make better marketing decisions and to reduce the risk of failure. Choice C is the best answer. Although predicting sales revenue may come from research, Choice D does not summarize the overall objective of market research. Similarly, analyzing data is an aspect of market research but not the primary goal. Choice A is too vague and is a distracter.

32. B: The first step in marketing research is defining the problem, which involves setting research objectives and identifying possible marketing actions. Choices C and D are part of the second step, while collecting information is the third step. The fourth step is to develop findings by analyzing data. The final step is to take marketing actions and evaluate the results.

Copyright © Mometrix Media. You have been licensed one copy of this document for personal use only. Any other reproduction or redistribution is strictly prohibited. All rights reserved.
This content is provided for test preparation purposes only and does not imply an endorsement by Mometrix of any particular political, scientific, or religious point of view.

33. A: Secondary data is the group of facts collected in the past, such as census data or Nielsen ratings. Secondary data is not specific to a particular project, so choice D is incorrect. Census data is collected every 5 or 10 years, so secondary data is not current, which means choice D is wrong. Observing a person's reaction to a product is observational data. Observational data is a type of primary data. Therefore, the best answer is choice A. Since the information has already been collected, time can be saved. In addition, Census reports can be attained for free or for a very small fee.

34. C: A marketing information system is any process of collecting, analyzing, and reporting market research information that managers then use to make marketing decisions. The best answer is choice C because managers take the information and then analyze the data in order to make changes to the product or marketing methods. For example, a computer system can track where a customer acquired a product coupon and where it was redeemed. Such information would help managers know whether coupons are a viable sales promotion. Supplier costs and stockholder information are not directly affected by an MIS, so choices A and D are wrong. Sales personnel should already be familiar with a product before an MIS, so choice B is wrong.

35. D: Marketing mix refers to product, price, promotion, and place. All of these factors are under the control of the marketing department of an organization, so choice D is the best answer. Derived demand refers to the demand for industrial products that is driven by consumer demands, so choice B is wrong. Customer value is the collection of benefits enjoyed by buyers, such as quality, price, and convenience. Although marketing departments consider customer value, they cannot control perceived value. Market share cannot be controlled by the marketing department, although it is an important factor considered by marketing managers.

36. B: Insignificant point of difference refers to the idea that a new product is not different enough from other products to convince consumers to use them. Consumers will not purchase a product that has low quality, so choice C is incorrect. Sometimes new products are released too soon or too late, or when there is no need for the product, so choice D is incorrect. The best answer is choice B because generating ideas for a product does not necessarily lead to product failure.

37. D: During the screening and evaluation state of the new product process, products are evaluated both internally by a firm and externally with consumer groups, so choice D is correct. Market testing involves testing new products on a limited scale in the actual marketplace. Business analysis refers to making financial projections of the product's success before investing capital for a prototype. Idea generation occurs in the early stages of a new product's life cycle when concepts for the product are discussed.

38. B: The FTC states that the word "new" can be used on products for six months, so choice B is correct. The problem with the restriction is that the phrase "regular distribution" is not clearly defined by the FTC. A new product could be distributed in certain areas of the country before being distributed nationwide, for example. In such cases, the product might be labeled "new" for longer than six months.

39. C: The diagram depicts a monopolistic competition where many sellers compete over price, product features, and advertising, so choice C is correct. In a pure monopoly, one seller sets the price for a unique product. In an oligopoly, few sellers exist, and they try to avoid competing on price. In a pure competition, many sellers follow a price established by the marketplace, such as occurs with corn or grain.

Copyright © Mometrix Media. You have been licensed one copy of this document for personal use only. Any other reproduction or redistribution is strictly prohibited. All rights reserved.
This content is provided for test preparation purposes only and does not imply an endorsement by Mometrix of any particular political, scientific, or religious point of view.

40. B: The price of the Nintendo system is $50 less than the Sony, so Nintendo was using penetration pricing. Penetration pricing involves setting a low initial price on a new product. Skimming pricing occurs when a firm introduces a product at the highest price it thinks customers will pay, so choice A is wrong. Prestige pricing occurs when a price is set high to appeal to status-conscious buyers. Bundle pricing is incorrect because Nintendo is selling only one item. However, if Nintendo offered consumers a DS carrying case, an extra stylus, and a free game cartridge at a price less than the cost of the individual items, then Nintendo would be bundle pricing. Therefore, choice B is the best answer.

41. A: A firm establishes pricing objectives, so choice D is incorrect. A company can change the price of its product based on supply and demand, so choice C is incorrect. The amount a company pays for labor is somewhat within its control, so choice B is incorrect. A firm has no control over its competition, so choice A is the best answer.

42. B: Product mix refers to the number of product lines offered by a company. Procter & Gamble sells a wide range of products including dishwashing detergent, coffee, toothpaste, and food products. As a result, Procter & Gamble has an opportunity to increase the amount of goods the firm sells, but also has to support each different product. Although IBM, Kawasaki, and Barnes & Noble sell more than one type of product, Procter & Gamble has a wide range of products that it sells.

43. C: Choice D is wrong because Land's End sells directly to consumers without using a wholesaler or retailer. Chevrolet uses a retailer but not a wholesaler, so choice A is incorrect. Wal-Mart is a big box retailer that is able to buy in large quantities from producers. Frito-Lay sells its line of chips to wholesalers, who then break down cases for retailers. Therefore, the best answer is choice C.

44. D: Environmental factors have an effect on the marketing channel used by a firm. For example, Kroger has eliminated wholesalers and started buying fresh-cut flowers directly from producers. Growing, transporting, and storing flowers has become simpler because of technological advances, so Kroger no longer needs flower wholesalers. The condition of a product does not necessarily relate to the wholesaler, so choice A is wrong. Retail sales and a product's life cycle may have an impact on which marketing channel to use but do not necessarily exclude wholesalers.

45. B: Sales promotions, such as coupons, rebates, and sweepstakes, are very flexible because they can be implemented to stimulate sales at any time, so choice D is wrong. The costs of sales promotions vary, but they can offer a quick return in a short time, which means choice A is incorrect. Database management may or may not be necessary depending on the type of promotion, so choice C is wrong. The best answer is choice B. If a sweepstakes lasts a long time, or if coupons are available every week, then the promotion loses its effectiveness.

46. A: Direct marketing refers to telemarketing, direct response advertising, direct mail, and catalogs. People are increasingly concerned with protecting their privacy, which has resulted in a decline in areas such as telemarketing. Choice B is wrong because the messages are typically very consistent, such as when a sales person calls someone and recites a sales pitch from a script. Feedback is easy to track because either the sales call or infomercial earned a sale or it did not. Direct marketing has been one of the fastest growing promotional methods because it does not involve huge costs, especially compared to developing an advertising campaign, so choice D is wrong.

47. C: In the maturity stage of a product's life cycle, the goal of promotion is to remind consumers about a product. Consumers know that the product exists, but they may to be encouraged to continue buying the product. In the introduction stage, the public needs to be informed about a new

Copyright © Mometrix Media. You have been licensed one copy of this document for personal use only. Any other reproduction or redistribution is strictly prohibited. All rights reserved.
This content is provided for test preparation purposes only and does not imply an endorsement by Mometrix of any particular political, scientific, or religious point of view.

product. In the growth stage, consumers need to be persuaded to buy a product instead of a competitor's product. In the declining stage of a product's life cycle, very little money is spent on promotion because the product may be replaced.

48. B: Push strategies involve a push of marketing campaigns, such as advertisements, discounts, and promotionals through retailers to make the product visible. In this strategy, the retailer acts as the primary selling point and takes a margin of the profit.
Direct selling involves bypassing intermediary parties and selling directly from the manufacturer to the consumer. A pull strategy occurs when demand from the customers necessitates that retailers and wholesalers order products from a manufacturer to meet the demand. Value-added reselling involves a similar flow, but where the product is incorporated into a service or product which the retailer offers.

49. A: Competitive institutional advertisements promote the benefits of one product class, such as dairy, over another. America's dairy farmers want people to drink milk rather than other beverages, so choice A is the best answer. Pioneering institutional advertising is used when a firm wants to inform consumers about what they have to offer. For example, Bayer ads state that the firm makes products other than aspirin. Public relations campaigns seek to change opinions but without direct payment, which means choice B is wrong. Choice D is wrong because sales promotions are typically short-term and intended to spur sales with coupons or with gifts.

50. B: Frequency refers to the average number of times a person in the target audience is exposed to a message, so choice B is correct. Reach refers to the number of different people or households exposed to an advertisement, so choice A is incorrect. Ratings measure the percentage of households in a market that are watching a particular TV show. Although cost is always a factor in advertising, expenditures do not relate to the target audience.

51. C: Magazines provide advertisers with plenty of room to give detailed information, and they have specific target audiences. Teenagers read magazines, such as *Teen People*, so a product geared towards teenagers would find a captive audience in the publication. Radio ads can target local audiences, but not necessarily by age group, and time restrictions would not allow for conveying much product information. Although extensive information could be given in a newspaper ad, the audience of a newspaper is wide ranging. Television ads are very effective at reaching large audiences and could be shown during shows watched by a specific group; however, time limitations might prevent product details from being provided.

52. C: The correct order of the personal selling process is described in choice C. Prospecting is the first stage when a list of possible customers is gathered. The prospects are researched and a decision is made by a salesperson regarding the best way to approach the potential client. After approaching the possible customer and stimulating interest from the prospect a sales presentation is given. Afterwards, a salesperson asks for a purchase and then follows up with the customer to ensure satisfaction.

53. C: If a prospect's objection is based on misinformation, then a salesperson needs to clearly state that the information is wrong before moving forward in the presentation. Objections should be ignored only if they appear to be the prospect's method of stalling. An objection can be changed to a reason for buying in some cases, such as when a prospect complains about the high price of a product. The salesperson could use the objection to point out the high quality materials used. Postponement is used when a prospect's objection is a topic that will come up later in the presentation, so choice D is wrong.

Copyright © Mometrix Media. You have been licensed one copy of this document for personal use only. Any other reproduction or redistribution is strictly prohibited. All rights reserved.
This content is provided for test preparation purposes only and does not imply an endorsement by Mometrix of any particular political, scientific, or religious point of view.

54. D: Choice D best describes the function of the Uniform Commercial Code. The purpose of the UCC is to standardize laws related to sales and other commercial transactions in all states in the US The reason for the standardization is that commercial transactions go beyond state lines in many cases. The UCC regulates the sale of goods, financial transactions, letters of credit, and the delivery of title documents. It outlines the rights and responsibilities of each party in a commercial transaction.

55. B: Exxon is changing its gasoline to make it appropriate for a country's climate, so Exxon is adapting an existing product. Product extension occurs when a firm sells virtually the same product around the world, such as Coca-Cola. Product invention occurs when a firm invents a product specifically to meet the needs of a particular area of the world. Choice D is not a marketing term related to global promotion.

56. B: When US dollar or products are less expensive for foreign customers, then US firms will export more products. If US products are more expensive for foreign customers, then US firms will export fewer products. The amount of exporting done by foreign nations is not necessarily affected by the US exchange rate.

57. B: Although a joint venture is not as risky as direct investment, it is financially riskier than the other options. Exporting provides the least amount of profit, but it requires the smallest commitment from a firm. Contract assembly and franchising are types of licensing. Contract manufacturing occurs when a US firm contracts with a foreign firm to manufacture goods according to certain specifications. US firms, such as McDonald's and Taco Bell, have franchises around the world.

58. D: Choice D best describes the global marketing strategy used by transnational firms. Choice B describes the marketing strategy used by international firms. These firms market their products the same way around the world. Choice C describes a multidomestic marketing strategy used by multinational firms. Choice A is somewhat like a multidomestic strategy because sometimes formulas are modified in different countries.

59. D: An independent travel expert writes a review about a hotel, so a hotel would have no control over the article. Reviews in guidebooks are sometimes favorable and sometimes not, so A is wrong. Choices B and C are wrong because hotels and restaurants do not pay to be mentioned in such guidebooks. The best answer is choice D because the publicity, either good or bad, is free. In addition, many people find the information in such guidebooks very reliable.

60. B: Adaptive selling occurs when a salesperson adjusts a sales presentation to match the needs of specific customers, so choice B is correct. Consultative selling is mostly used in business-to-business marketing when recognizing and solving problems is needed. For example, Xerox uses consultative selling to help customers solve business-related problems. Formula selling occurs when a canned sales presentation is used and no flexibility is involved. Suggestive selling occurs when a salesperson attempts one appeal after another hoping to make a sale.

61. C: The concept behind the need-satisfaction presentation format is that by asking questions and listening to customers, a salesperson can identify a customer's needs. By learning as much information as possible, a salesperson can help solve problems for the customer, so choice C is correct. Although handling objections is part of a sales presentation, it is not the primary focus of the need-satisfaction format. Gathering information about a client is needed before an approach is made, but the need-satisfaction format focuses on listening to customers. Choice D is wrong because the size of a client is not a relevant factor in how to make a sales presentation.

Copyright © Mometrix Media. You have been licensed one copy of this document for personal use only. Any other reproduction or redistribution is strictly prohibited. All rights reserved.
This content is provided for test preparation purposes only and does not imply an endorsement by Mometrix of any particular political, scientific, or religious point of view.

62. A: Communicating effectively with foreign clients involves understanding the cultural and societal expectations of that country. In Asia, for example, a person's name is treated with great respect, so business cards are handed to Asian customers using both hands. An American salesperson who is fluent in Japanese would be very effective; however, learning to speak the language fluently before a meeting is highly unlikely. Although choices C and D are important aspects of any sales presentation, learning a culture's business etiquette would be extremely beneficial.

63. A: Choice B is wrong because a cost focus strategy involves controlling expenses and lowering product prices when necessary. Choice D is incorrect because a differentiation strategy relates to charging premium prices for products when customers believe the products are worth it. A microsales analysis traces the source of sales revenue, such as sales representatives and geographical regions. A profitability analysis tells managers which products, promotions, or customer groups are responsible for the profits a product is making.

64. C: Return on investment marketing is a type of profitability analysis that uses technology to optimize money spent on a marketing plan. Computer models can collect data to determine if an e-mail promotion is reaching the intended target audience and if more products are being sold as a result. Choice A is incorrect because the program costs of a promotion would be one of the factors used to assess the return on investment. The structure of a sales force is not directly related to ROI, so choice B is wrong. Although advertising relates to how many products are sold, the validity of an ad campaign cannot be quantified.

65. B: The percentage of total revenue that is equal to total expenses is calculated by dividing total expenses ($3,000) by sales revenue ($10,000). Choice B is correct because 30% of the firm's revenue goes towards expenses such as rent, salaries, and utilities.

66. D: Markup refers to the amount added to the actual cost of an item to reach a selling price. Markup is a way to set a retail price. In this example, the cost of the item is $36. The AAA Company increases the price by $44 to reach a selling price of $80. The percentage markup is calculated by dividing the markup ($44) by the selling price ($80) and multiplying by 100. Therefore, the AAA Company has a 55% markup on the items it sells to consumers.

67. A: The diagram illustrates the formula used to calculate stock turn rate, so choice A is correct. The stock turn rate measures an inventory's movement. A slow stock turn may mean that a retailer is buying merchandise from suppliers than customers do not want. Supermarkets pay close attention to the stock turn of different product lines since shelf space is limited.

68. D: A click-only company does business through the Internet, such as Amazon, so choice D is correct. A click-and-mortar company maintains a storefront, but it also does business through its Web site. Wal-Mart, Sears, REI, and Pottery Barn sell goods to consumers at their stores, but they also sell items to consumers from their Websites. A brick-and-mortar company only sells goods from its store and does not have a Website from which consumers can shop. Choice A is a distracter, since it is virtually the same as choice B.

69. B: Marketspace refers to the Internet-enabled environment that allows buyers and sellers to interact. The two-way communication that occurs in the marketspace allows sellers to customize their products to meet the needs of consumers. On Godiva.com, for example, consumers can select the specific types of chocolate candy they want in a box of chocolates. Choices A, C, and D could occur in the standard marketplace, so they are wrong.

Copyright © Mometrix Media. You have been licensed one copy of this document for personal use only. Any other reproduction or redistribution is strictly prohibited. All rights reserved.
This content is provided for test preparation purposes only and does not imply an endorsement by Mometrix of any particular political, scientific, or religious point of view.

70. C: An interstitial is a Web page that is displayed prior to the display of another page. Online marketers often use interstitials to display advertisements. A banner ad is a type of Web advertising. A banner ad is embedded into a Web page and does not pop up. Contextual advertising is targeted for the specific person using the Website based on certain keywords. If a person is looking at a Website about dogs, then the contextual ad may be for dog food or pet supplies. A dialog box is a window that pops up requesting a response from the computer user.

71. A: The seven C's of effective Website design are context, commerce, connection, communication, customization, community, and content. Context refers to the site's aesthetic appeal and its layout, so choice A is correct. Customization is the site's ability to tailor to the needs of different customers. Communication refers to how buyers and sellers are able to interact. Community is how the site enables user-to-user interaction.

72. B: Permission marketing occurs when a consumer consents to receive e-mail and advertising based on the data they have provided to a firm. For example, Petco sends e-mails regarding sales and specials to customers who have opted to receive such information. Choices A, C, and D are actions employed by firms that use permission marketing with success. Although customers may receive discounts for providing feedback, surveys are not one of the guidelines followed by firms that successfully use permission marketing.

73. D: Viral marketing is the Internet version of word-of-mouth marketing. For example, Hotmail embeds messages with a marketing tagline, so when the message is forwarded the promotional information goes with it. Marketers also try to make the content on their Websites so interesting that viewers want to pass the information along. Marketers also use incentives to customers for referring their friends to a company's Website. Choice A is wrong because multichannel marketing refers to the blending of different communication methods. Promotional Websites are established by marketers to advertise and provide information about a product or service. Content sponsorship is the content on a Website sponsored by an advertiser.

74. C: Extranets use Internet-based technology to allow a firm to communicate with its partners, so choice C is correct. An Intranet is a Web-based network used within the confines of an organization. A Web community is a Website that acts like a community, such as MySpace or Facebook.

75. B: Multichannel marketing occurs when a firm uses more than one method of marketing their products or services. For example, Eddie Bauer customers can view clothing through the firm's Website or in printed catalogs. Eddie Bauer increases the likelihood of a sale by marketing through two channels. Although firms can monitor trends and customer data through the information gained from online purchasing, the main goal of multichannel marketing is to expose customers to a product through different marketing channels.

76. A: Magazines and journals, such as *Marketing Today*, can provide teachers with current information about the way marketers use technology as a tool in marketing products and services. Although helping a nonprofit organization with their marketing needs is a worthwhile activity, it would not provide an instructor with information about technology-based marketing trends. Interviewing local business people might provide some insight into marketing trends, but a magazine or journal would offer a broader range of information. A great deal of information about marketing can be found on the Internet, but not all of it is valid. A professional journal would be a more effective way to gather current marketing information.

77. C: Before planning meetings or elections, a marketing education teacher should determine if there is enough interest in DECA to begin a chapter. At least 10 students should be interested before

Copyright © Mometrix Media. You have been licensed one copy of this document for personal use only. Any other reproduction or redistribution is strictly prohibited. All rights reserved.
This content is provided for test preparation purposes only and does not imply an endorsement by Mometrix of any particular political, scientific, or religious point of view.

beginning the procedures to begin a chapter. After determining student interest, a teacher should receive approval from school administrators. The ideas presented in Choices A, B, and D are important considerations, but none are not the first step when establishing a DECA chapter.

78. C: *Entrepreneur* includes articles about marketing strategies, starting businesses, and technology, so it would be an invaluable resource to a marketing education teacher. *Forbes* focuses on the financial aspects of business, while *Newsweek* covers weekly news in all politics, business, and health. *The New York Times* would provide some useful information about marketing and business, but the narrow subject matter of *Entrepreneur* would be the best choice for a marketing teacher.

79. D: The purpose of curriculum guidelines is to maintain standards in the classroom. A marketing teacher should follow the guidelines to ensure that the marketing course is academically challenging and will prepare students for life after high school. The guidelines cannot guarantee high marks on standardized tests, although a rigorous course load should help students do well. Choice B is incorrect because teachers should not follow the curriculum guidelines in hopes of receiving school funding, although high scores may result in such. Choice A is too broad because the question is specifically related to marketing teachers.

80. D: An articulation agreement is an agreement between a high school and a technical or community college that allows the transfer of high school credit for qualifying students. Choice D is the best answer because a minimum GPA and a minimum number of marketing coursework would be relevant to earning college credit. Community service and SAT scores would be irrelevant, so choices A and C are wrong. Three hours of marketing is only one class and most likely insufficient for college credit.

81. B: If a high school's marketing department offers courses similar to those offered at a community college, then an articulation agreement can most likely be arranged. A community college would not give credit to high school students if their marketing classes were less academically challenging or covered different material. The best question to ask is choice B because the other questions fail to address the main purpose of an articulation agreement.

82. D: Local businesses will be more likely to continue supporting a marketing education program if they are shown appreciation for their efforts. Placing the names of businesses in the school newspaper or on a special display board provides the business with good advertising for their efforts. Although businesses may support the program with jobs and tours of facilities, both of these actions help the program more than the business. Choice A is incorrect because a business does not benefit from receiving marketing instructional materials. Therefore, the best answer is choice D.

83. C: Advisory committees support a marketing education program in a variety of ways including the assessment of instructional information and curriculum goals, so choices A and B are wrong. Members of a committee are often part of the business community, so they can help coordinate field trips and speakers. Although committee members may provide input in the classroom on occasion, they are not teaching on a regular basis. Therefore, the correct answer is choice C.

84. A: Choice A would provide marketing students with an opportunity to use their skills to help a local charity. The strategy would also promote a positive relationship between the local community and the marketing education program, which could have long-term benefits for the program.

85. A: Joining a group such as the American Marketing Organization would enable a marketing instructor to have access to current marketing information. Members can attend conferences and make professional contacts that could provide valuable information for future classroom usage.

Copyright © Mometrix Media. You have been licensed one copy of this document for personal use only. Any other reproduction or redistribution is strictly prohibited. All rights reserved.
This content is provided for test preparation purposes only and does not imply an endorsement by Mometrix of any particular political, scientific, or religious point of view.

Choice B is not feasible given the fact that teaching is a full time job. Helping a charity or an advisory group would provide an opportunity to use marketing skills but not necessarily learn more about marketing.

86. B: Training plans for work-based programs require a description of work-based instruction. The work-based instruction should relate to the state standards and class instruction. The purpose of the training plan is to ensure that students receive marketing instruction while working. The training plan enables the business and the classroom instructor to maximize a student's learning. Choice A is wrong because some work-based learning programs involve payment while others do not. Choice D does not relate to work-based training. Choice C is tempting, but study assignments are not the responsibility of businesses.

87. D: The purpose of most student organizations is to guide and encourage students so that they have ownership of the group. Although an advisor may assist students with finances, fund raising, and employment, the ultimate goal is for an advisor to teach students how to do these activities themselves. Therefore, the best answer is choice D.

88. A: The best answer is choice A because a data miner collects and analyzes data about buying preferences and consumer trends. A media buyer chooses advertising media while an industrial salesperson sells supplies to businesses. A supply chain manager deals with distribution issues.

89. D: Sales positions offer the chance to earn high salaries, especially when commissions are combined with base salaries. Salespeople work independently many times, so they have the flexibility to schedule sales calls and presentations when it is convenient for them. Sales positions offer the chance for salespeople to advance into management or to expand their sales territories. Therefore, choice D is the best answer. Although salespeople need to be creative in their presentations, personal selling is not an area for people who are especially creative or artistic.

90. C: The first step in the job process is performing a self-assessment. A student should consider his or her interests, strengths, and weaknesses before embarking on a random job search. Identifying job opportunities, writing a resume, and preparing for interviews are important, but should not occur until a student has a strong understanding of his or her own abilities. If a student lacks the skills, personality, or education for a particular job path, then the student should reconsider their job objectives.

91. D: Roleplaying a job interview is an excellent strategy for teachers who want to prepare students for interviews. Asking students typical interview questions and helping them become comfortable will boost their confidence before the actual interview. Choices A, B, and C may occur before the interview, but only roleplaying helps prepare for the real thing.

92. B: Work-based learning programs are intended to train students and prepare them for life after high school. Studies have shown that students are not obtaining the skills needed for a modern workforce, and work-based learning programs can help fill that gap. Not all programs pay students, so choice A is not necessarily true. Some programs may offer college credit, but not all, which means choice D is not correct. Students can use the program to determine their aptitudes, but the overall goal is to prepare students for college and work. Therefore, choice B is correct.

93. C: A workplace mentor trains and guides students to help them have a beneficial experience in the workplace. A mentor may be an employee or someone outside the firm who has been approved to mentor the student. Responsibilities include instructing and reviewing the student in regards to job performance. The mentor also works with the teacher and employer. A mentor should not help students with assignments, so choice C is the best answer.

Copyright © Mometrix Media. You have been licensed one copy of this document for personal use only. Any other reproduction or redistribution is strictly prohibited. All rights reserved.
This content is provided for test preparation purposes only and does not imply an endorsement by Mometrix of any particular political, scientific, or religious point of view.

94. D: The main goal of organizations such as DECA is to provide opportunities for students to develop leadership and occupational skills through activities and programs, so choice D is the best answer. Choice A is tempting because work ethics are an important element of DECA, but social skills are not as important as leadership abilities in the organization. Choice B is wrong because not all teachers offer extra credit for competing in DECA competitions. Working for local firms is a benefit for some DECA members, but it is not the primary purpose of the student organization.

95. A: Choice A is the best answer because students would be practicing their public relations and public speaking skills while discussing DECA functions. Researching information and searching for employment opportunities are minor aspects of a marketing class, so choices C and D are wrong. Setting up a DECA fundraiser might integrate the curriculum into a DECA activity, but inviting people to the fundraiser is not an element of the marketing curriculum.

96. C: Performance-based assessments typically assign students a task that involves applying skills used in the classroom in the creation of something new. Choice C is the best answer because students would have to come up with an idea for a retail store and then develop a retailing strategy. Researching information and administering surveys fail to force students to apply information in a new situation, so choices A, B, and D are wrong.

97. C: The most reasonable first step to take is to brainstorm problems and solutions with the marketing students who run the store. The students may already know why sales are slow, and a group brainstorming session may generate good ideas. In addition, businesses often use group brainstorming to find solutions, so the activity serves to model real-world business practices. A survey of needs from the student body may need to be performed, but it would not be the first step. Monitoring inventory is always important in a retail store, but it will not resolve the issue immediately. Asking for money from the administration would not teach students about the realities of retailing, so choice A is wrong.

98. D: Marketing education allows for the integration of skills and concepts learned in other academic areas, especially math and language arts. Choice D is the best answer because writing a press release helps students realize that the skills they learn in language arts are applicable in the real world. Although some writing is involved in a magazine ad, writing a press release requires writing that is more formal. Researching ethical issues and evaluating Websites both relate to reading comprehension skills, but they fail to integrate the writing element of language arts.

99. A: Choice A is the best activity for students after a personal selling unit. The activity would allow students to try out personal selling techniques and receive feedback from peers. Aptitude tests may assist students who are considering sales as a career choice, but might be a waste of time for other students in the class. Talking to salespeople about sales presentations would be less effective than actually developing a sales presentation, so choice C is wrong. Choice D would make an appropriate test question but not a very interesting culminating activity.

100. D: The purpose of a spreadsheet is to manipulate numbers easily and painlessly. A spreadsheet would be useful for students comparing pricing strategies because mathematical equations can be set up on the spreadsheet. Design elements such as newspaper layouts and packaging are not suited for spreadsheets, so choices B and C are incorrect. Choice A may be tempting, but life cycle analysis would not require number manipulation. Therefore, the best answer is choice D.

Copyright © Mometrix Media. You have been licensed one copy of this document for personal use only. Any other reproduction or redistribution is strictly prohibited. All rights reserved.
This content is provided for test preparation purposes only and does not imply an endorsement by Mometrix of any particular political, scientific, or religious point of view.

How to Overcome Test Anxiety

Just the thought of taking a test is enough to make most people a little nervous. A test is an important event that can have a long-term impact on your future, so it's important to take it seriously and it's natural to feel anxious about performing well. But just because anxiety is normal, that doesn't mean that it's helpful in test taking, or that you should simply accept it as part of your life. Anxiety can have a variety of effects. These effects can be mild, like making you feel slightly nervous, or severe, like blocking your ability to focus or remember even a simple detail.

If you experience test anxiety—whether severe or mild—it's important to know how to beat it. To discover this, first you need to understand what causes test anxiety.

Causes of Test Anxiety

While we often think of anxiety as an uncontrollable emotional state, it can actually be caused by simple, practical things. One of the most common causes of test anxiety is that a person does not feel adequately prepared for their test. This feeling can be the result of many different issues such as poor study habits or lack of organization, but the most common culprit is time management. Starting to study too late, failing to organize your study time to cover all of the material, or being distracted while you study will mean that you're not well prepared for the test. This may lead to cramming the night before, which will cause you to be physically and mentally exhausted for the test. Poor time management also contributes to feelings of stress, fear, and hopelessness as you realize you are not well prepared but don't know what to do about it.

Other times, test anxiety is not related to your preparation for the test but comes from unresolved fear. This may be a past failure on a test, or poor performance on tests in general. It may come from comparing yourself to others who seem to be performing better or from the stress of living up to expectations. Anxiety may be driven by fears of the future—how failure on this test would affect your educational and career goals. These fears are often completely irrational, but they can still negatively impact your test performance.

Elements of Test Anxiety

As mentioned earlier, test anxiety is considered to be an emotional state, but it has physical and mental components as well. Sometimes you may not even realize that you are suffering from test anxiety until you notice the physical symptoms. These can include trembling hands, rapid heartbeat, sweating, nausea, and tense muscles. Extreme anxiety may lead to fainting or vomiting. Obviously, any of these symptoms can have a negative impact on testing. It is important to recognize them as soon as they begin to occur so that you can address the problem before it damages your performance.

The mental components of test anxiety include trouble focusing and inability to remember learned information. During a test, your mind is on high alert, which can help you recall information and stay focused for an extended period of time. However, anxiety interferes with your mind's natural processes, causing you to blank out, even on the questions you know well. The strain of testing during anxiety makes it difficult to stay focused, especially on a test that may take several hours. Extreme anxiety can take a huge mental toll, making it difficult not only to recall test information but even to understand the test questions or pull your thoughts together.

Copyright © Mometrix Media. You have been licensed one copy of this document for personal use only. Any other reproduction or redistribution is strictly prohibited. All rights reserved.
This content is provided for test preparation purposes only and does not imply an endorsement by Mometrix of any particular political, scientific, or religious point of view.

Effects of Test Anxiety

Test anxiety is like a disease—if left untreated, it will get progressively worse. Anxiety leads to poor performance, and this reinforces the feelings of fear and failure, which in turn lead to poor performances on subsequent tests. It can grow from a mild nervousness to a crippling condition. If allowed to progress, test anxiety can have a big impact on your schooling, and consequently on your future.

Test anxiety can spread to other parts of your life. Anxiety on tests can become anxiety in any stressful situation, and blanking on a test can turn into panicking in a job situation. But fortunately, you don't have to let anxiety rule your testing and determine your grades. There are a number of relatively simple steps you can take to move past anxiety and function normally on a test and in the rest of life.

Physical Steps for Beating Test Anxiety

While test anxiety is a serious problem, the good news is that it can be overcome. It doesn't have to control your ability to think and remember information. While it may take time, you can begin taking steps today to beat anxiety.

Just as your first hint that you may be struggling with anxiety comes from the physical symptoms, the first step to treating it is also physical. Rest is crucial for having a clear, strong mind. If you are tired, it is much easier to give in to anxiety. But if you establish good sleep habits, your body and mind will be ready to perform optimally, without the strain of exhaustion. Additionally, sleeping well helps you to retain information better, so you're more likely to recall the answers when you see the test questions.

Getting good sleep means more than going to bed on time. It's important to allow your brain time to relax. Take study breaks from time to time so it doesn't get overworked, and don't study right before bed. Take time to rest your mind before trying to rest your body, or you may find it difficult to fall asleep.

Along with sleep, other aspects of physical health are important in preparing for a test. Good nutrition is vital for good brain function. Sugary foods and drinks may give a burst of energy but this burst is followed by a crash, both physically and emotionally. Instead, fuel your body with protein and vitamin-rich foods.

Also, drink plenty of water. Dehydration can lead to headaches and exhaustion, especially if your brain is already under stress from the rigors of the test. Particularly if your test is a long one, drink water during the breaks. And if possible, take an energy-boosting snack to eat between sections.

Along with sleep and diet, a third important part of physical health is exercise. Maintaining a steady workout schedule is helpful, but even taking 5-minute study breaks to walk can help get your blood pumping faster and clear your head. Exercise also releases endorphins, which contribute to a positive feeling and can help combat test anxiety.

When you nurture your physical health, you are also contributing to your mental health. If your body is healthy, your mind is much more likely to be healthy as well. So take time to rest, nourish your body with healthy food and water, and get moving as much as possible. Taking these physical steps will make you stronger and more able to take the mental steps necessary to overcome test anxiety.

Copyright © Mometrix Media. You have been licensed one copy of this document for personal use only. Any other reproduction or redistribution is strictly prohibited. All rights reserved.
This content is provided for test preparation purposes only and does not imply an endorsement by Mometrix of any particular political, scientific, or religious point of view.

Mental Steps for Beating Test Anxiety

Working on the mental side of test anxiety can be more challenging, but as with the physical side, there are clear steps you can take to overcome it. As mentioned earlier, test anxiety often stems from lack of preparation, so the obvious solution is to prepare for the test. Effective studying may be the most important weapon you have for beating test anxiety, but you can and should employ several other mental tools to combat fear.

First, boost your confidence by reminding yourself of past success—tests or projects that you aced. If you're putting as much effort into preparing for this test as you did for those, there's no reason you should expect to fail here. Work hard to prepare; then trust your preparation.

Second, surround yourself with encouraging people. It can be helpful to find a study group, but be sure that the people you're around will encourage a positive attitude. If you spend time with others who are anxious or cynical, this will only contribute to your own anxiety. Look for others who are motivated to study hard from a desire to succeed, not from a fear of failure.

Third, reward yourself. A test is physically and mentally tiring, even without anxiety, and it can be helpful to have something to look forward to. Plan an activity following the test, regardless of the outcome, such as going to a movie or getting ice cream.

When you are taking the test, if you find yourself beginning to feel anxious, remind yourself that you know the material. Visualize successfully completing the test. Then take a few deep, relaxing breaths and return to it. Work through the questions carefully but with confidence, knowing that you are capable of succeeding.

Developing a healthy mental approach to test taking will also aid in other areas of life. Test anxiety affects more than just the actual test—it can be damaging to your mental health and even contribute to depression. It's important to beat test anxiety before it becomes a problem for more than testing.

Study Strategy

Being prepared for the test is necessary to combat anxiety, but what does being prepared look like? You may study for hours on end and still not feel prepared. What you need is a strategy for test prep. The next few pages outline our recommended steps to help you plan out and conquer the challenge of preparation.

Step 1: Scope Out the Test

Learn everything you can about the format (multiple choice, essay, etc.) and what will be on the test. Gather any study materials, course outlines, or sample exams that may be available. Not only will this help you to prepare, but knowing what to expect can help to alleviate test anxiety.

Step 2: Map Out the Material

Look through the textbook or study guide and make note of how many chapters or sections it has. Then divide these over the time you have. For example, if a book has 15 chapters and you have five days to study, you need to cover three chapters each day. Even better, if you have the time, leave an extra day at the end for overall review after you have gone through the material in depth.

If time is limited, you may need to prioritize the material. Look through it and make note of which sections you think you already have a good grasp on, and which need review. While you are studying, skim quickly through the familiar sections and take more time on the challenging parts.

Copyright © Mometrix Media. You have been licensed one copy of this document for personal use only. Any other reproduction or redistribution is strictly prohibited. All rights reserved.
This content is provided for test preparation purposes only and does not imply an endorsement by Mometrix of any particular political, scientific, or religious point of view.

Write out your plan so you don't get lost as you go. Having a written plan also helps you feel more in control of the study, so anxiety is less likely to arise from feeling overwhelmed at the amount to cover.

Step 3: Gather Your Tools

Decide what study method works best for you. Do you prefer to highlight in the book as you study and then go back over the highlighted portions? Or do you type out notes of the important information? Or is it helpful to make flashcards that you can carry with you? Assemble the pens, index cards, highlighters, post-it notes, and any other materials you may need so you won't be distracted by getting up to find things while you study.

If you're having a hard time retaining the information or organizing your notes, experiment with different methods. For example, try color-coding by subject with colored pens, highlighters, or post-it notes. If you learn better by hearing, try recording yourself reading your notes so you can listen while in the car, working out, or simply sitting at your desk. Ask a friend to quiz you from your flashcards, or try teaching someone the material to solidify it in your mind.

Step 4: Create Your Environment

It's important to avoid distractions while you study. This includes both the obvious distractions like visitors and the subtle distractions like an uncomfortable chair (or a too-comfortable couch that makes you want to fall asleep). Set up the best study environment possible: good lighting and a comfortable work area. If background music helps you focus, you may want to turn it on, but otherwise keep the room quiet. If you are using a computer to take notes, be sure you don't have any other windows open, especially applications like social media, games, or anything else that could distract you. Silence your phone and turn off notifications. Be sure to keep water close by so you stay hydrated while you study (but avoid unhealthy drinks and snacks).

Also, take into account the best time of day to study. Are you freshest first thing in the morning? Try to set aside some time then to work through the material. Is your mind clearer in the afternoon or evening? Schedule your study session then. Another method is to study at the same time of day that you will take the test, so that your brain gets used to working on the material at that time and will be ready to focus at test time.

Step 5: Study!

Once you have done all the study preparation, it's time to settle into the actual studying. Sit down, take a few moments to settle your mind so you can focus, and begin to follow your study plan. Don't give in to distractions or let yourself procrastinate. This is your time to prepare so you'll be ready to fearlessly approach the test. Make the most of the time and stay focused.

Of course, you don't want to burn out. If you study too long you may find that you're not retaining the information very well. Take regular study breaks. For example, taking five minutes out of every hour to walk briskly, breathing deeply and swinging your arms, can help your mind stay fresh.

As you get to the end of each chapter or section, it's a good idea to do a quick review. Remind yourself of what you learned and work on any difficult parts. When you feel that you've mastered the material, move on to the next part. At the end of your study session, briefly skim through your notes again.

But while review is helpful, cramming last minute is NOT. If at all possible, work ahead so that you won't need to fit all your study into the last day. Cramming overloads your brain with more information than it can process and retain, and your tired mind may struggle to recall even

Copyright © Mometrix Media. You have been licensed one copy of this document for personal use only. Any other reproduction or redistribution is strictly prohibited. All rights reserved.
This content is provided for test preparation purposes only and does not imply an endorsement by Mometrix of any particular political, scientific, or religious point of view.

previously learned information when it is overwhelmed with last-minute study. Also, the urgent nature of cramming and the stress placed on your brain contribute to anxiety. You'll be more likely to go to the test feeling unprepared and having trouble thinking clearly.

So don't cram, and don't stay up late before the test, even just to review your notes at a leisurely pace. Your brain needs rest more than it needs to go over the information again. In fact, plan to finish your studies by noon or early afternoon the day before the test. Give your brain the rest of the day to relax or focus on other things, and get a good night's sleep. Then you will be fresh for the test and better able to recall what you've studied.

Step 6: Take a Practice Test

Many courses offer sample tests, either online or in the study materials. This is an excellent resource to check whether you have mastered the material, as well as to prepare for the test format and environment.

Check the test format ahead of time: the number of questions, the type (multiple choice, free response, etc.), and the time limit. Then create a plan for working through them. For example, if you have 30 minutes to take a 60-question test, your limit is 30 seconds per question. Spend less time on the questions you know well so that you can take more time on the difficult ones.

If you have time to take several practice tests, take the first one open book, with no time limit. Work through the questions at your own pace and make sure you fully understand them. Gradually work up to taking a test under test conditions: sit at a desk with all study materials put away and set a timer. Pace yourself to make sure you finish the test with time to spare and go back to check your answers if you have time.

After each test, check your answers. On the questions you missed, be sure you understand why you missed them. Did you misread the question (tests can use tricky wording)? Did you forget the information? Or was it something you hadn't learned? Go back and study any shaky areas that the practice tests reveal.

Taking these tests not only helps with your grade, but also aids in combating test anxiety. If you're already used to the test conditions, you're less likely to worry about it, and working through tests until you're scoring well gives you a confidence boost. Go through the practice tests until you feel comfortable, and then you can go into the test knowing that you're ready for it.

Test Tips

On test day, you should be confident, knowing that you've prepared well and are ready to answer the questions. But aside from preparation, there are several test day strategies you can employ to maximize your performance.

First, as stated before, get a good night's sleep the night before the test (and for several nights before that, if possible). Go into the test with a fresh, alert mind rather than staying up late to study.

Try not to change too much about your normal routine on the day of the test. It's important to eat a nutritious breakfast, but if you normally don't eat breakfast at all, consider eating just a protein bar. If you're a coffee drinker, go ahead and have your normal coffee. Just make sure you time it so that the caffeine doesn't wear off right in the middle of your test. Avoid sugary beverages, and drink enough water to stay hydrated but not so much that you need a restroom break 10 minutes into the

Copyright © Mometrix Media. You have been licensed one copy of this document for personal use only. Any other reproduction or redistribution is strictly prohibited. All rights reserved.
This content is provided for test preparation purposes only and does not imply an endorsement by Mometrix of any particular political, scientific, or religious point of view.

test. If your test isn't first thing in the morning, consider going for a walk or doing a light workout before the test to get your blood flowing.

Allow yourself enough time to get ready, and leave for the test with plenty of time to spare so you won't have the anxiety of scrambling to arrive in time. Another reason to be early is to select a good seat. It's helpful to sit away from doors and windows, which can be distracting. Find a good seat, get out your supplies, and settle your mind before the test begins.

When the test begins, start by going over the instructions carefully, even if you already know what to expect. Make sure you avoid any careless mistakes by following the directions.

Then begin working through the questions, pacing yourself as you've practiced. If you're not sure on an answer, don't spend too much time on it, and don't let it shake your confidence. Either skip it and come back later, or eliminate as many wrong answers as possible and guess among the remaining ones. Don't dwell on these questions as you continue—put them out of your mind and focus on what lies ahead.

Be sure to read all of the answer choices, even if you're sure the first one is the right answer. Sometimes you'll find a better one if you keep reading. But don't second-guess yourself if you do immediately know the answer. Your gut instinct is usually right. Don't let test anxiety rob you of the information you know.

If you have time at the end of the test (and if the test format allows), go back and review your answers. Be cautious about changing any, since your first instinct tends to be correct, but make sure you didn't misread any of the questions or accidentally mark the wrong answer choice. Look over any you skipped and make an educated guess.

At the end, leave the test feeling confident. You've done your best, so don't waste time worrying about your performance or wishing you could change anything. Instead, celebrate the successful completion of this test. And finally, use this test to learn how to deal with anxiety even better next time.

Review Video: Test Anxiety
Visit mometrix.com/academy and enter code: 100340

Important Qualification

Not all anxiety is created equal. If your test anxiety is causing major issues in your life beyond the classroom or testing center, or if you are experiencing troubling physical symptoms related to your anxiety, it may be a sign of a serious physiological or psychological condition. If this sounds like your situation, we strongly encourage you to seek professional help.

Copyright © Mometrix Media. You have been licensed one copy of this document for personal use only. Any other reproduction or redistribution is strictly prohibited. All rights reserved.
This content is provided for test preparation purposes only and does not imply an endorsement by Mometrix of any particular political, scientific, or religious point of view.

Online Resources

Due to our efforts to try to keep this book to a manageable length, we've created a link that will give you access to all of your online resources:

mometrix.com/resources719/gacemarketed

It's Your Moment, Let's Celebrate It!

Share your story @mometrixtestpreparation

Copyright © Mometrix Media. You have been licensed one copy of this document for personal use only. Any other reproduction or redistribution is strictly prohibited. All rights reserved.
This content is provided for test preparation purposes only and does not imply an endorsement by Mometrix of any particular political, scientific, or religious point of view.